To

MY WIFE HELEN
AND OUR CHILDREN
MARTHA AND
GREGORY

GREGORY
ROCHLIN, M.D.

Associate Clinical Professor of Psychiatry,
Harvard Medical School, Boston

GRIEFS
AND
DISCONTENTS

THE FORCES
OF CHANGE

LITTLE, BROWN AND COMPANY
Boston

Published in Great Britain
by J. & A. Churchill Ltd., London

PRINTED IN THE UNITED STATES OF AMERICA

GRIEFS AND DISCONTENTS

THE FORCES OF CHANGE

PREFACE

In this book it is my purpose to show that not only do our griefs and discontents begin early in life but that our reactions to them have a lasting effect. In addition, I have tried to make plain that in the deeper roots of the psychology of everyday life are the conflicts which become associated with our disappointments as well as our efforts to offset them.

We fill the discrepancy between our wishes and our satisfactions with our doubts along with our expectations. The uncertainties of fulfillment, however, coupled often with the failure to be satisfied, leave burdens of displeasure that demand relief. Psychoanalytic studies of many such commonplace experiences are provided in this book. They demonstrate the enormous significance of being deprived of what we may value and the effect of a confrontation with our own limitations. We, for our relief, erect defenses against these experiences. These defenses may become a source of pleasure. Moreover, the studies show our compelling unconscious need to compensate for imagined and real deficiencies. They show, for example, how from our feelings of ignominy we promote noble deeds; how we find that making a necessary and thus a desired relationship with another person, even though at the cost of our egocentric aims, has a profoundly civilizing influence, making us social creatures. From our failures, we often make gains. Where we had losses, we may find an impetus to creativity. From our fears of dying, we fashion convictions on immortality. In short, the book is to convey that our disappointments, failures, deprivations and losses generate dynamic forces with a powerful impetus, indispensable to our emotional development, and, while essential in effecting some of our highest achievements, they are also the basis from which many of our pathological states derive.

The plain fact that we pursue our pleasures and avoid pain frequently leads to a common misconception: the belief that, except for the perverse comfort which pain may provide, we profit little from it. But often obscure and hence overlooked is the way in which our achievements may be goaded by our discontents. This is not to suggest that there is a plausible claim to virtue in a Spartan existence that makes pleasure a vice and pain a value. Our efforts toward independence, autonomy, and freedom (for instance, the skills that we master and the versatility that we show in adapting to and then influencing our environment), no less than the faiths we nurture, indicate how obliged we are to attempt to transcend our limits, to find reparations for our deficiencies, and thus to earn some relief from our frailties. It appears, therefore, that the development of character and behavior and their rewards may depend at least as much upon our failures and anguish as upon our satisfactions.

Are we not impelled, in the course of finding relief from our pains, to change and influence our world? And are we not also obliged to alter and affect our environment when circumstance deflects our pursuit of pleasure? These questions refer to governing principles of mental functioning. They are that reality regularly forces us to defer a possible immediate pleasure or a respite from our discomfort for later relief that is more certain. This is the replacement of what Freud called the pleasure principle by the reality principle. It represents a profound change in the thought processes from the infantile mere wishing for pleasure to the more mature striving for satisfaction. Hence, our instincts, while altered neither at their source in biology nor in their aims at gratification, are subject nonetheless to the variable dictates of social and physical reality for their appeasement. The point of both questions is that our gratifications are also forged by discontent. These questions are probably as old as the condition and as clinical in their implications as they are philosophical. This book attempts to explain the clinical problem. It may also illuminate the philosophical one.

One theme predominates in all the chapters. It is that often we lose what we most value, and, as we do not really accept our losses, it is an invariable aspect of the human condition, therefore, to attempt to remove the dilemma. Our greatest achievements frequently come from these efforts.

Griefs and Discontents is intended for the reader who, enjoying his curiosity about himself, overcomes his strenuous resistance to the Delphic maxim "Know thyself." It is hoped that the reader will learn something more of himself and something new about others.

G. R.

Cambridge, Massachusetts

ACKNOWLEDGMENTS

A work solely of creative imagination perhaps would not be as directly dependent as this one upon the help of others. I wish to acknowledge, as a clinician, that my patients have taught me a great deal and that I am indebted to them. I could not have worked long at this book without an awareness of my debt to my students and colleagues, who have taught me far more than they realize. Two of my teachers, who have generously made me their colleague and who have become dear friends, made basic contributions to my own views. To them I am therefore especially grateful. They are Helene Deutsch, M.D., and Ives Hendrick, M.D. Their foremost and unique contributions as clinicians to ego psychology have become so much a part of contemporary psychoanalysis that many of my own views of the emotional development of late childhood and of the psychology of women stem largely from the work of Helene Deutsch, and those on the functions of the ego are, after Freud, based upon the work of Ives Hendrick.

My long friendship with Nancy Lyman Roelker, Associate Professor, Tufts University, Department of History, allowed me to call on her scholarship and her great talent as a teacher as well as on her boundless patience to help me with the preparation of some parts of the manuscript. She was lavish in her generosity to me. I am profoundly grateful to her.

My gratitude to Robert Lee Wolff, Coolidge Professor of History, Harvard University, for his help in the preparation of the manuscript cannot be adequately expressed. We are old friends who habitually exchange manuscripts. He has the mind of a scientist who is a historian and a historian who is a psychologist. He generously placed these gifts at my disposal.

The preparation of the book depended upon the liberality of Jack Ewalt, M.D., Bullard Professor of Psychiatry, Harvard Medical School, who spared me many tasks and thus gave me freedom to work on the material for the manuscript. I am grateful to him.

In a special sense, Judith A. Schoellkopf, Ph.D., of Buffalo, Cambridge, and Ravello has my deep affection and gratitude for her support and encouragement in connection with this work.

Mrs. Antonia Gerald Ellis has been so valuable a help in preparing the book that her work with me on the manuscript has been indispensable.

Throughout the undertaking, my wife has had her own essential part in the work represented here. She would not want me to speak of her share in any detail, but without her support in getting on with the task, it might not have been done.

Acknowledgment is made to Basic Books, Inc., Publishers, New York, for permission to quote from *Collected Papers of Sigmund Freud,* 1959.

Several chapters of this book are based in part on writings and lectures of mine. These are: Chapter 1, a paper in *The Psychoanalytic Study of the Child* (Vol. 16, 1961); Chapter 2, a paper in *Journal of the American Psychoanalytic Association* (Vol. 7, 1959); Chapter 3, a lecture delivered at the Western New England Psychoanalytic Society, January, 1964; Chapters 4 and 5, a series of lectures delivered at the Polish Academy of Science, Warsaw, May, 1964; Chapter 7, a lecture delivered at the Albert Einstein College of Medicine, Yeshiva University, November, 1964.

G. R.

CONTENTS

CONTENTS

INTRODUCTION

Freud's discoveries, those beginning with the neuroses, soon led him to a wealth of original findings in normal mental life. Whether his discoveries, and those of other psychoanalysts since he began, illuminated the neuroses more than the psychology of everyday life would be extremely difficult to determine. There is, however, a growing general inclination, even among many who are well informed, to disregard the distinction between what is applicable to neuroses and what is applicable to "the psychopathology of everyday life." Admittedly the difference is frequently very difficult to establish, but if it is ignored the result is that the behavior and alleged motives in daily life tend to be increasingly and loosely regarded as neurotic. On the other hand, viewing clinical pathology as dissociated from everyday life does little service to the effort to make the distinction, because it merely separates the two, just as the running together that obliterates the lines of differences contributes little if any understanding of either condition. We have much to gain from recognizing that there are discernible distinctions to be made and that all the aberrations in mental life that we have become familiar with are disorders of phenomena that normally exist. It is the aim of this book to present the development of a common, ordinary, yet central psychological conflict — the *loss complex* — in its everyday normal aspects, to describe its clinical aberrations, and to indicate the features that distinguish the normal from the aberrant manifestations.

Psychoanalytic research has increasingly been focused, in recent years, upon young children. Not only has it contributed to an understanding of many aspects of the psychology of the young child, but it has clarified previously obscured features of the emotional life of the adult. It is the purpose of this book to present, as completely as brevity permits, psychoanalytic studies of adults and young children and illustrations from the culture of everyday life that bear upon a unifying theme throughout the life of the individual. Other nuclear conflicts of emotional life have been written about extensively. The one presented here has not.

The book begins with work that I have recently restudied and revised. It is based in part upon my previous publications. It attempts to show the early emergence of specific emotional conflicts that are associated with important personal object relations and the significant vicissitudes of these conflicts throughout life. The dread of abandonment and the conflicts associated with loss develop as factors of prime importance, which on regularly becoming manifest in young children and by their subsequent persistence demonstrate that they have a critical role in the maturation of a wide variety of mental functions. The two factors have a continuing, lifelong, profound effect upon relationships that are personally important and upon the nature and quality of the adaptation to reality. Conventionally, they are usually regarded as negative influences with little good coming from them; and when it does, it is in spite of these occurrences rather than because of them. In the chapters on restitution and on creativity, the conflicts associated with abandonment and with loss may be seen to be related, each having a part in bringing on those elements in emotional experience and mental functions that are in the service of psychological development, rather than simply calling for regression as has been generally supposed because it is usually conspicuously present. These invariable experiences, the dread of abandonment and the experience of loss, whether occurring in fact or in fantasy, are not responded to as merely distressing events, later to be recollected on reflection. They are also revealed to be engines of change.

Experiences in life require no large catalogue to show us that our personal losses have a profound effect on us. We shall see that the process of loss is never unrelated to another one, restitution. The controversy as to when restitution may begin is perhaps not important, particularly since it seems not to be a real question. It is valuable, however, to understand when the cycle of loss and restitution is demonstrably established. Highly important is the fact that it has a lifelong course and produces effects that are significant for the person as well as for his society.

Our sense of worth will be shown to have its taproots in this cycle, not always drawing, however, upon satisfaction because previous pleasures that do not meet the expanding desires of the needs of growth and development may thus become limitations. We shall see that the discontent which results may become an important source of appetite. Thus it may lead to making change and novelty desirable rather than threatening. We may mature from the restrictive narrow needs to expanding ones because we are not tolerant of our unrequited wishes, frustration, or the finality of our losses. We may observe from direct clinical material cited that we are obliged to alter reality throughout our lives. It makes creativity a common human quality.

When we think of failure as a social fact, we see that the one who has failed has disappointed his own and others' expectations for him. He has sunk in his own and in the general esteem; this usually involves a moral judgment. Or, if we grasp its importance as expressing unconscious wishes, we tend to regard failure as a clinical symptom of neurotic origin. But we seldom recognize that failure — although it may be based on an underlying or unconscious conflict — carries with it an important psychodynamic impetus, related to everyday experience and to particular inevitable encounters in every life. By limiting ourselves to the social-moral or to the conventional interpretations of neurotic failure, we overlook the question whether failure itself is at times not an enormous and perhaps even an essential incentive to succeed. Much has been written about success, little about failure. In this book we try to redress the balance.

Our religious beliefs may stamp and characterize us in a fashion that few other convictions we harbor can. Yet what beliefs we acquire and how our religious life commences in relation to them as psychological experiences, important in transcending our limitations encountered in everyday life, have received little study or scrutiny for inexplicable or indeterminate reasons. Unique data are offered the reader to illumine some of these questions.

The illustrative clinical material presented in Chapter 7, The Loss of Function, aims at showing that the experience of an actual as well as a supposed physical disability relates to the unconscious meaning of a significant loss to the ego. Psychoanalytic views of the importance of personal losses, the impairment of function, or the presence of disabilities favor explanations in terms of the libidinal aspects, to the neglect generally of the effect on the ego and its mechanisms of defense.

The far-reaching psychological implications of a loss of function may become explicit when they are studied in the context of the experience of a loss of what has been valued. For example, the psychoanalytic study of the emotional experience of a trivial physical disorder reveals that its unconscious significance is that of an impairment in many ways indistinguishable from a serious one. The disquiet of limitations of function, whether they are transient and inconsequential or malignant and fatal, will be shown to have a common meeting place — in conflicts expressing loss and an indispensable need for restitution.

Conflicts in relation to loss gain special prominence among those who are aging. The clinical studies presented in this work will show that some generally held views of psychological development may need to be modified. The role of the reality of degenerative processes coupled with the loss of both objects and physical functions gives rise to conflicts in narcissism. The efforts to resolve the conflicts that are aroused and associated with loss lead to dynamic psychological changes that are related to an intensification of particular defenses. They constitute consolidating this period as a further phase of development. Paradoxically, the intensified defenses of this period are more attached to the fantasies of loss than to the reality of losses.

Little abstract theory will be offered to explain the dynamic processes that are involved in the phenomena presented. The theory that will be provided is closely tied to what may be clinically and empirically observed and studied to confirm it, albeit psychoanalytic conditions would often be required to obtain the findings. In other words, conditions that are conducive to eliciting material from the unconscious are often necessary to establish a working situation comparable to what is described in this book.

I shall assume no rhythms or laws that underlie the development of the human problems that are presented. There are, however, some uniformities that invariably appear. They are the regularities that are detectable or discernible in the psychological and the related social life of the individual. For example, I shall attempt to show that it is predictable that the sense or experience of loss will invoke processes that bring on attempts at restitution of the loss, whether it occurs in fact or in fantasy.

It is not regularly predictable to what degree these efforts will be effective to bring about a resolution of the conflict over the loss in respect to the altered self-esteem, nor can the social circumstances in which such efforts will be made be foreseen. Hence, it is not possible to make a long-range prediction as to the effectiveness of either the efforts or their outcome. Nonetheless, it is possible to draw certain general conclusions because the phenomena are not unique; on the contrary, we shall show that they are common and thus they may be regularly observed under the conditions described. They thus represent certain "laws of process, of change, of development—not pseudo-laws of apparent constancies or uniformities" [2].

The book is an occasion to present some of "the mind's less obvious, less logical, less conscious aspects" [1], which are deeply and permanently affected by its attentiveness to particular and inescapable conflicts associated with the experience of losses that result in discontent and prove a need for restitution.

REFERENCES

Röshlin's key source + teacher of ego psychology

1. Hendrick, Ives: *Facts and Theories of Psychoanalysis* (New York: Delta Books, 1963), p. vii.
2. Popper, Karl R.: *The Poverty of Historicism* (Boston: Beacon Press, 1957), p. 45.

GRIEFS AND DISCONTENTS

THE FORCES
OF CHANGE

I
THE DREAD OF ABANDONMENT

Olav

Though we often appear to be slaves of our material possessions, actually they may not be what we most fear to lose. When some of us are pressed by poverty, we may find it particularly difficult to perceive that there may be more severe privations than lack of goods and comforts. Nevertheless, to lose someone we love, or a substitute for one, or to lose our own self-esteem is more likely to be the hardest blow that life deals us. Such losses may lead to despair. The experience of a loss is common, and often a fancied loss creates as much havoc as a real one, though of course the distinction between the two remains important [26]. "Object loss" in the psychoanalytical sense means the forced abandonment of a desired and valued personal relationship. Grief at such a loss — whether real or fancied — usually affects one's image of oneself, sometimes pathologically.

The relationship that an infant develops with the person who cares for him represents the most archaic form of an object choice. The baby, being completely self-centered, forms a relationship in which he displays his solely hedonistic aims. The young child, because of his immaturity, can make no other connection with a person. For most of his infancy, the child insistently demands satisfaction of his needs and is not content with anything less. With time and maturity, the relationship of the infant to his mother undergoes a profound change. The alteration, especially significant to him, is expressed in a beginning concern with the wishes of another. He is no longer exclusively egocentric. He still clings to narcissism and to the archaic forms of a relationship, but later they will be relinquished though, under special conditions, he may revert to them.

From the point of view of psychological development, it is important to recognize that there is a clear distinction between a relationship to a *person* and a relationship to an *object*. Each is determined by the nature of the libidinal investment the young child can put into it. The child establishes the *person* relationship on the basis of his need. Who satisfies him is of secondary importance to fulfillment of his wants. In the *object* relationship, the child's need is as great, but it is coupled with a preference for an individual whose wishes are recognized. In the earlier phase, a substitute can be relatively easily accepted because infantile emotional life is governed essentially by need. The person is important only to the extent that he satisfies the need. An object choice, however, is governed by an additional emotional commitment whose significance goes far beyond a primitive need fulfillment.

Countless provocations in life strain and temper the self-esteem of an individual as he grows up and continues to live. (Chastening events affect self-esteem and narcissism.) The necessary attention that is paid to a younger brother, an admonition expressing a parent's disapproval, an illness which may impair temporarily the control of sphincters, are everyday examples from a multitude of childhood experiences in which the self may feel devalued. The circumstances and experiences in which self-esteem is hurt multiply as the child grows older.

The self, when demeaned, produces conflicts and responses similar to those that may be observed in object loss. In fact, where there is a loss, self-esteem invariably is affected. Loss and hence damage to self-esteem remain

bound throughout life from early childhood onward. Therefore, in the dissolution of a meaningful relationship, a
satisfying image of the self tends in part to be given up and
the experience of loss becomes intensified. It is no less true,
however, that loss is always followed by attempts at restitution. In the spectrum of the experience of loss, narcissism plays a basic part. Irrespective of the cause, as the
sense of loss is experienced, it brings a set of reactions that
involve narcissism. But the variations in mood, the momen-
tary despair and elation, so frequently experienced are
generally ignored or attributed to simple external realities
and thus rationalized as though narcissism were not regularly in the balance [24].

Vain people are especially prone to narcissistic injury.
They are likely to suffer severely from a loss of self-esteem
when they experience object loss. Ruled primarily by self-
interest, the young child also reacts to object loss with
heightened narcissism. He has, however, a readiness to
accept a substitute for the object that is lost. Only later in
psychic development, as object libido — even though it may
be immature — is established, is object loss met in fact or
fantasy, with a lowering of self-esteem and, under certain
conditions, with emerging guilt. The critical difference between the adult's and the child's reaction is in emotional
development. Since the lowering of self-esteem always depends upon "a criticizing faculty of the ego and the ego as
altered by identification" [1], the reactions reflected in
changes in self-esteem can become apparent only when the
more organized functions of the ego resulting from identification evolve.

This step marks the development of the superego. With
the acquisition of its self-critical faculty, the child's ego
holds him accountable to himself in a way that he cannot
hold others, particularly his parents, as he was previously
inclined to do. His disappointments and his frustrations
now become firm evidence, in the light of self-criticism, to

convince him of his own worthlessness. In order to spare himself these painful reactions, he keeps them removed from consciousness by *negation,* a very effective defense. This device has "a way of taking cognizance of what is repressed" [15], thus blocking the realization that much of his disillusionment comes from his own thwarted aspirations in the failure of his oedipal wishes. The disappointments are heaped upon an awareness of his own limitations. Both confirm him in the conviction of his lack of value. His reactions therefore focus upon questions of self-esteem in this period. Hence, a lowered self-esteem is of special importance in the phase of recovery from the oedipal conflicts.

During the oedipal period, the self is subject to severe criticism. The identification with the authority of the parental figures generates it. The deep and persistent concern over one's worth would have considerably less urgency were not doubts about self-esteem residually held. They stem from both erotic and aggressive sources as wishes. The wishes, having intensely egocentric aims, are expressed in fantasies of great expectations. Furthermore, because of their extravagance, they carry self-doubts of their being realized. The uncertainties about oneself are thus drawn on the one hand from inner conflicts resulting from the lack of satisfaction of unconscious wishes in the oedipal period, and on the other hand from the force that a multitude of circumstances convey to reveal one's limitations. The disappointments experienced in this phase are plainly expressed in the aspirations of the next one, latency.

The timelessness and the universality of conflicts over self-esteem are reflected everywhere in tales that essentially demonstrate that the human reach exceeds the grasp. In order to prevail over the uncertain outcome of wishes and events, special pleading or favor needs to be solicited in a world conceived to be ruled by authority and not governed by chance. These are common and persistent beliefs, to judge from the remarkable similarity in meaning given to religious rituals that carry pleading for special privilege, whether they are Buddhist, Brahmanic, Judaic, or Christian. We all know the story of Moses, whose abandonment is turned into triumph: he does not drown or starve; he is rescued, he overcomes ignominy and obscurity, he wins a place of honor, he attains nobility. Restitution of a demeaned self is completed on being accorded a noble station in place of ignominy. The variations on this imperishable and dateless theme are countless.

If the epic merely related a successful encounter with adversity, it would be but a tale of high adventure. What is significant is not that Moses is abandoned and then spared an uncertain fate by a rescue, or that he became a heroic leader. The significant element is that his entire fate was reversed on being chosen. Given this distinction, he was to lead a people who themselves asserted their uniqueness in being privileged, that is, chosen: "For thou *art* an holy people unto the Lord thy God: the Lord thy God hath chosen thee to be a special people unto himself, above all people that *are* upon the face of the earth." [1]

It would indeed be a naïve oversimplification to reduce the entire process to its oedipal components, though they may be easily discerned; or to dismiss the importance of the aspirations, destined to be thwarted, as merely a part of the family romance or the oedipus complex; or to merely generalize the observation that everyone wants to be favored. The need to be designated as special or enthroned as chosen and the wish for an advantage are regularly seen not only in the crises of life and in those occasions that evoke fears of the present and apprehensions of the future, but also in the quite ordinary events of everyday that leave their dissatisfactions, unrequited wishes, and unfulfilled expectations. No great mishap is required for us to feel troubled or hurt and, while awaiting the unpredictable outcome of an event to wish and pray for a favored solution.

[1] Deuteronomy 7:6.

People everywhere and always have been confronted with an inscrutable future that gives rise to apprehensions. In the course of history, therefore, humanity has wished to be favored or to be chosen. The wish to be chosen, even though undeserving, is nowhere more forcefully or more eloquently expressed than in a parable from Isaiah in which man is revealed as obstinate, base, and idolatrous. The Lord inveighs against him by declaring, "I *am* God, and *there is* none else: I *am* God, and *there is* none like me." [2] With His supreme powers, unique and as the Chosen One, He turns to man and addresses him: "Behold, I have refined thee but not with silver; I have chosen thee in the furnace of affliction." [3] We can here discern that God asserts His own uniqueness and superiority. He is chosen. Then He makes His choice, that of stubborn and heedless man, and in so doing He rectifies man. Both are elevated. God is given His due and man is redeemed. People who wish to be chosen may vary the details of the saga, but the theme will remain unchanged. Its most important aspect is that the entire device operates to elevate an otherwise doubtful or precarious self-esteem.

Some of the ordinary practices and beliefs of childhood found everywhere indicate the prevalence of the wish to be chosen and to be favored. (There are similar wishes among adults.) Probably the most intolerable conviction that a child may bear is that he is not wanted. It is an oppressive and alarming belief. It makes the child feel worthless and sink in his self-esteem — the sense of loss — and it arouses in him the anxiety that he must fend for himself and cannot expect favor or fortune. In the struggle against his distress he develops special and characteristic emotional reactions as defenses. He may depend upon denial: supporting his vanity by grandiose and extravagant fantasies that assert the opposite of what he feels to be true and make him feel

[2] Isaiah 46: 9.
[3] Isaiah 48: 10.

worthy and important. Although he still holds his disquieting convictions, they will remain ineffective so long as the
repressed conviction of feeling worthless does not return. If
it does, despair follows. The child's conflicts reveal that self-
esteem is central to them. The defenses show the same fact.
Narcissism is assigned a critical role.

The narcissism of early childhood, despite its central importance, is compelled to give way by two forces: first, by
the child's dependence and thus the indispensability and
value placed upon another person; and second, by the increasing awareness of fantasies, wishes, and the sense of
omnipotence that reality contradicts, frustrates, and denies.
Self-esteem that appeared impregnable is eroded, reduced,
and reversed into an esteem for an object to whom the qualities are attributed that one wants for oneself. As these
changes take place, the enormous value placed upon an object like a parent is brought in to be then associated with
fears of abandonment and loss. In the eagerness to be chosen
lies the pernicious fear of not being favored. Children at this
time are concerned with what may appear to be a remarkably banal question: ''Who will love me when I am left?''
Just as regularly their fear that they may indeed be left is
expressed in the thought: ''No one may want me.'' Such an
insidious question is regularly associated with fears of not
being loved and its extension to being hated.

These reactions and their corresponding fantasies are
part of the daily mores of childhood. Gradually we learn
that the burdensome exactions of life are lifted only in part
through wishing for the opposite. We partially give up cu-
pidity and, in so doing, trust that the present and the future
may be more assured. The belief that there will be one
who cares and who watches out provides a measure of relief
from the fears of being abandoned as worthless, not without good reason, because the young child learns very
quickly to become familiar with his own disappointments,
frustrations, hostility, envy, and greed and he knows that

these qualities in himself are subject to the criticism of others, as he would criticize them, although not as yet himself. It is the child's veiw that there is little danger except if one is worthless. What is no good is given up. To be angry and hateful is to be no good.

The cardinal virtues of prudence, fortitude, temperance, justice, and well-doing are hardly more than minimally observed by the child of five or six years. It is therefore no marvel that man's enduring dilemma in part may be manifested in his assertions and in his beliefs of being privileged or belonging to a chosen people. In this sequence of psychological development, because of the necessity of being privileged, as a defense, wishes gain expression that give way to assertions of worth, which in turn become beliefs, which are finally made a creed of faith. Hence he who resigns himself to the Divine Will, renouncing the aggressive instincts and practicing pity, kindliness, and patience, will thereby achieve his salvation. Then there will no longer be the perhaps well-deserved persecutions for aggression and hostility that are both conscious and unconscious, but instead enduring love for everyone will prevail. The problems of self-esteem would thus be resolved. These ideas embody the world's great religions and its little beliefs.

Self-esteem, whether expressed in fact or fantasy or legend, is rarely supported or elevated in the absence of objects. The myth of the epic hero is a later phenomenon in human development. Psychoanalytic studies of emotional development have shown that the formation of meaningful relationships is a principal psychic process in the formation of object relations of childhood. Thus family relationships become the prototypes of subsequent relationships throughout life. When a central psychic process supports life from the outset and thus becomes a principal developmental process, its serious impairment produces profound and often lasting effects upon the individual.

Not only is the process of forming object relations itself

of primary importance, but the object per se is also of central significance. Whatever threatens such an object invites an assault upon the process by which object relations are established. The individual risks lowering his self-esteem when he puts the object in jeopardy by making it a focus of his aggression. The sources of such a danger may be from within the self or they may be from without. In either case, the ensuing conflicts are remarkably similar. The fact that the child is in the unique situation of depending upon an object for relief from his tension, and that he thus depends upon an object that is indispensable for his maturation, brings the object immediately into close relation with the elemental problems of life and development. Without an object relationship maturation cannot proceed in an orderly fashion, nor can conflicts be reasonably resolved. Without a person the young child does not survive. Moreover, if deprived of adequate object relationships in later periods, the child will show either little emotional maturation or severely impaired development. (See Chapter 6.) This suggests that another person plays a special role which may insure not only life but growth and development as well. The need for a relationship to support life points to the helplessness that is characteristic of man in childhood. The child cannot alone relieve his discomfort, nor can he reduce his tension without the fostering or nurturing care of an adult. Ego and libidinal development are, by definition, processes of maturation. Although this development cannot be entirely attributed to an interaction of drives and environment, these processes cannot evolve in a reasonably plastic fashion unless there is an object outside the self to support them.

The realization of instinctual needs, the adaptation to the environment, and the formation of critical judgment about oneself are the later processes which show signs of failure when a necessary or desired relationship with primary objects (parents or surrogates) in a phase of development has not succeeded. For example, the mother who infantilizes her older child succeeds with him in his infancy, but when he is no longer an infant and she carries out her need to continue the period of infancy, the child's development begins to fail. The reverse is also true; when the parent's narcissistic expectations require a precocity of the ego of the child before he has developed sufficiently, the signs of failure begin to set in. The required physical care administered the child insures his survival. It also introduces the other person who is associated with providing the necessary comfort or relief.

Physical care alone, however, is not adequate for the young child's well-being. Comparisons that are frequently made between the human and other animals that, when young, are dependent upon care for their survival lose their validity in that the child will not thrive on physical care only, without another essential element, a relationship based upon a mutual need. Moreover, physical privation, when an emotional relationship with a parent is satisfying or flourishes, is tolerated well. The opposite is not the case. The inadequacy, withdrawal, or loss of a relationship with another brings about serious emotional impairment which mere physical care, however good it may be, will not prevent. (See Chapter 6.) The most significant disruptions of emotional development throughout later phases appear to be associated with object loss and thus indicate that in all periods of life, from the early developmental stage to the final one, object loss constitutes a serious and often dangerous threat to the self. When an important object is lost, there is an unconscious wish to give up object cathexis and to react further with an increase of narcissism; despite this tendency, however, even in the most narcissistic states, objects are still sought, although in greatly modified or pathological forms. A valued relationship, therefore, never seems to be entirely relinquished. It endures even though the means to secure or hold to it may change beyond ordinary recognition, as exemplified in the substitution with inanimate objects in early childhood or in the extreme to be observed in the common persecutory auditory hallucinations of psychotic adults in which the voices are recognizable as the parental figures [22].

Study of the intrinsic role accorded the object in the course of human development reveals that despite all that has been said about object relations, one aspect of the principle involved is often unnoticed: namely, that the principle of "constancy," stability, or homeostasis cannot be carried out as an independent operation in the human organism. Freud and those few authors following him who have written on the subject of homeostasis and the functions of the ego seem not to have questioned the hypothesis that the task of meeting the aim of constancy fell on the ego and its defenses and that the ego could not meet it alone. Descriptions of the aims toward a dynamic equilibrium that hold for all living creatures (expressed in the self-contained regulatory physiological mechanisms that facilitate achieving a balance) make clear that the ultimate goal in man is to achieve a reduction in tension, which is defined as the psychological aspect of disturbed homeostasis [12, 19].

Herbert Spencer maintained that equilibrium was the goal or aim of all evolution. His contemporary, Fechner, no doubt under Spencer's influence, arrived at a parallel psychological hypothesis [5]: decrease in mental tension is the goal; increases are felt as displeasure, decreases as pleasure. Freud needed only a short logical step to make this principle of constancy an important part of his own principles with regard to the functioning of the mind. From work in physiology, Cannon [2] too proclaimed the principle of homeostasis the maintenance of a dynamic equilibrium in all living tissue. Zipf [28] has viewed homeostasis as an economic device to make survival more certain. He thus does not contradict Cannon but puts forward his work as an extension of Cannon's, that all is directed at a conservation of effort making for stability, constancy, homeostasis, or the conservation of energy by the least work. When carried over into considerations of ego functions, for instance by Menninger [21] and others [12], the point is overlooked that for human beings the principle of stability or constancy, however defined, cannot function, meet its aim, goal, or termination, without a valued relationship to another person. The loss or absence or lack of an object or something that represents such a relationship precludes the achievement of stability. Hence the concept of homeostasis, the tendency of organisms to achieve this condition, is in man inseparable from an object relationship. Our entire conception of the organism striving toward constancy, however it may be applicable to man, must include an object in order to approximate its aims.

We know from common observation that the lack of an object is associated with discomfort. The younger the child, the greater is the dependence. The lack of an adequate relationship correspondingly fosters discomfort; relief is not available without a person or an object. The concept of homeostasis applied to man is coupled with a relationship to an object that provides care and thereby reduces tension. We may conclude that even on the most elemental level, a relationship to an object is indispensable to the operation of the principle of constancy as well as to survival. The most disrupted states of inconstancy and instability are observed in children who have been deprived of a relationship [25]. The lack of a valued object is throughout life associated with discomfort. This formulation does not suggest that discomfort always signifies the loss or deprivation of an object. It does, however, suggest that the loss of a meaningful object cannot take place without discomfort.

A sense of abandonment does not always go back to the child's beginning, for such an assumption would imply that the child had, at the outset or soon thereafter, some preconceptions of object relationships. There is nothing to suggest that this is the case. There is much to support the observation that, like many similar processes associated with relationships, the sense of abandonment evolves, develops, and prevails.

It remains to show some of the early forms that the dread of abandonment takes; the later forms are common enough to need no exposition here. A failure to provide for the neonate's pleasure or a neglect to relieve his discomfort would hardly mean abandonment to the baby. The infant requires care and it can sense neglect, as is demonstrated by ample clinical instances and common-sense observations. It is not likely that the young infant conceives of frustrating experiences as anything more than a lack of pleasure. However, to explain this developmental step, that is, the relationship of the infant to the mother, as relieving and satisfying, several writers have introduced into the mental life of the infant such concepts as good and bad objects; moreover, they imply that the infant moralizes over his mother. Such ideas, although having a certain popularity, tend to preempt development itself.

The absence of pleasure or the persistence of displeasure in turn plays a critical part in activating the constancy principle. It is this operation, in conjunction with a person or primitive object choice, which places the two in an inseparable association. The pleasure principle and an object relationship with narcissistic libido make a binding primary connection for the child upon which all subsequent experience is built. A child has no original sense of abandonment. To understand the dread of abandonment, one must realize that its origins rest in the three elements that are related to gratification — the child's need, the person or object, and the activated constancy principle. Pleasure, gratification, or reduction of tension is contingent upon the child's need being met by the person or object. The lack of the object and discomfort are but a short gap away from the anxiety and fear of being without the object. The dread of abandonment in its earliest form is the coalescence of discomfort unrelieved, the absence of the object, anxiety, and the child's inability, in the final analysis, to provide his own comfort and hence his own stability.

The child's experience of care is immediately so mixed with pleasure and the relief of discomfort and tension that to forgo it constitutes pain. In this way, perhaps, the pain-pleasure principle is introduced and with it inextricably bound, of course, is an object, upon whom the realization of the pleasure principle depends. The simplest care of the infant introduces the object. Here an archaic fundamental association, which remains throughout life, is formed: primitive object relationship, homeostasis, and pleasure principle. This means that object need and relief and the relationship of object loss to discomfort are imbedded deep and early in psychic development.

At no point in later life is physiology so closely related to mental functioning or to an object as in infancy. The early psychological disorders associated with object relationship typically reveal themselves in developmental emotional retardation, in physical dysfunction of sleep, and in gastrointestinal-tract disorders. The latter are the most common forms of emotional somatic disorder found throughout later life. This correlation in early childhood represents a prototype for the somatic effects that are commonly observed in adults who during and after grief develop clinical depression and insomnia, motor disturbances, and systemic disorders. Hypochondriacal complaints, characteristic in states of heightened narcissism, are in later life often associated with object loss. The prototype has been shown to exist in infancy. Clinical experience abounds in examples of the chaotic emotional states in which the aims of the activated constancy principle are wide of their mark when object relationships have been seriously impaired.

The tendency of all living tissue is to right itself. That

living creatures aim to establish an equilibrium led Freud to believe in the "dominance of the pleasure principle in mental life"; it also led to his hypothesis that the mental apparatus endeavors to keep the quantity of excitation present in it as low as possible, or at least it thus makes an attempt at constancy. Although this thesis is often taken as axiomatic, it remains, I believe, an incomplete statement. Man is in the unique position that the first principle of his mental functioning — that is, to find relief from tension is found in the tendency that aims at constancy — is directly associated with object relationship. Thus the need for an object enters into the development of mental functioning in such a way that the relationship to another person is part of that functioning. In man, therefore, the principle of homeostasis includes an object without which its aims cannot be achieved. The tendency toward constancy, the achievement of the pleasure principle, and the adherence to the reality principle, man cannot gain alone. He can succeed in these aims only through the society of another person.

We merely can speculate how early in the infant's life there occurs the dimmest recognition of his dependence upon another person for the relief of his discomfort from without and his frustration from within. The significant way in which this influence is expressed is seen in the first phase of development, in which being loved and cared for are most important and take precedence over loving. The person is indispensable, valued but not loved. When loss occurs, self-interest is heightened, a withdrawal of interest from the frustrating object takes place as well, and a readiness for a substitution occurs.

The inseparable association of lost self-esteem with abandonment comes only as some maturity of the ego takes place. In the earliest years this significant association does not make its appearance; instead we see that abandonment seems to evoke frustration, anger, and perhaps even hatred. When an object relationship is still regarded from the view of primarily relieving discomfort and satisfying need, and when love has but a small part to play, the aggressive instincts predominate. In the phases of emotional development which have yet to come, when the libido will have evolved sufficiently and significantly from narcissistic to object libido, familiar and distinct phenomena of mourning and depression can be seen to emerge with object loss.

Depression is the psychology of disappointment. A common and naïvely proposed assertion is that depression is a reaction to frustration, simple aggression or deprivation. Psychoanalytic studies of children who have experienced object loss, in fact or fantasy, through separation or deprivation, or in whom an adequate object relationship has failed to develop, have shown that the clinical picture is ruled by the infantile vicissitudes of aggression which are associated with unfulfilled expectations [17, 20]. When these governing elements include a severely self-critical faculty, depression ensues.

The child's commonplace equating of being left and being worthless does not depend solely upon the countless little circumstances of reality or upon desertion and separation. These incidents in early life evoke aggression, frustration, and hostile responses in the very young child. His tears and fury are directed toward those who frustrate or deny him his wishes. The devaluation of the self occurs in later development when the object itself is valued [6]. Then these same incidents, occasions, or circumstances come to represent abandonment. They evoke aggression and lead to sadism that turns on the self. The process can be observed in masochistic attacks. By directing hostility to the self, wishes to destroy the disappointing object may be avoided. The tendency to direct the aggression against oneself comes about when the object has assumed an importance beyond its nurturing functions. As the object begins to have more value, the self has correspondingly less. The implications are significant because, as the narcissistic libido gives way to a measure of object libido, with emotional development, the fantasies of being left or abandoned become equated with being worthless. In other words, a sense of worthlessness occurs only when the object that may be lost is worthwhile. The loss of a worthless object is the loss of a trifle. It evokes neither aggression, a sense of devaluation, nor masochistic attacks.

Man is the only creature who knows that death is his inevitable end. He acquires this knowledge remarkably early in life and he applies it not only to himself but also to the objects he has learned to depend upon. Thus, far from adding to the stability of his world, this insight makes for even greater uncertainty. The more clearly the child learns the plentiful facts of the instability of his world, the more uncertain the future seems. Ordinarily, all children learn these lessons very early and never forget them. How little is currently written about the influence that such insight brings to bear is thus all the more remarkable. Awareness of death is a viable idea in very young children, two to three years old, who still have only inadequately evolved sentiment, altruism, and pity. They are the "little sadists and animal tormentors" who fear they themselves may become objects of scorn and hurt [9]. And if we add to these convictions the awareness of dependence that a child has upon being cared for by an adult, the world of the child is more uncertain than it is stable.

A substantial basis for the dread of abandonment seems to be well established by experiences in reality as well as by dreams and fantasies. Aristotle, observing that man begins life in utter social dependence, called him a political animal who does not live on his own but in a society. Childhood is full of a need for people, and of fears of being left by them. There was never a child who did not need an adult, nor was there a child who did not fear losing an adult he had. It is axiomatic that this contention is the human condition. Freud [14] wrote that the weak and immature child's ego is permanently damaged by the strain of the child's efforts to ward off the dangers which are peculiar to that period in life; moreover, the child pays for the security of his parents' protection by the fear of losing their care and love, which he tends to equate. Hence, whatever disrupts a relationship represents an exposure to danger and evokes a sense of helplessness. The reaction continues throughout life. This "feeling [of helplessness] is not simply carried on from childhood days but is kept alive perpetually by the fear of what the superior power of fate will bring" [13]. If we couple this commonplace fear of what might happen and the apprehensions over being left or isolated to cope alone and helplessly with the demands of reality on the one hand, and the no less urgent inner forces of aggressive impulses on the other, two great inseparable fears that we harbor are joined: the dread that we shall be abandoned, and our fear of not surviving or death.

Substantial evidence indicates how man deals psychologically with fears of abandonment and death and the despair which is evoked. Vying against the comprehension of death, the durable knowledge that existence has its limits and that intolerable losses will be experienced, is the defense of denial. Before it enters into the service of some of man's highest aesthetic experiences, however, the use of the mechanism of denial is readily seen in the very young child. As a well-developed faculty the defense, through unconscious denial, deals with unpleasant realities. By its operation, a conviction of the fulfillment of wishes gains. Denial is thus perhaps the earliest defense to emerge in psychic development. It is also the most persistent. The denial of one's own dying, death, or inevitable death together with certain other irreversible vicissitudes of life, as a personal experience, seem to be a normal state.

It is inevitable that such primordial conflicts, which are actively conveyed throughout life, should find rich expression or lead to and utilize certain early mental mechanisms.

As indicated above, it is imperative and inevitable that a substitution for the lost object take place in the young child. In fact, if he cannot find such restitution in another person, inanimate objects are used, in part at least, to govern or control and to represent those who escape him [25]. In the older child, psychic development has carried him to the point where the significant relationships, the parental figures, are internalized objects of identification. He holds them within himself. They are a permanent part of himself. A loss of them or abandonment by them, in fact or in fantasy, is apt to take a different course than at an earlier period. Before, when the figures were given up, the child did what was done to him. He abandoned those whom he lost and took up with others. Now that he is older, he cannot relinquish these central figures as he previously might have done. The extent of the identification with them is also a measure of the tenacity with which they are held.

The difference between the earlier and the later period lies in the fact that with development narcissistic libido has been altered into object libido. Ego development is signified in this change. With this maturation taking place, the superego evolves. The growing superego is "not merely a deposit left by the earliest object-choices of the id," [12] but is a powerful institution that cannot be readily relinquished. Through it the object choices are retained. Hence, object losses and the dread of abandonment at this phase of development and throughout later life tend to direct the superego (associated with the objects) against the ego. (See Chapter 2.) The classic clinical examples are readily seen in depressions, which are characterized by "a cleavage between the criticising faculty of the ego and the ego as altered by the identification [superego]" [10]. The wish to rid oneself of the loss by disengagement from the object, as one might once have done in early childhood, unfortunately raises old antagonisms, frustrations, disappointments, and now guilt. This results in hostility and ambivalence to the objects. But the superego does not permit abandonment, since wishes to relinquish the objects are felt historically as dangerous and disloyal intentions. Hence conscience resorts to attacks on the self.

The internalized figures, that is, the personally important people, permanently imbedded in the matrix of the character, partly serve, among other functions, to insure against losses in reality as well as against hostility from within, whether conscious or unconscious. This appears at best to be only a partial solution. It is a fixation on the object in order never to be left alone or abandoned. The tendency to project and to transfer these internalized objects to outside ones seems to be in the service of maintaining an equilibrium by creating surrogates outside the self that represent the primary figures. Toward the same ends the mobile or labile libido of childhood becomes increasingly fixed in the process of maturation [14].

This important finding seems to bear out the theory that the fixation which takes place is in the development of object libido, and that this development in turn results in solidifying identification. The primary figures are thus secured against the vicissitudes that they are otherwise subjected to. Freud furnished from his own experience the classic example, in which a child invents a game wherein the absent mother is represented by a reel tied to a string. The child, by throwing the reel so that it disappeared and then pulling it back at will, encompassed and solved his problem temporarily. Freud [11] used this observation as an expression of the pleasure principle. In addition, this example shows that renunciation of an object which leaves the child is short-lived. If it occurs at all, it is no more than partial. The giving up is countered by a mechanism that holds the figure. Otherwise the game might have been simply to throw the reel; but keeping it tied and controlling its return are of central importance. The child cannot relinquish the object. Although, through his game, he seems to master his loss, he does so only by tying it to himself. There are countless illustrations of the same mechanism, not only in childhood but throughout life, in which figures who appear to be given up or lost are permanently held with bonds that are impervious to being severed.

Many studies verify the conclusion that severe loneliness, isolation, or separation from others can be tolerated only temporarily without profound psychic changes taking place, regardless of the phase of development or of the age at which they may occur. Probably loneliness does in fact occur as an intrinsic part of mental illness. One source of confirmation is found in the psychoses which develop in people undergoing an experience of enforced isolation; another, in the psychosis-like states induced experimentally, as states of loneliness, and states involving sensory deprivation [27]. The process of internalization of important objects, therefore, although serving a variety of ends, including that of not giving up objects, is of itself insufficient. The need to project and to transfer object relationships is equally indispensable toward retaining objects in reality.

An important discovery is to find similarities to ourselves in another person. The process begins very early in life. The young child may be observed to be actively searching for them in a prototype, his parents. We look for qualities in others to which we aspire, or that we possess and that we hope to find in others. The child is eager to take qualities from the adults who are important to him. The more nearly he can be like the adults, the closer he feels to them. Others having characteristics that are similar to those within himself make him feel less an alien, less strange. This process of identification is a lifelong process. In each phase of development it is important to rediscover that we are like others. Holding an identification that was important in one phase over to another, however, can be anachronistic. The following are two clinical fragments that illustrate this point: (1) The father who is eager to be home from work, who dismisses his occupation as merely an unpleasant means to the end of pleasure, should not be dismayed that his son finds no gratification in labor and seeks only fun and learns only with difficulty. He has a good identification with his father. (2) A young woman who adores her father is not content with being a housewife and mother. She still longs to fulfill her father's wish that she practice medicine as he does. He always hoped she would go to medical school. When she was a little girl, he went to great lengths to take her on his calls to see patients. He told her tales about his practice. He fostered her fantasies of being a physician. Her identification with her father was so satisfying that she was unable to be free of her childhood aspirations. Her large brood of children and a devoted husband have not served to make her give up her identification with her father. She has selected unconsciously which of her little daughters will become a physician. From an identification in the past and by a projection of it into the future, she hopes to find satisfaction that may take a generation to realize.

Similarities and identities with others are common qualities that are both conscious and unconscious. We transfer them to a variety of people. Some people bear the characteristics that we prize. Some are attributed qualities that are not present which we wished they possessed. Certain aspects of our identification we would deny, and others we would exhibit. When we couple what we project onto others with the identification that we form, we may become aware how this elaborate system of mental experiences binds us into relationships that have not only internal representation, but important external representation also. Both aspects operate to retain relationships.

Freud showed that even those processes which yield a pathological product — for example, a delusional formation — are "in reality an attempt at recovery, a process of reconstruction" [7]. As illustrative, Freud quotes Goethe's Faust, who, having uttered the curses that free him from the world, is immediately exhorted to remake it [7]:

> . . . more splendid
> Build it again,
> Build it up in thy bosom [7]!

Restitution, a process toward recovering a balance, may commonly be observed in restitution of an object by identification, or in the search for the idealized object as in Conrad's *Lord Jim,* described by Helene Deutsch [3]. We observe the use of projection as a defense against destroying a valued object. The destructive wishes are ascribed to the object instead of to oneself.

In a footnote in his "Ego Development and Certain Character Problems," Ives Hendrick wrote that there are certain economic gains in projection. The principal points that relate to our discussion of this phenomenon here are his comments that

. . . there is less anxiety associated with the idea of being hated by the object, than with the idea that the object will retaliate the subject's unprojected hostility. That is to say, the experience of hostility, and therefore the associated anxiety, is less intense when it is referred to an external agency than when it is perceived as one's own primary impulse. This may be due to the fact that projection accomplishes a division of mental presentations of the hostile impulse; . . . projection is a successful defense as long as it is incomplete, and the hostility is experienced as though originating both in the ego and the other person. This is supported by the fact that when projection is most complete, the intense anxiety of paranoid panic occurs [18].

From the considerations entertained here, a further conclusion may be drawn: the inability of the ego to tolerate the destruction of an object without itself being significantly affected.

Hendrick states in effect that the primitive ego depends upon projection as one of its principal defenses when it experiences frustration and hatred in its conflict with a primary object. In the process of development the object is incorporated and it thus becomes part of the self. As destructive fantasies and wishes are attached to this internalized object, a danger to the self is thereby brought about. The object, it is feared, may retaliate. As part of the self is threatened, a part of the self may attack. The indispensable and now incorporated object is on the one hand a source of gratification and hence pleasure, and on the other hand disappointing, a source of discomfort and a menace. There seems to be no final resolution to this conflict. As further organization of the ego takes place with development, identification with the object occurs. The development of identification with the object therefore precludes its destruction. The old enmity cannot be gratified without its representing an attack and even destruction of the object now incorporated. Self-attacks and self-destructive or sadistic tendencies directed at this part of the self are possible. The form appears manifestly as masochism. It represents the only possible partial solution. Identification with the object compels that existing hostility be taken out of consciousness, as a disquieting destructive element, by repression. Identification becomes a substitute. An affectionate object choice has succeeded the hostile aggressive attitudes which are now held in abeyance. But it has not replaced them. The importance of the object has been reinforced by repression of hostility, and consequently the preservation of the object has been further insured. This alteration in the character conserves the object [12]. An enforced peace with the id is thus partially achieved. In the metaphor of current affairs, coexistence rather than a permanent peace is made possible. The archaic conflict between the self and a significant, and therefore indispensable, object results in retribution to the self. The ego shows poor tolerance for supporting destructive wishes, especially when the identification with the object, while heightened, is at the same time threatened.

There are two generally well-known states of emotional disorder which best reveal how the ego is affected when hostile wishes, destructive impulses, and aggressive fantasies are directed toward a significant object. There is a wide variation of the symptomatology within each condition and between the two conditions. In respect to a loved object, they bear in principle a remarkable resemblance which has not been given enough attention and which has special importance here. In both conditions, when a previously loved object is believed to direct its criticism, reproaches, and hatred against one who loved, the sense of loss is experienced as a lowered self-esteem coupled with object loss and is perceived as love replaced by hostility. The anger, hostility, and frustration that are mobilized and accorded archaic power, destructive by its mere existence, reverse an affectionate object choice which, we noted, had previously succeeded hostile and aggressive attitudes. In order to arrive at an affectionate state toward the object, the ego disavowed criticism and reproaches, repressed hostility, and was thus able to love without censoring. The split in the ego, making alliances, so to speak, with both sides, is characteristic and moved Freud to remark:

The ego can take itself as an object, can treat itself like other objects, can observe itself, criticize itself, and do Heaven knows what with itself! In this, one part of the ego is setting itself over against the rest. So the ego can be split; it splits itself during a number of its functions — temporarily at least. Its parts can come together again afterwards [16].

Now all is reversed, the formerly loved one is the persecutor and demeans the self; this is expressed in "the lament of the paranoiac [which] . . . shows that at bottom the *self-criticism of conscience is identical with, and based upon, self-observation''* [8]. [Italics added.] In the clinical depression the *criticizing faculty of the ego is directed against the ego,* "so that the latter could henceforth be criticized by a special mental faculty like an object, like the forsaken object" [10].

In other words, we see that a return of anger, frustration, or hatred for a previously loved object results in a withdrawal of libido, heightened narcissism, a return of the repressed, unconsciously wished-for attacks by the object, a resurgence of hostile wishes and destructive impulses that had been repressed, and a stream of persecutory abuses directed at the self by one who was once loved. In these respects the two conditions, the paranoid and the depressed states, are indistinguishable. They both show, in ways that leave no room for doubt, that attacks on the previously loved object result in assaults on self-esteem, while heightened narcissism notably turns to support the ego; the superego has its sadistic aims satisfied by its severe self-criticizing faculty. Although the love object is rejected or reviled, it turns out nevertheless to be supported, while the ego is belittled and demeaned.

When attacks upon a loved object take place the relations between ego and superego appear to undergo changes. The superego is critical of the ego. There is an important difference, however, which occurs when the object choice and the self are of the same sex, as in paranoid conditions. The psychodynamic aspects of homosexuality need no elaboration here. But its importance lies in the fact that the narcissistic libido is heavily invested in identification with such an object — the ego ideal. In no other condition is the attack on an object more nearly an attack also upon the self as when it is directed toward a homosexual object. Aggressive wishes in such cases aim to destroy the ego ideal, that narcissistic aspect of the self which is most valued. This represents so serious a danger to the ego that it dissociates itself from such wishes toward a valued object and particularly toward one in its own image. Through repression narcissism is exaggerated; the ego disclaims its hostility and attributes it to the previously loved object. Its own anger is explained as a reaction to the hostile object that reviles and slanders the ego. Thus it appears that the characteristics of the object are internalized. Although the defenses that the ego finds useful under these circumstances are primitive, they can be understood as occurring in a highly organized ego that in the face of threatening conditions resorts to early developmental or immature forms as well as mature ones.

As Hendrick [18] shows, panic ensues when the balance of relations between the ego and the object is shifted in favor of predominantly destructive wishes without retaliation, or when the abuses are directed solely toward the object. This is a very useful observation in the study of the self and its objects. The self is then, it appears, in the greatest danger from its own attacks, which are often expressed as suicidal wishes and impulses. This suggests that to entertain destructive wishes toward a meaningful object cannot be endured. In the presence of such wishes the self must take the abuse even though its recourse is to project the source of hostility onto another. The object must be spared. Conservation of the object is an essential characteristic in all these conditions, even though often contradicted in the manifest content. To these ends, it seems evident that just as internalization is essential, so is its opposite: the externalization of the relationship. Were total internalization possible and then sufficient, it would perhaps prove to be satisfying, but then it would probably lead to isolation and would contradict rather than serve the ends of social need.

Hence, we take into ourselves the important figures not only to be like them but also to have them; then we set about finding their counterparts in others. In this way we retain in perpetuity the significant figures both within ourselves and in the world about us. Thus, the feelings of help-lessness and the early conflicts in relation to objects and their inconstancy are not simply carried over from child-hood but are kept viable throughout life. Those experiences which substantially contribute to form the sense of help-lessness and dependence are probably among the earliest organized concepts in man's existence. They sink their roots very early into the matrix of psychic development, and the dread of abandonment by an object is an invariable outcome. Hence the fear and the act of abandonment have in common fantasies of being lost and losing, of destruction and of aggression toward objects, of grief and of death.

These timeless problems are not basically cultural. They merely find different expression socially and culturally. Moreover, in principle, these differences are not significant. Joseph Campbell writes: "And why should it be that whenever men have looked for something solid on which to found their lives, they have chosen not the facts in which the world abounds, but the myths of immemorial imagina-tion?" [1]. The answer is that reality offers little comfort even though the lifeless things of the world are most permanent. Men do not relate themselves to things primar-ily, but to people, and to things only insofar as they represent people. The solidity of life evidently does not rest on *matériel*. It does depend upon relationships with other people. However strong they may be, they are nevertheless realistically temporal. To mitigate the risk of loss there appears to be a need for insurance which will provide against the catastrophe of irrevocable loss. Hedging the future with insurance regularly brings man to the market place as a trafficker in myths and fantasies to ease the afflic-tion of abandonment.

One of the most powerful, persistent, and timeless myths, paradise, found everywhere, serves to defend man against his deepest and earliest fears in relation to his objects. These defensive attempts have two aims. They are never really separate but, for convenience, may be described as if they were. The first is to protect oneself from having to abandon all that is cherished; the second is to quell the fear of death by a continuity of life. The individual's early infantile wishes of omnipotence to exercise control give way to the weight of reality. But later in psychic development life is linked to eternity, Earth is bound to Heaven. In this way the future may be foretold, its evil uncertainty is warded off, and the superior force of a precarious fate is mollified. In commonplace observation, the human condition of wishing to be together forever is a better way than singlehandedly to defend oneself against the dreaded outer world, and so is that of combining with the rest of the human community and taking up together the attack on nature and fate [13]. The paradisal existence tries to lift the oppressiveness of separation, loss, and death. A study of the paradise myth affords an excellent illustration. "We encounter the paradise myth all over the world in more or less complex forms . . . it has a certain number of characteristic elements, chiefly the idea of immortality. The entire religious history of man shows it" [4]. In the paradise myth, which rests entirely upon restitution, it is not left to the individual to work out his fate. His efforts being too puny, like the child's, it is left to the more superior beings and forces to take over. Abandonment and death are no longer separation but are, through myth, turned into just the opposite, a joining with others, with what is wished for, to be a chosen one or a chosen people. Thus, not only is immortality achieved but also a continuum from this world to the next, to the happy garden where our first parents lived. By giving up nothing really, by substitutes and surrogates, abandonment and loss are thwarted. This theme has countless variations which stretch from the present to prehistory.

It follows that the wish for another chance at life is expressed in the rebirth ritual, in the Resurrection, and is seen in the discovery of the Neanderthal skeletons interred with supplies for another life. The little Neanderthal child standing at the graveside would not experience the elementary idea (*Elementargedanke*) directly figured in mythology. Since it is rendered by way of local ethnic ideas or forms locally conditioned (*Völkergedanke*), we must take this process into account when looking for the general principle [1]. We do not know what mythological ideas were incorporated in the remote Mousterian-Neanderthal period of the Dordogne. The discovery of an individual interred in a small natural depression oriented east and west, accompanied by shells, some Mousterian flints, the remains of a woolly rhinoceros, horse, reindeer and bison [1], suggests that the mystery of death, the extreme in separation and abandonment, had been encountered. In short, then, a prodigious continuum has been identified, deriving in time at least from the Riss-Würm interglacial period, about 200,000 B.C. The daily task of dealing with death and the anxiety about an uncertain future had to be resolved by mastering a system of defenses against the importance of death, not the least of which is to develop a mythology of the continuity of life.

Throughout time and from first to last the conflicts of childhood are not simply delivered to adult life as recollections or associations of an uncertain and precarious past existence. They give a morphology to the foundation of a relationship to others, superior beings — the parental figures. As reality renders their proportions less colossal and their existence temporal, the conflicts remain. Further solutions are sought. First they are seen in the transference to others and then in the obeisance to the superior forces of the gods of man through whom his temporal nature is mitigated.

The profound effects of the experience of loss appear to have their roots in the dread of abandonment. Its beginnings are in the earliest relationship to a person that activates the never-ending principle of constancy or homeostasis. In man, unlike all other creatures, the degree to which an object serves these ends makes him forever dependent for his comfort upon a society of which he is a part and which becomes part of himself. One of the most civilizing influences is another person. When we cannot realize this political existence in fact, we reconstitute it in fantasy. In either case we do not allow ourselves to be alone.

In the child's emotional development, in which the formation of meaningful relationships is the principal psychic process, there rests the matrix of the dread of abandonment. The childhood fantasies of omnipotence and immortality, and the tenacious concern with origins and kinships, evolve in adult life into formal myths with a similar content. In these beliefs and in material accomplishments are found permanent defenses which help ameliorate both the inevitable experience of the dread of abandonment and the realization of external losses. In neither respect is there a stable solution. A constant modifying and developing of both material achievements and psychic defenses continues whose foundations reach into the earliest relations to the primary objects.

REFERENCES

1. Campbell, Joseph: *The Masks of God: Primitive Mythology* (London: Secker & Warburg, 1960), pp. 130, 324, 354.
2. Cannon, W. B.: *Bodily Changes in Pain, Hunger, Fear and Rage* (New York: Appleton, 1929).
3. Deutsch, Helene: The Character of Lord Jim, a Restitution Process. (Presented at Edward Bibring Memorial Meeting of the Boston Psychoanalytic Society and Institute, Inc., April 14,

1959.) In *Neuroses and Character Types,* by Helene Deutsch (New York: International Universities Press, 1965), p. 353.

4. Eliade, M.: The Yearning for Paradise in Primitive Tradition. Myth and Myth-Making. *Daedalus,* Spring, 1959, 255, 267.

5. Flugel, J. C.: *Studies in Feeling and Desire* (London: Duckworth, 1955), p. 116.

6. Freud, A.: Aggression in Relation to Emotional Development. In *The Psychoanalytic Study of the Child* (New York: International Universities Press, 1949), III–IV, 41.

7. Freud, S.: Psycho-Analytic Notes upon an Autobiographical Account of a Case of Paranoia. In *Collected Papers* (London: Hogarth Press, 1948), III, 457.

8. ———. On Narcissism: An Introduction. In *ibid.* (1948), IV, 53.

9. ———. Thoughts for the Times on War and Death. In *ibid.* (1948), IV, 296.

10. ———. Mourning and Melancholia. In *ibid.* (1948), IV, 159.

11. ———. Beyond the Pleasure Principle [1920]. In *The Complete Psychological Works of Sigmund Freud,* Standard Edition (London: Hogarth Press, 1955), XVIII, 14–15.

12. ———. *The Ego and the Id* (London: Hogarth Press, 1947), pp. 37, 44, 50.

13. ———. *Civilization and Its Discontents* (London: Hogarth Press, 1946), pp. 21, 29–30.

14. ———. *An Outline of Psychoanalysis* (New York: W. W. Norton, 1949), pp. 112, 24.

15. ———. Negation. In *The Complete Psychological Works of Sigmund Freud,* Standard Edition (London: Hogarth Press, 1961), XIX, 235.

16. ———. The Dissection of the Psychical Personality. In *ibid.* (1959), XXII, 58.

17. Hartmann, H., E. Kris, and R. M. Loewenstein: Notes on the Theory of Aggression, in *The Psychoanalytic Study of the Child* (New York: International Universities Press, 1949), XVI, 19, 21, 22, 26, 27; A. Freud: Aggression in Relation to Emotional Development, in *ibid.* (1949), III–IV, 39; B. Rank: Aggression, in *ibid.;* (1949), III–IV, 43–48; and M. S. Mahler: On Symbiotic Child Psychosis, in *ibid.* (1955), X, 200, 201, 211.

18. Hendrick, Ives: Ego Development and Certain Character Problems. *Psychoanal. Quart.,* 5 (1936), 329, footnote 2.

19. Kubie, L. S.: Instincts and Homeostasis. *Psychol. Med.*, 10 (1948), 15.

20. Mahler, M. S.: On Symbiotic Child Psychosis. In *The Psychoanalytic Study of the Child* (New York: International Universities Press, 1955), X, 200, 201, 211.

21. Menninger, K.: Psychological Aspects of the Organism under Stress. Part I. Homeostatic Regulatory Functions of Ego; Part II. Regulation Devices of Ego under Stress. *J. Amer. Psychoanal.* 2 (1954), 67, 280.

22. Modell, A. A.: The Theoretical Implications of Hallucinatory Experiences in Schizophrenia. *J. Amer. Psychoanal. Ass.*, 6 (1958), 475.

23. Rank, B.: Aggression. In *The Psychoanalytic Study of the Child* (New York: International Universities Press, 1949), III–IV, 43–48.

24. Rochlin, G.: Disorder of Depression and Elation. *J. Amer. Psychoanal. Ass.*, (1953), 438–457.

25. ———. Loss and Restitution. In *The Psychoanalytic Study of the Child* (New York: International Universities Press, 1953), XVIII, 288–309.

26. ———. The Loss Complex: A Contribution to the Etiology of Depression. *J. Amer. Psychoanal. Ass.*, 7 (1959), 315.

27. Zilboorg, G.: "Loneliness," *Atlantic Monthly,* January, 1938, 45–55.

28. Zipf, G. E.: *Human Behavior and the Principle of Least Effort* (Cambridge, Mass.: Addison-Wesley Press, 1949).

2

THE LOSS COMPLEX

Like anxiety, despair is neither a disease nor a disorder, yet it is the commonest ill that mankind suffers. It may last for long or short periods. The sufferer may recover fully. But he may also experience as an aftermath an unrelieved depression or a brief period of elation that appears simply as being in good spirits. Careful psychoanalytic investigation shows that in onset, content, and its disappearance, everyday fleeting moments of despair — usually unnoticed clinically — have the same basis as the serious disorders, the clinical depressions, that they resemble and which they may herald. They do not last so long or necessarily remove the sufferer from reality, but otherwise, even in the course of recovery that they follow, are identical.

Despair in its clinical dimensions is known as melancholia. While the symptoms of depression were sufficiently well known to the Greek clinicians of antiquity to prompt Aristotle to describe both Plato and Socrates as being of a "melancholic temperament" [20], it was only in this century that Freud penetrated beyond its description and classification to the psychodynamics. He made the major contribution to understanding the etiology of depression. It is his definition that generally prevails.

At first, depressive states were considered adult disorders. The development of psychoanalysis brought with it many studies of depression. But the psychoanalytic studies of adults indicated that the origins predated adult years.

Some psychoanalysts have suggested that pathological depression affects very young children as well as the aged. The focus of research has naturally been shifted to the youngest subjects, by which it is hoped that the issue of etiology, genesis, and onset would be clarified. Despite extensive clinical experience, the chronology of the psychic processes in depression is still very elusive. A question of central importance, which has a bearing on emotional development as well as on the evolution of depressive states, has given rise to a great deal of speculation in psychoanalysis: How early in psychic development does a clinical depression appear?

It is the purpose here to show that clinical depression, whose "distinguishing mental features are a profoundly painful dejection, abrogation of interest in the outside world, loss of capacity to love, inhibition of all activity and fall in self-esteem" (which is how we understand the disorder psychoanalytically), does not occur in childhood [7]. Central to this problem is the universally regarded trauma, the experience of loss. This is true only in the narrowest and most oversimplified definition, however. In fact, the experience of a meaningful loss produces a highly organized sequence of reactions and manifestations, and a particular effect upon behavior. When all these consequences of a loss are taken together, they are best understood as a *loss complex*.

The *loss complex* probably shows itself in its simplest form as an expression of a universal fear in man, the dread of abandonment. This has its beginnings with the infant's dimmest recognition of its dependence upon another person, or object, for the relief of its discomfort from without and its frustration from within. It then advances to the even more complex responses related to the child's recognition of his utter dependence upon an object. It is very likely that the impelling emotional need and incentive to mastery and maturation find a constant source of impetus in the fear expressed in the defenses that are primed against dependence. The fears of dependence manifest themselves in various ways at different phases of emotional development. They produce profound changes. The alterations that come about tend to have a lasting effect, although they are not necessarily the same from one period of development to another. Children do become sad, grief-stricken, and dejected. They thus appear to present some of the features of depression in their behavior, as their experience with losses will show. They may also revile themselves. But these reactions in young children before the superego is formed with the "passing of the oedipus" do not lead, as they will later, to depressive states, which by definition are beyond the "preoedipal" child's development.

A unique mental content present in clinical depression, which on close examination reveals a specific unconscious conflict, was defined by Freud in 1917. He wrote in his classic paper, "Mourning and Melancholia," that "mourning was regularly the reaction to the loss of a loved person or the loss of some abstraction which has taken the place of one such as fatherland, liberty, an ideal and so on. As an effect of the same influences, melancholia instead of a state of grief develops in some people" [7]. When a loved person or some abstraction has been lost (and it will be shown in later chapters that similar reactions prevail with any loss) the reproaches harbored against the loved object become turned into self-reproaches. "Thus the shadow of the object fell upon the ego." The self-critical faculty or the superego now in conflict with the ego is the "key to the clinical picture." This is the core or the key, as Freud called it, to clinical depression. In the vast subsequent literature on the psychodynamics of depression, neither his empirical observations nor his interpretations based upon them have been fundamentally improved upon. The noteworthy contributions by others to the subject have used Freud's work as a basis.

The most significant feature of depression is the sense of loss, whether in fact or fancy, and its psychic effects at whatever age or phase of development. Although there are other constant findings, none are as essentially significant as the experience of loss. Clinical experience compels us to look for loss where we find depression. But does the opposite hold as well — do we find depression regularly as a reaction to loss? There appears to be less doubt when such a problem is posed about the adult than about the child patient. Some form of mourning or grief over the loss does occur, and in certain instances melancholia or even absence of overt grief [3] may develop as a reaction. The evidence is clear enough, derived as it is from extensive analytic investigation of adults. The child's reaction to loss has not been studied thoroughly. There is a tendency to assume that what experience has shown to be true of adults applies also to children. (This leads to the frequent assertion that the adult disorder is present in the child.) The basis for such assumptions is derived from the inference that a young child's behavior, resembling in some respects those of adults in depression, must therefore harbor the conflicts common to adults. But the content of the child's conflicts that would bear out the inference has not, as a rule, been either studied or demonstrated. Those who believe that the young child suffers clinical depression as a result of object loss apparently do not take into account that a child in the preoedipal level of development cannot at that time develop from a portion of the ego, the superego, the self-critical faculty that is necessary to the psychodynamics of depression. Nor have they explained how the disorder can appear without regard to the mechanisms necessary to produce it to the level of the patient's psychological maturity.

A substantial reaction to loss seems hardly to have importance unless it carries with it another normal characteristic, an identification with that which is lost. Even if what is lost is but an abstraction like freedom, or some symbol

representing what is valued, or a part of one's body or
changes in the body as in the loss of function (see Chapter
7), it is the identification which bestows a value and thus
makes an object (or what represents one) a part of the self
which, when forfeited, gives importance to what we lose.
Losses are commonplace experiences. What gives them
their added significance and poignancy is that, by making
what we value a part of ourselves, we invariably and unconsciously have invested it with our narcissistic interest. With
that increased commitment, losses have profound effects
that are dictated in large measure by the extent of the narcissistic involvement associated with them.

The following incident is an illustration of a severe reaction to a seemingly trivial loss. The irrationality of the
response lies in the narcissistic element that is clearly ex-
hibited. A young woman was precipitated into a serious
episode of pathological depression when a well-meaning,
fastidious photographer removed an inconspicuous mole
from her new portrait. She became deeply concerned over
its loss despite the fact that she admitted the mole was un-
attractive. The paradox was resolved when it became clear
from the analysis of her rage at the photographer that by
removing her mole, even though only in the picture, he had
taken away a part of her as if he were a surgeon, and that
she had lost an important member. The loss of the mole was
significant only in what it represented. It was a part of an
unconscious identification with a beloved father. Removal
of the mole brought about a reactivation of the fantasy of
being mutilated. The photographer had castrated her. She
was horrified at her injury and depressed, not simply at the
loss of the mole, nor at being unmanned. What had happened
to her meant a loss of her identification with her father.
Her narcissism was in a central role in the relationship.

In an earlier publication [13], I attempted to show some
effects of a serious object loss with its attendant problems
of identification in early childhood. A normal, healthy boy

in the latter half of his first year had been left, through unfortunate circumstances, in the care of servants who were indifferent to his emotional needs. The best physical care was lavished on him for two years. The mother, because of her enforced frequent absence, remained a lost figure even after she resumed his entire care nearly two years later. By this time, he had developed a type of disorder that has been variously described as autistic, or atypical, or schizophrenic, or "primal" depression. More significant than this variety of classifications was the effect of the object loss and the attempts of the child's ego at restitution through a series of archaic forms of identification.

Freud in one of his most important papers, "On Narcissism" [9], showed the way in which object loss may be compensated by heightened narcissism. It has been generally assumed that this reaction would adequately make up for the loss. In other words, some equilibrium is unconsciously attempted and it is believed to be achieved this way. Further clinical experience, as indicated in the case just described, suggests that increased narcissism is inadequate to the task and that object cathexis is still sought even though in a modified or pathological form. Noteworthy was the apparent inability of the ego to content itself with heightened narcissism. An object to be identified with, albeit an inanimate one, was still necessary. I attempted to show that taking oneself as an object characteristically meets only some of the narcissistic wishes. But a more significant, and a neglected, essential consideration is that the need to have an object is ineradicable.

This basic concept of Freud's has in some respects been taken for granted, perhaps because the more obvious response of the individual shows a heightened narcissism, overshadowing the other. Analysts have been inclined to overlook that in such patients the necessity for object relations, even when an object is relinquished manifestly, is not met altogether by taking an increased interest in oneself, that is, by taking oneself as an object, which leads to the exaggerated narcissistic reaction. An extreme example may be taken from psychotic patients who seem to have divested themselves of everyone in reality. Their hallucinations may be observed to be an expression of object relations in which the restitution for lost figures is regained, albeit in a bizarre fashion [15]. It appears that the effort to establish object relations is so inherent a human characteristic that even when the disturbance in the ego is so great, through object loss, as to produce the most regressive forms of response we know, psychosis, the need for establishing a relation to an object is not actually relinquished, as is generally assumed.

It seems that the young child exists exclusively in relation to an object, and that it is one of the central functions of the ego to sustain this relationship. One of the chief ways to do it is by the process of identification. When this process is seriously interfered with, as by separation or loss, the child does not continue alone. He appears often to do so, but closer examination reveals that this is not the case. He finds some representation of the lost object to make restitution for his loss. He may often choose an inanimate object, such as his mother's fur coat, over which he can exercise control, and by the substitution hopefully mitigates the risk of deprivation [13].

The first such scientific observation was Freud's upon his grandson when the child's mother had left him briefly in the care of his illustrious grandfather, during which time the child played out the mother's going and returning [8]. Freud's interest in what he observed was that the child's game to retrieve his mother was an expression of the pleasure principle. It also marked the beginning of the era when a child's play could no longer be regarded as without unconscious meaning. Moreover, the episode has historical significance because it is the first study of object loss in a young child by a psychoanalyst. Another important aspect of this episode is that it illustrates a facet of the process of identification. Elsewhere, Freud refers to the demands that pleasure makes in the same way that he referred to objects: ". . . we never can relinquish anything; . . . When we appear to give something up, all we really do is to adopt a substitute" [6].

In a child the immediate reactions to loss are often the usual ones, such as howling to get back what is gone. But the manifest symptoms in the child characteristically are temporary. The permanent effects are less easily seen, and in a child what is not in evidence is not usually searched for by the adult. It is not readily accessible. Moreover, the child easily dissembles his "griefs and discontent." The processes in relation to object loss and identification in infancy are most rudimentary. They are difficult to discern. It seems that withdrawal from living objects does take place. The infant produces this reaction as the adult often does. The adult, however, through a differentiated ego, has many more resources with which to respond to a loss; the child does not have such an elaborate and complex structure. The young child may commonly withdraw from others and develop its libidinal attachment toward inanimate objects instead. Retardation in development — that is, an arrest of executant functions of the ego — and the relinquishment of previous ego achievements are often observed in the form of regression. Although such processes may provide gratification, they do not replace what is lost. The need for the object is not any less, although that has been thought to be the case because of the manifest withdrawal. On the contrary, the heightened narcissism in such children indicates that the need is greater rather than less, but the means to satisfy it are lacking. The craving for the object, no longer able to take its usual course, often takes a bizarre one. In the case of the boy left without his mother for two years, a restitution of the mother was gained through rubbing her fur coat. The child gave her up ostensibly, and became attached to her coat instead.

Object loss in the young child finds expression manifestly in withdrawal, often with regression and a disorder in the process of identification. Instead of looking for signs of pathological depression, it appears more fruitful to follow the process of identification in relation to the loss. The younger the child, the more severe may be his withdrawal on experiencing an object loss. Consequently regression in the young child serves as an index of the narcissistic reaction. As identification with inanimate objects increases, the identification process becomes distorted.

Object loss and the process of identification in a later phase of psychic development are illustrated by the following clinical example. A young mother brought her three-year-old girl for treatment because the child had severe temper tantrums and was difficult to bowel-train. The mother was an obsessional type, and the uncontrolled, anal behavior of her child was especially distressing to her for obvious reasons. The early phase of the child's analytic play sessions was characterized by controlled and organized behavior. Much of the little girl's play was thinly disguised sadistic behavior that alternated with exhibitionism. She made every effort to be admired. Some time later she abandoned herself to reveal her underlying conflicts. She found in the playroom a book with a child's picture on the front cover. She threw the book to the floor and made the noise of a flatus over it. I suggested she could do as she wished with the book. She threw it about the room, then kicked it, jumped on it, bit it, said that it stank. She sat on it and continued to pretend to emit flatus-like sounds, spat on it, said it was no good, bad, that it smelled. She grunted as if she were having a stool over it, meanwhile shouting that she hated the book. She would not stop until virtually exhausted, even though I would plead with her that the child in the picture was not really so worthless as she insisted.

The play abated only when she had destroyed the image by reviling it. On later occasions she played more directly, with a doll, saying she was the mother and hated the child. When I attempted to modify her statement to the effect that perhaps she was only angry because the child was not obedient, she said, "No! I am the mother and I hate her, I just hate her." Many other hours indicated in similar fashion how the child wished to be dirty and deserved to be hated. She would swallow large quantities of air and belch them up, waiting for my disapproval. She would smear and soil herself until she was covered with dirt, expecting me to be as disgusted with her as her mother often would be.

A commonly held misconception would suggest that the child was identified with the excrement and was rejected forthwith by an obsessional, overly clean mother who had an abhorrence for dirt. It is true that the mother was neurotically concerned with cleanliness, but also that the child, identified with this facet of the mother's character, loses her own approval when she wishes to be, and is, dirty. As the clean mother that she is identified with, she reviles and attacks herself. As the dirty creature that she also is, she loses the good will of the mother, whose wishes she does not meet. It is by the identification with the obsessional mother that she attacks herself on the one hand, and then partially retains the object on the other. This is an example of object loss in which the identification with the object is rather complete: that is, the object is an ideal whose wishes are not met and whose hatred is incurred. The object is thus lost and regained. But the behavior is directed at the same time toward the object outside (the mother) as well as toward the self. This ordinary case shows that clinical depression does not set in when object loss has occurred, even at a phase of development later than that in the case previously cited, despite the fact that a feeling of worthlessness is present with self-denigrating acts and an ambivalent relationship to the object which are classic criteria for adult depression.

Another child, a girl, approximately the same age, was characterized as being closely "tied" to her mother. The child would become violently ill as soon as the mother left her. She was very destructive in her play at home. The mother was an infantile, hysterical woman who was very dependent upon her own mother; she was clinging to her passive husband upon whom she made infantile demands. After this child was briefly studied, her play showed that she believed babies have to be good and that if not good they should be thrown out. When I said this shouldn't happen because the baby would be frightened, she said it had to be: "The mother wants something to happen to her and wants to punish her." No amount of pleading on the baby's behalf would alter the baby's fate. When I suggested that the mother made the baby angry, "No," she retorted, "she made the mother mad." The child said, "The baby gets sick because it is bad, she ought to get sick. She is wanted only if she is good."

The early agoraphobic behavior of the child no doubt expresses her enormous hostility and thus her ambivalence toward the mother. But at the same time a deep attachment is present that produces a strong identification on the one hand, and a constant threat of loss from her own hostility toward the mother on the other. The mother is an object hated and devalued, but at the same time valued and identified with. The mother had abandoned the child to the grandmother and rejected her for not being good and for being so aggressive.

This child, like the previous one, reviles and attacks herself, feels that she is worthless, hates herself, develops a type of common defense wherein the mother is depicted as excessively good and the child as correspondingly bad. Self-accusations are coupled with an object that is hated and yet identified with as good. The child feels that the needed object is lost, but then restores it by identification with it.

The foregoing examples show that with a loss of affection or of a loved person a fall in self-esteem occurs and the reproaches against the loved object are shifted onto the child's own ego [7]. A narcissistic relationship to the object and heightened ambivalence are present in all aspects to a greater or lesser degree. The critical difference between the cases cited appears to be in the period of emotional development at which the object is lost. This, in turn, shows the affects upon the process of development in which identification takes place. In other words, loss at the earliest phases of development evokes a reaction in which the ego fails to adequately differentiate, that is, to mature. Such experiences hamper development. When the loss of an object occurs in a later phase of ego development, the reaction differs but also hampers maturation.

There is a type of disorder which seems to occur particularly in boys.[1] The children in a group studied were generally between two and five years old. The commonest complaint was that they were hyperactive. Some of them seemed to have been overactive from birth. The mother, in a few instances, claimed that the child had seemed to be overactive *in utero* and continued to be overactive thereafter. Others complained that the activity began as soon as the child started to walk, whereupon he began to run and had been doing so ever since. The mothers were constantly tormented by the activity, which did not abate from one day to the next or from one year to another. Another characteristic was the children's unalterable destructiveness as a way of life. All the games and relations with objects, whether in fact or fantasy, were destructive and sadistic. There seemed to have been no period in the child's life in which hatred, destruction, and sadism did not play a major, conscious

[1] Based on studies conducted at The James Jackson Putnam Children's Center, Roxbury, Massachusetts.

role, let alone an unconscious one. The child in his play, in his expressions, and in his ruminations always depicted himself as being bad and correspondingly hated the parents, especially the mother. Identifying himself with her as bad, he was preoccupied with playing this out in his games of destruction. The object was always being lost or destroyed and he was being abandoned. The father, often an object of abuse by the child, was a man whose passivity was strikingly prominent. There was no contentment; the play was given up only through exhaustion and revived again as soon as recovery from fatigue took place.

One boy, aged three and a half, illustrates this behavior in a characteristic way. When his mother would bring him, he seemed to be dangling from her hand as she gripped him, while he was tugging and shouting, often cursing as she was threatening him with whatever punishment sprang to her mind at the moment: for example, that she would beat him, strap him, send him away, or lock him up. Her threats often brought out abusive, vulgar, anal language from the boy. He would be released or tear himself away and come rushing into my office. Week after week he made a shambles out of it, pulling things off shelves, throwing toys against the walls, spilling and stumbling about the room, playing momentarily with a toy and then tearing it to pieces. Everyone and everything seemed to be bad: father, mother, himself; toy cars, soldiers, clay — whatever he played with was dashed to the floor as no good or slammed into the wastebasket. If he ate candy I gave him, it too was bad and he smeared it into his face. When he played with clay, he fashioned it into stools, shrieked that it "smelled," and threw it out. Everything about him was vile; what he was related to or a part of was equally worthless. The child was in a constant state of losing his object, but since it was a bad one, and yet the principal object for identification, the process of loss and restitution continued.

There were, of course, individual variations between one

child and another, but as a group their similarity was striking. The relationship to objects was characteristically destructive and sadistic, aggressive without any respite, and the same impulses were directed toward the self, which was typically devalued, denigrated, and pronounced worthless.

On the basis of these and previous studies [13, 14], it appears that object loss and a hated narcissistic relationship with an object, in the young child, have led to no behavioral picture which corresponds to clinical depression. Although many of the same psychological elements as those of clinical depression in adults are clearly in evidence, they do not seem to produce this common disorder in young children. So far, the clinical examples cited deal with object loss in fantasy and in the unconscious. Unfortunately, there is no dearth of instances which illustrate what develops when the losses are more realistic.

The immediate loss of a loved or central and important object, or even an abstraction like liberty or an image of oneself, is often followed by grief or mourning and in some cases by melancholia. Although this is true for adults, there seems to be some question as to what effect such a misfortune has upon a child. A study of young children who have had acute recent losses is not an altogether new effort. Anna Freud and Dorothy Burlingham have described some of the effects of separation or object loss on very young children during World War II when children were evacuated from London. They found that regression was the outstanding characteristic. "Regression occurs while the child is passing through the no-man's land of affection, i.e., during the time the old object has been given up and before the new one has been found"[5].

The observations of Freud and Burlingham that regression is one of the more immediate effects of loss have been confirmed. It seems to be a constant finding in both the young and the old, and occurs far more often than is generally recognized. Naturally, it will be more apparent in the young. However, regression is not the only process involved.

Another significant difference between the young child and the adult which may be commonly observed, but neglected as a subject of study, is the rapidity with which regression and fixation take place in the young. Obviously, the explanation lies in the disparity of their emotional development, which specifically means that the child's superego, unlike the adult's, is not yet a developed function, nor at this time are the ego defenses set as they will be later. Therefore, when a child experiences a loss, the effect is very different from the effect on an adult of the loss of a loved person, or an abstraction that has taken the place of one, or an ideal that represented one and that has been lost.

For the young child, the needed object is neither abstracted nor transformed into an ideal, nor is the needed object internalized and thus made an essential part of the self. These aspects of character formation must await the further development which comes with the process of a more complete identification with the loved object, from which there will begin to emerge the ego ideal and the superego. The young child's narcissism will then have been sufficiently forfeited to deflect its aims from primarily self-gratification to efforts at satisfying another person or an ideal. This process, which involves "the formation of the ideal, increases the demands of the ego and is the most powerful factor favoring repression" [9].

The experience of loss regularly calls on regression. When the repressive forces are not fully developed, regression and fixation are readily resorted to as our experience and study of the child, and the work of Freud and Burlingham [5], reveal. In point of fact, adults whose repressive defenses are not strongly developed, or who are subjected to severe conditions of loss and deprivation, show readiness, like the child, to regression and to levels of early fixation as a reaction to loss. It is significant that the incompletely developed superego in the child experiencing a loss permits, on the one hand, a quick necessary replacement of objects, expressed as a ready tendency to accept substitutes, and on the other hand contributes to rapid regression and fixation. The child's ego thus makes restitution for its losses more quickly and directly than the adult's. The young child's frailty is compensated in defending itself against object loss by the swiftness with which it can institute a replacement.

The more pathological children, the "autistic," "atypical," so-called schizophrenic types, turn to inanimate objects to replace their losses, like the child who chose his mother's fur coat as a substitute for her. They probably do so no more than other young and deprived children may, but they are conspicuously different in the uncompromising way in which they adhere to their inanimate objects. They show a corresponding inability to establish a relationship with another person, even when one may have once existed. There seems no inclination to revive a previous relationship or to form a new one. Once the renunciation of others has been made, the relations that are sought seem to be exclusively narcissistic, and none of the narcissism is forfeited for the sake of another person. Little deviation appears. This clearly shows the parsimony of narcissism.

An adult, having a more fully developed superego, holds to a lost loved object with a greater tenacity than a child. Neither restitution nor substitution for the lost object is desired or pursued as readily by the adult as by the child. The forfeit of narcissism to the loved object, now lost, may have been so great as to leave the adult inconsolable. His need to strengthen narcissism as a defense results from the loss. It has been observed to be similar to that of the child, whose narcissism rules early object relations. It alters only slowly. Narcissism also governs those adults whose ego development in respect to object relations has not been significantly modified from the egocentricity of an earlier period. The infantile vanity in such adults betrays the narcissistic quality of their relationships.

A further phenomenon in children, not so easily observed as regression, is identification with the lost object. We know that making objects a part of oneself is both an early and a deep process, and also that it is subject to development. Hence, losses when one is young should affect the process of identification in one way, and when they occur later, affect it in another. It is by object relations that the principal psychic development of childhood takes place. We have observed clinically that in the young child, when this process is seriously disrupted, ego development is correspondingly impaired. In later phases of childhood, an object loss impairs superego development and its functions.

Some colleagues [17, 18] and I have had a common experience in recent years. We have studied children in pre-oedipal, oedipal, and latency phases who have suffered a severe acute object loss.

Direct analytic studies of children who have experienced serious object loss have not been reported except for one case of a five-year-old boy. The chief emphasis in this instance was on the failure of the oedipus complex to be resolved as a result of the father's death a year earlier [16]. Meiss could draw no further conclusions from her clinical material than that the boy's emotional development had been affected so that an "analysis was essential to a normal resolution of the oedipus complex" [16]. In the period since Meiss's report, the subject of object loss in children has received scant clinical psychoanalytic exposition even though problems of separation, depression, and mourning in infants have been given considerable study in recent years. Active controversy has arisen that is focused on theoretical concepts and terminology rather than on fresh clinical data derived from actual psychoanalytic studies of children [1].

Object loss through the death of a parent or a sibling is a

relatively common experience in childhood. The following account shows the effect upon two sisters of their encounter with a sudden death. An eight-year-old girl and her five-year-old sister were in a motor accident with their parents. The father was instantly killed. The mother suffered injuries from which she steadily recovered. The children were unharmed but they were emotionally disturbed and within a short period the mother and her two children were studied. Until the accident the older child, developing as an intelligent, competent little girl, was in a fierce and unremitting rivalry with her sister and mother for the father, in which she did not feel herself to be successful. She seemed rarely to be other than a morose, cheerless child, who was disgruntled and complained often and bitterly. Little seemed to suit her. Following the accident she would not mention her father's death, and the principal reaction to be noted was that she had stopped her old complaints, took increasing pride in her competence, and became more independent than she had ever been. Her younger, warmer, affectionate sister cried and became more "babyish" as the older one "matured."

The older sister showed in her therapeutic play that she was in a rage at being dependent upon the mother, and also that she felt she was not good and would not be loved and therefore would be abandoned. Turning this around, the child said to the objects she played with, "I'll kill you if you don't love me. If you make me lose you, I'll hate you." She then turned these attacks on herself out of conscience. She became increasingly strict with herself as she developed an unconscious satisfaction in fighting against the regressive wishes, which gave way to the mastery of control that was excessive. Her obsessional characteristics, such as orderliness, organization, and ritual, became intensified. In her superego development lay the solution to the trauma of loss. Superego development seems to have been promoted even though there were many regressive wishes expressed in her fantasied play. There was also an intensification of her rivalry with her younger sister who collapsed into re-gressive behavior under the effects of the trauma.

But no indication of the *sine qua non* of depression was in evidence during the two years she was studied. Depres-sion did not develop. She restored the father's wishes for her — identified with her father in this way. She fought her younger sister, whose regressive behavior represented wishes she deplored in herself, but which were her own repressed wishes. The fear expressed in her play was that her mother would hate her if she was not good enough. Superego functions were consolidated further to meet this fear and thus to gain her mother's praise. She now identi-fied herself with her mother more successfully than before, thus completing a strong double identification.

It appears to be significant that the younger child showed in her behavior and in her therapeutic play her sadness, grief, and loss by regression to helplessness and infantile oral erotism — she became "babyish," as her dead father had often encouraged her to be — while the older sister went into an opposite mode of behavior. Both children car-ried out what they supposed to be the dead father's wishes. The younger sister, because of the father's death, lost part of what is destined to be her superego. By contrast, the older one, in a later phase of psychic development, showed a readiness to reinforce her superego when a part of it is in danger of being lost. The older sister responded in a way which is characteristic of superego formation that is reach-ing maturity. The younger sister took an opposite course that impedes it.

The importance of object loss in those periods which follow early infancy, in terms of the phase of psychological development in which it occurs, has been given remarkably little study. Studies of the effects of separation of an infant from a mother have been numerous in the decades since World War II. The effect upon the infant may in part be judged from observation but, of necessity, much must be inferred. When data are meager, speculation tends to be rich. For reasons that are not clear, the wealth of clinical material that children, beginning with those three years old, would provide for studies of object loss has generally been neglected.

When the focus is changed from studies of infants to older children, there is an inclination to put together a conventional catalogue of signs and symptoms of depression. They are usually related to grief rather than representing a work on the dynamic conflicts, associated with loss, that are present and which effect basic aspects of development.

We have seen, for example, that a young child's loss of her father represents not only a deprivation of an important object relationship, but also, very specifically, the loss of a part of what is to be shaped into a significant mental structure. While there will be other sources that she may call upon to make restitution for that part of the superego she loses as a consequence of her father's death, until she does accomplish it, her proclivity to regression and fixation will be her source of gratification. The older child experienced the same misfortune but its occurrence coincided with a period in development when the superego is typically severe, which she shows to be the case. She draws strength from it to obviate the threat of succumbing to the regressive wishes she sees her sister acting on. The reaction she has to the increased strictness of her superego is that it carries her further along into latency; she is hence nearer to sublimating the wishes that she wanted to carry out but which her superego would not condone. The father's death seemed to have promoted this daughter's development, while the younger one was affected in the opposite direction.

Neither child could be said to be depressed or melancholic, although they had suffered the loss of a loved object. It might be argued that the matrix of the relationship to

their father was not pathological to begin with, and therefore the reaction to his death was not a disordered one. But
this would be a rationalization *post hoc*. Both children show
their characteristic narcissistic object relationship to him,
their ambivalence, their infantile identification with certain
aspects of a father who wished and encouraged one child to
free herself of him, which she took to mean in part rejection, and the other to be more dependent, which the younger
child understood as an encouragement to infantilism. These
are the considerations which usually are taken into account
in the etiology of depression and melancholia. Neither of
these children, nor the others who have been cited here, can
be said to show a depressive state.

The onset of typical depression and melancholia beginning in adolescence and adult life is a phenomenon common
enough to require no exposition here. It is important, however, to note that depression or melancholia although not as
frequent a finding in adolescence, as it is in adult life,
occurs as a clearly defined entity. Perhaps the intensification of the conflicts of narcissism during this period plays
as critical a role in the emergence of this disorder as it does
in others that occur during the adolescent phase of development.

An attempt to consider the development of depression
would indeed be incomplete without comments on mania or
elation. Interest in mania or elation is probably as old as
interest in despair. However, clinical studies of the elations
are scarce compared with the voluminous studies on the
depressions. It is of interest that although depression in
childhood has received considerable attention in recent
years [19], elation and mania get no reference. As far as I
can determine, no clinical analytic work on the subject of
mania in children exists. I have never seen a case myself.
Such extensive bibliographies as Fenichel's [4] and the
thoroughness of Lewin's work [12] fail to reveal that
mania exists in childhood. The twenty years of publication

of *The Psychoanalytic Study of the Child* since 1945 disclose no single clinical work or theory referring to mania or elation in childhood. Sadness, grief, or even temporary depressive episodes occur in childhood but children evidently do not become elated, just as they do not become depressed in the clinical sense. It seems that mania or elation as a *clinical pathological state* in childhood is not found. One hypothesis forces itself: namely, that the elations, at least those of clinically significant proportions, do not occur until relatively late in the psychic development of the individual. Denial is an essential mechanism in the elations or mania. It functions as a defense, in those conditions, against the underlying depression [2]. The reasons that elations are absent in children, or occur late in psychic development, may lie in the fact that denial, on which these disorders rest, acquires a special function in a highly structured or developed ego. It would therefore not be found in young children. The child's form or use of denial, unlike the adult's, is relatively undifferentiated. Through development it becomes an elaborate defense.

An increasingly important place in psychoanalytic literature has been given in the past thirty years to direct psychoanalytic work with children. As a result, those who have not engaged in it have naturally depended heavily on the few for some of the newer views on childhood disorders that studies of children would reveal. Nowhere is this borne out better than in the current views held by many who have written on depression in childhood. No satisfactory theory of childhood depression has evolved, perhaps because theories of depression in adults have been applied too generously. The views having most currency are based upon certain manifest behavior encountered, in cases, in very young, deprived, and disturbed children [19]. But the dynamics of depression can no more be assumed from manifest behavior in children than in adults. The content of the child's experience is left to speculation drawn from conflicts studied in later periods of life. The clinical data are often far too meager, leading not to substantial theory but often to repeated assertions, as in Melanie Klein's work [11]. Critical evaluations by analysts have periodically appeared, but the major ones are by analysts who have not themselves worked directly with children. As a result, most critique has been on theoretical grounds and has consisted of debates on the major changes in, or abandonment of, basic psychoanalytic concepts by Melanie Klein *et al.*

Another strong influence over the past twenty years has been a tendency on the part of some psychoanalysts to conclude that the manifest behavior of certain deprived infants illustrates and reaffirms concepts of basic Freudian theory of melancholia [19]. Their wish is to demonstrate the validity of the dynamic importance of object loss during infancy. But this does not, however, perform the service it sets out to. If infants were affected by object loss in the same way that adults are, then a child's development would have little meaning. The clinical facts of the unconscious are asserted, not demonstrated, in these efforts. Characteristically, the further we stray from clinical data, the harder is the way back to verification and the greater are the speculations.

On the subject of depression, and particularly depression in early childhood, these two trends continue to exert an inordinately strong influence, but we have reached the point where it is more important to evaluate what we can from verifiable data than to continue to speculate.

There seems to be agreement that object loss, no matter at what period in life, provokes serious consequences. Furthermore, the younger the individual, the more likely it is to produce profound alterations. In the young child, when executant functions of the ego are in the ascendancy, they are apt to be gravely affected by a loss. Regression is one of the most characteristic results; and in some instances even an arrest of development of certain ego functions, particularly in respect to object relations, has been demonstrated. There is also a tendency for the child to develop animism[2] to a greater than usual degree. The course that identification takes is also more apt to have pathological characteristics. An increase in narcissism or its intensification in object relations is another common sequel. In other words, any and all the structural and functional changes of the developing ego are affected.

If the infantile character has a strong fixation in certain pregenital phases, these phases are likely to be reinforced by object loss, with the result that further fixation develops. If the object loss occurs during the phallic period or when the castration complex is at its height, these phases, too, are correspondingly prolonged to a degree that they would not otherwise be. Regression takes place in effect to the point at which the identification with objects was fixed.

Later the same effect is to be seen in superego development, as illustrated above. At any phase of development or period, insurance against loss is to a degree acquired by an identification with that which may be lost (that is, by unwittingly making what is valued a part of oneself), and thus the separation, the distance, and the difference are reduced. The result is that the person not only is unconsciously *like* the object, but unconsciously has partially *become* the object. The effect of the loss of so valued an object, or the loss of an abstraction which has taken the place of one, is correspondingly manifested by a disturbance in the process of identification. The disorder in identification does not fail to affect the self or ego.

The clinical manifestations of mourning and melancholia presuppose certain phases of psychic development to have occurred. We see many partial or rudimentary signs, indications, and symptoms in the young of depression or even

[2] This important aspect of psychic development has been grossly neglected and should be studied. It is beyond the scope of this book to deal with it.

elation, and commonly what appears to be an absence of grief [3] — for example, laughing, joking, and playfulness as a reaction in the presence of the death of a personally important object. What adults in analysis have reported about serious object loss when they were young is confirmed in the frequent reactions to be observed in the children studied. But we do not obtain in childhood the clinical findings, that is, the typical conflicts, of the common disorder or pathological depression or elation that are ordinary in adult life. If we would believe that these disorders occur in childhood, the clinical data to support such views are not convincing. They remain to be demonstrated. It is worth repeating that manifest behavior without analysis of its corresponding conflicts is a notoriously unreliable index to an understanding of psychology on a level that is beyond behaviorism.

This caution should in no way suggest that young children are not affected seriously by losses. It does mean, however, that the effects should be sought in clinical phenomena other than those that are appropriate to adults. The effects in children are seen in the processes of identification, fixation, narcissism, regression, and in the developmental changes that, as a result, take place in the character. This is in keeping with the developmental process in mental life which psychoanalysis rests upon.

Particular and highly organized reactions are evoked in each period of development by the experience of object loss, regardless of whether the defenses that develop in response to it are founded in fact or on fantasy. The entire process is encompassed by a *loss complex*. Its function is to provide, through a developed system of defenses, some security against the constant uncertainty, threat, or liability that the loss of a personally important object, or even some abstraction of one, represents. The *loss complex* is an elaborate differentiating system of defense mechanisms developed by the ego, in which the processes of narcissism and identification are the keystone. Thus the preparations for a defense against object loss are fashioned well in advance, usually before the actual event. (Under ordinary social conditions, if a very young child in fact loses its mother, it has scarcely had time to develop its defenses and a substitute for the mother is readily received. In this way the young child is not devastated by the loss, which may have very serious consequences when there is no adequate replacement, as has been demonstrated above.)

What is valued may be lost, what is beautiful may fade, what is satisfying may displease, or what is interesting may become boring. Nothing escapes change, and to rail against transience is but to make "a demand for immortality too unmistakable a product of our wishes to lay claim to reality" [10]. Regrettably, perhaps, the experience of transience is left neither to the poet, the philosopher, nor even to the clinician to muse upon, but actively occupies the thoughts of the three-year-old child. He is always deeply moved by this experience which he encounters daily. (See Chapter 3). He shows a revulsion against losing or forgoing something needed, someone valued or loved, and he does not usually meet the moment of misfortune without some prior anticipation. Transience and losses are reviewed by the child countless times. He is compelled by his private encounters in fantasy, by events and by circumstances, to make preparations, in advance, to alleviate his anguish. As a result, from anticipation, the child's ego weaves a web of defenses that will elaborate with psychic development to meet his conflicts.

Unlike other conflicts, those entailed in losses and transience apparently are not resolved; instead, defenses are raised against them. One of the commonly observed pathological adult forms of these conflicts, when the defenses are inadequate, is clinical depression. The childhood forms, although not identical with the adult, are no less significant. Each represents a different expression of the universal conflict derived from the fear of abandonment and related directly to object loss. The reactions cited indicate that they are disorders of what we all develop — *a loss complex.*

REFERENCES

1. Bowlby, J.: Grief and Mourning in Infancy and Early Childhood; A. Freud: Discussion of Dr. John Bowlby's Paper; M. Schur: *ibid.;* R. Spitz: *ibid.* In *The Psychoanalytic Study of the Child* (New York: International Universities Press, 1960), XV, 9, 53, 63, 85.

2. Deutsch, Helene: Psychologie der manisch-depressiven Zustände insbesondere der chronischen Hypomanie. *Int. Z. Psychoanal.,* 19 (1933), 358–371.

3. ———. Absence of Grief. *Psychoanal. Quart.,* 6 (1937), 12–22.

4. Fenichel, O.: *The Psychoanalytic Theory of Neurosis* (New York: W. W. Norton, 1945), pp. 592–664.

5. Freud, A., and D. Burlingham: *War and Children* (New York: International Universities Press, 1943), p. 85.

6. Freud, S.: The Relation of the Poet to Day-Dreaming (1908). In *Collected Papers* (London: Hogarth Press, 1925), IV, 173–183, 175.

7. ———. Mourning and Melancholia. In *ibid.* (1925), IV, 152–170, 153, 158.

8. ———. Beyond the Pleasure Principle (1920). In *The Complete Psychological Works of Sigmund Freud,* Standard Edition (London: Hogarth Press, 1955), XVIII, 7–64, 14–16.

9. ———. On Narcissism: An Introduction. In *Collected Papers* (London: Hogarth Press, 1948), IV, 30–59, 52.

10. ———. On Transience. In *The Complete Psychological Works of Sigmund Freud,* Standard Edition (London: Hogarth Press, 1957), XIV, 305.

11. Klien, M., P. Heimann, and R. I. Money-Kyrle: *New Directions in Psychoanalysis* (New York: Basic Books, 1955).

12. Lewin, B. D.: *The Psychoanalysis of Elation* (New York: W. W. Norton, 1950).

13. Rochlin, G.: Loss and Restitution. In *The Psychoanalytic Study of the Child* (New York: International Universities Press, 1953), VIII, 288–309.

14. ———. Disorder of Depression and Elations. *J. Amer. Psychoanal. Ass.,* 1 (1953), 438–457.

15. Modell, A. A.: The Theoretical Implications of Hallucinatory Experiences in Schizophrenia. *J. Amer. Psychoanal. Ass.,* 6 (1958), 442, 443, 462.

16. Meiss, M. L.: The Oedipal Problem of a Fatherless Child. In *The Psychoanalytic Study of the Child* (New York: International Universities Press, 1952), VII, 216, 229.

17. Scharl, A.: Regression and Restitution in Object Loss. In *ibid.* (1961), XVI, 471.

18. Shambaugh, B.: A Study of Loss Reactions in a Seven Year Old. In *ibid.* (1961), XVI, 510.

19. Spitz, R. A.: Anaclitic Depression. In *ibid.* (1946), II, 313–341.

20. Zilboorg, G., and G. W. Henry: *History of Medical Psychology* (New York: W. W. Norton, 1941), pp. 55–56.

3

FEARS OF DEATH: ORIGINS OF RELIGIOUS BELIEF

The realization that death may occur at some unpredictable moment gives man a zeal for living rather than despair at dying. His is the psychology of rising expectations and endless hope. Note his countless efforts to extend life. In a tiny Moravian village, excavations in the nineteenth century revealed that man had been carefully buried with the remains of mammoths and implements which represented prosperity and good fortune as insurance for a safe journey. How little different, essentially, is this crudely arranged grave from the elaborate tombs of Egyptian pharaohs whose existence was similarly to be extended from this life to another. Only the eons distinguish them; the high purpose remains the same. The same principle may be observed in the ancient Chinese pharmacopoeia, still in use, with its ten thousand recipes for the elixir of life; or in the endless pursuit to find a fountain of youth to put off the final end. History is colored with limitless excursions and forays indicating man's efforts to prolong life or to postpone death. Man learns of his unpredictable moment remarkably early in life — far sooner than is generally supposed. As with any knowledge, its real significance lies in how it is applied, how it governs his behavior.

Man is the only animal that possesses a mirror in which he never ceases to examine himself and those about him. Seeing their fate reflected in his own, he persistently demonstrates his endless self-absorption. His searching curiosity reveals a lifelong interest in the human condition. Man's concern with his own end, expressed in fear, or with the end of others, expressed as sorrow, stems directly from his individual experience. As nature abhors a vacuum, man abominates isolation, separation, and loss. Countless examples in daily life convince him that whatever lives also dies. The cumulative knowledge about dying and death, some of it conscious, much of it relegated to stores at various lower levels of consciousness or degrees of awareness, spills into everyday life an element of critical importance which produces profound effects that have a governing influence on man's behavior.

Man's wish to live is precisely his reason for not coming to terms with death if it means accepting his own end. There is no evidence to support the contention that man ever accepts his own death. His long history indicates the opposite. Because of Freud's speculation about a death instinct, some people still hold that man wants his own destruction or his end, and that his aggressive capacities show it. In fact, however, a scrutiny of man reveals that although he is aggressive, destroys others, and may turn some of his apparently limitless aggressiveness on himself, there is no firm evidence that this is his aim. The opposite is the case.

Man has no wish for his own death, whether such impulses are conceived of as an instinct or as a principle or as reality. His self-destructive wishes and acts have an altogether different meaning. Careful studies (by Freud, Zilboorg, and others) have shown that suicidal tendencies and acts are really aimed at others. These destructive impulses are always poorly tolerated, and one who harbors grievances against another regularly turns his fury on himself, often in the form of suicidal wishes and acts. We are therefore in great danger from our hatred of others, which we unwittingly take out on ourselves. Man's license to murder others or to fight to his own death occurs when he is relieved of the burden of guilt, and of the anxiety in carrying out his own impulses, by provocation or what he believes to be just cause for his acts. Regardless of how destructive his inventions or impulses may be judged to be, man's entire history shows that his efforts are to prolong life. To escape death rather than to submit to it is his aim.

The evidence of man's conflict between the realization that he will die and his unwillingness to accept it is both universal and timeless. The study of every culture or civilization, however archaic, shows that man does not wish his end and that he does not fail to make an effort to prolong his life. When life is nearing its end, he still finds ways to prolong it through his beliefs. He makes life on earth a rite of passage to another life. Death becomes significant and meaningful as a conveyance to resurrection; this is evident in both the archaic and the developed forms of religion. Their aims seem not to differ. Hence the wish to live, to prolong life, and to attain a life after death is not simply a doctrine. It is a pragmatic conviction built up by reason out of contending with danger and out of uncertainty about life [10].

It would seem absurd to affirm that, above all, man wants to live if there were not prevalent so much ill-conceived conviction that man wants destruction either for its own sake or to destroy himself. "Man has lived his life in the shadow of death and he who clings to life and enjoys its fullness must dread the menace of its end. And he who is faced by death turns to the promise of life" [10]. The denial of death has led to another set of beliefs which show little evidence of being relinquished — beliefs in immortality. Man's conviction that life will continue does not come from a wish for death or lack of direction in his aims.

Man's fears over his own end, or the end of others important to him, come from his experience, which when formalized or standardized by religious institutions and practices makes him a communal partner in the struggle to live. The conscious fear of his own death, well in advance of its occurrence, is a part of man's unique awareness. This knowledge affects him more deeply than any other information he acquires. Social, cultural, physical, and geographical experiences provide some basis for variations in the expressions of the particular beliefs held, but these different expressions of the wish to live, to extend life, and to achieve some kind of immortality reveal many more similarities than they do differences.

Since life is carried on in the shadow of death it is not usual to await the final threat or the last breath to begin to wish to prolong life. It follows, in Mircea Eliade's words, "that immortality should not be conceived as a survival post-mortem, but rather as a situation one is constantly creating for oneself for which one is preparing, in which one is even participating from now onward and from this present world" [2]. The need for immortality is not simply some abstract fancy. It is commonly to be found in our daily efforts to prolong life, to ward off death. It is to be observed both as a conscious and unconscious emotional experience, as in the repetition of a little prayer, the muttering of a fleeting wish, the habitual carrying of a small charm, and the myriad other ways that ordinarily escape our scrutiny.

Religious beliefs have always expressed human needs, the most important of which is the desire to stay alive. A religion which failed to make some provision against disaster or to provide a passage to another life would be too frail a rod to lean upon. Religion aims to sustain, prolong, and extend life. Man has always demonstrated that he possesses powerful aggressive wishes, and he has harnessed them in the service of developing those social institutions which would shield him from a final end. Aggression is too often regarded as a negative force rather than as an engine of change. With it man has transformed the face of the earth and in the near future will bring outer space as well within his reach. These are his works. Religion is also one of his most ingenious inventions. Through it he has contrived to extend himself beyond his limits. It serves as an enormously civilizing influence even though in its employ some of the bloodiest conflicts have been fought. In some parts of the world it still continues to take a heavy toll in lives. But this only attests to the strength of man's beliefs and his unwillingness to relinquish them.[1]

Malinowski wrote that religion "simply was from the beginning." He fails to explain how it comes about. Since man is the only creature who knows that death invariably follows life, it sharpens the question to ask when in his life he learns this awesome truth.

My own studies have shown that the knowledge of death, including the possibility of one's own death, is acquired at a very early age, and far sooner than is generally supposed. By the age of three years the fear of one's own death is communicable in unequivocal terms. How much earlier than three years of age this information is acquired is a matter of tenuous speculation. Communication with a younger child on the subject is unlikely. It also would be much too fragmentary. What is more important is that in a child three years old death as a fear, as a possibility, has already begun to produce significant effects.

The institutional or ceremonial life of a society as expressed in its religious forms is of supreme importance both to the community and to the individual. Through these conventions the past and the present are pressed historically and mythically into the service of solving the present conflict, which is daily living, and that of the future,

[1] Note the theft in 1965 of an alleged hair of Mohammed and the bloody riots which ensued in India.

which is dying. Man knowingly lives his existence in the presence of death, clings to life, and abhors what threatens it. His unique intelligence solves these dilemmas by developing certain beliefs within himself, by organizing a society which is committed to relieving the grind of the present, and by assuring himself of a future reward. In these beliefs, Freud discovered a basic principle of human mental functioning: it is possible to put off satisfaction of a present need for a later reward. This profoundly civilizing influence will be easily recognizable in everyone's childhood as it will in each religion. This is not to say that religion is built up of a child's developmental blocks, but rather that both the child and the man depend upon a principle that is applied in early childhood. The principle extends throughout life. The great social institution of religion, which invariably depends upon this principle, exercises it through a ceremonial life that mitigates the fear of death and the uncertainty of life, and offers solace in the present and a reward in the future while an oppressive or hazardous life is endured.

Many complexities in the young child's life have been unraveled during the past sixty years. What not long ago were regarded as outrageous assumptions about young children are accepted now as self-evident clinical facts. While we have discovered and learned a great deal about the early erotic life of the child, we know as yet remarkably little about his religious development or religious life during this period, or even whether it exists.

It has only rarely been suggested that little children have a religious life; that children hold religious beliefs and that their behavior is governed to a significant degree by them. What a young child, three, four, or five years old, holds as religious beliefs has not been understood because neither systematic nor careful investigations have been carried out.

The religions of the world generally pay little or no heed to a young child's capacity for religion. The fact that such a child is exclusively bound to his immediate family and

that he has as yet only a limited capacity for social participation may have a bearing on this issue. The child's
contribution to society may be considered too meager.
When puberty is reached, however, nearly universal recognition is given to children through initiations or rites which
are both religious and civic. The child is accorded a capacity he previously was not thought to possess. He is accepted
as a full member of the community, both religiously and
socially. Puberty marks the full entry into the community,
and with that the prior claims, among them that a child's
elementary duty is to his mother, are terminated. While
puberty may well be the time when the child is ready to be
claimed by the community, it may not be the time when his
religious life commences.

"As it is practically impossible to rear a child apart
from all contacts with the religion of his elders, we cannot
accurately determine how much of one's religious growth is
due to social influences and how much to one's own spon-
taneous impulses. It is safe to say, however, that the individual is as dependent upon others for his religious as
for his moral attitudes" [7]. Since all attitudes of the child
are subject to development, the real problem concerning the
genesis of individual religion is therefore: What is it that
calls out the early genuinely religious responses?

It is characteristic of the young child to be avidly concerned with causality. The child's interest in the search for
explanations of phenomena and experiences begins very
early in life. The answers that he seems to prefer, whether
his own or those furnished by others, tend to have certain
common characteristics. They are outside of logic and are
not testable. They are often dependent upon the power of
wishes and magic. To the child all is governed by law and
ruled by a higher authority or force, whose favor needs to
be courted. Accident, caprice, or chance being thus elimi-
nated, a childhood source of apprehension, the fear of what
might happen or the unpredictability of the future, is con-

siderably altered and stabilized. A sense of security is increased as the uncertainty of events is diminished. Relationships with people, inanimate objects as they represent them, and events ruled by such principles make the struggle against errors, irrationalism, and superstition both arduous and not always successful. The child conceives of the world as directed by forces which are subject to persuasion. The conflict thus lies between the governing power of wishes and the laws of causality. The two are best reconciled in religion, where both hold sway but in which explanations or causes are intimately related to wishes. Given these conditions, the child is ready for religious responses. Taken in this light, religious beliefs serve as a certain or particular and essential type of explanation of events, phenomena, and causes. The child's practices are in accord with his beliefs. His beliefs are of a religious nature; that is, he believes in a higher power, and that all phenomena are ordained. There are no natural causes. The child is actively engaged in religiosity.

Commonplace observation and the careful scientific studies of Freud, Piaget, and others show that the child is concerned almost exclusively with himself and his immediate relationship to the environment. The earliest stages of this period "precede language or are contemporaneous with the first spoken words, and any effort to reach the child's consciousness during these stages is fruitless, if one claims to go beyond mere hypothesis" [12].

One way a child displays interest in his environment is by endowing it with his own characteristics, to make it alive. For example, he will give his own qualities to a toy, which will then have wishes, motives, speech, or whatever attributes are important modes of expression to the child. The young child's play with objects readily reveals how alive a stick, a piece of mud, a stream of water, a leaf, or a toy can become. The reverse takes place in an emotionally troubled child, who then takes on the characteristics of an inanimate thing. While it is generally believed that this process represents the earliest form of identification, closer study reveals a more far-reaching and perhaps more fundamental concern. To endow all things with life is to make them like oneself — alive. Hence animism, besides being a phase of development, seems also to be filling a function. A wish to make no distinction between what is alive and what is not, or to remove the distinction that is present, is to create an exclusively animate world.

Remnants of this process may be observed among the most sophisticated people, who, for example, not only animate ships, planes, and winds but often give them as well a specific gender. Thus endowed with life, objects or forces magically may be subject to influence and hence to the power of wishes. Animism prevails. Existing in various degrees of refinement at all levels of society, it serves both to explain and hopefully to master phenomena.

It should be added here that none of it is the result of deliberation; each child learns and practices it chiefly by himself, making his own discoveries, though subject to the prevailing social influences. Hence a society may help extend one aspect or another and limit one phase that encourages a second. No child will develop without having gone through the entire course to a greater or lesser degree. A child in a pastoral community will negotiate his development in a different coin from one in a fishing community; a child in our highly mechanized society will have different toys to speak to from those of a child living in a rain forest at the foot of the Andes. In substance, however, it is doubtful if they would say different things; the similarities would be more striking than the differences.

The child not only regards his interpretations as true, but regards his own experience as universal rather than unique. This makes for a stubborn adherence to his belief that his own experience reflects the way things are. He neither wishes nor needs to test the validity of beliefs. Experience promotes two related developments, learning or knowledge, and what constitutes faith. A child's constant reaffirmation of what is believed encourages an orthodoxy. It goes without saying that the child does not perceive the world as pure phenomena and that his mind is ruled only by the physical reality he perceives [12]. It is, however, ruled by his experience with reality, which is an altogether different matter. It has been said that reality undergoes a progressive transformation with age. While the perception of reality continues to modify with experience, some of the old perceptions affected by earlier experiences seem not to be always relinquished by the accumulation of new experience or even enlightenment.

A modifying factor which denies experience and resists enlightenment appears to be regularly present. It may be that our oldest or most archaic wishes are the most difficult to relinquish. We need hardly to be reminded how often and readily, in adult life, early childhood wishes may be aroused. An abhorrence of changes or of what is foreign and alien, the death of someone personally important, often a minor illness or injury, or even a disappointment, are experiences in which childhood apprehensions are mobilized and before which adult knowledge and repeated experiences are brushed aside as though they were non-existent. In their place arise answers that do not rest on either logic or knowledge, which are influenced by egocentricity, childish principles of causality, and a resort to magical thinking and wishing.[2]

The realization of how much the young child is affected by his experience tends to focus the attention of those who are concerned with the child's complex psychology on physical reality, often at the neglect of the child's perception of himself. The child is never far removed from an egocentric interest in his own existence, no matter what he

[2] This discussion is developed further in Appendix I to this chapter (page 96).

learns or acquires from the world about him. Even as an adult, this core of egocentricity shows through the enveloping qualities of character. These remarks refer to the child's narcissism and not to his instincts. The child's ideas of causality are self centered. Piaget showed that a child may provide answers to questions put to him about what makes clouds move, the wind blow, or birds fly. Piaget seemed not attentive to the child's motives. The child's replies reflect, as do his own questions, a profound wish to respond to an unwitting egocentric need to know what makes his own heart beat, his chest heave with breath, his eyes see, his ears hear, and his legs move. These, to the child, are his vital processes. The use of locomotion and the powers of perception, together with his sexual organs, hold his interest. He projects concern with his functions in the form of questions about other creatures and other things.

Thus the world of causality is closely bonded to his own functions and perceptions of himself and his own motor actions. The world is explained in terms of the self that he knows.

This in no way suggests that the child merely transfers his inner experience to the outside world by projection alone. Rather, what occurs is the result of the child's encounter with reality, his egocentric orientation as he engages with the outside world. This encounter then helps produce that elaborate system of thinking which leads to what we observe as projection, animism, and magic. The child's emerging ego defenses and his relationships to others are all operating together to produce for the child a changing and expanding universe. Despite the constant search and acquisition of new and contemporary beliefs, the child, and even the adult, as we have learned, never altogether gives up some of his most most archaic beliefs.

Freud refers to the child's curiosity, especially in gifted children, as passing through a period, beginning about the age of three, which he called a time of infantile sexual researches. He did not believe that it arose spontaneously, but that it was awakened by some important event — "by the actual birth of a little brother or sister, or by a fear of it based on external experiences in which the child perceives a threat to his selfish interests." He stated that the child's sexual interest led him to oedipal wishes. But such wishes are coupled with the recognition that they, together with begetting a child, are beyond his capacity. It leads to the child's abandoning the entire venture. This failure, Freud thought, the first attempt at intellectual independence, appears to be of a lasting and depressing kind [4]. These conclusions were drawn from his "Analysis of a Phobia in a Five Year Old Boy (Little Hans)" [3], and from "The Sexual Theories of Children" [6]. "This brooding and doubting becomes the prototype of all later intellectual work directed toward the solution of problems, and the first failure has a crippling effect on the child's whole future." A large body of clinical facts has accumulated to corroborate Freud's conclusions.

In view of present studies, his deductions appear too limited. The young child's discovery of death has an equally singular effect. I would not suggest that it has greater importance than those infantile researches Freud refers to, but I do assert that the child during the period in question attempts to solve other important problems: those that are attendant on the discovery of death. These investigations, or researches, as Freud calls them, have a far-reaching and significant effect, especially since they occur at the same time in development as the child's discovery of death evolves. These investigations or problems which the child contends with lead to solutions; the child's deep concern with living and with death leads him to form and practice a religiosity which becomes an active part of his life for the rest of his days. I do not believe that the effect of these discoveries is necessarily crippling. Freud himself has on many occasions shown that latency is ushered in as a result of the oedipal wishes being disappointed. At this time many new achievements are gained. The disappointment that erotic wishes are not gratified marks the beginning of a sublimative process. In a parallel fashion, when the discovery of death leads to the knowledge of its finality, it marks the beginning of a highly creative process opposing finality.

The persistent interest in causality is an extremely viable one. It normally continues to gain momentum, in large measure, because the child's explanations — as well as those which are offered him in response to his questions — seem always to lag behind events and experiences. The answers seem not to be adequate for long, especially as, on the one hand, the child's universe continues to expand with his growth and development, while, on the other hand, events do not comply with the rules and laws previously believed to be ordained. The child who fails to question or is content with answers fails to thrive and has begun to show a conservatism that suggests he wants no change, or cannot tolerate it, or that he wishes to ward off the uncertainty that questions express. He wants no challenge to his dogma or to his orthodoxy. And whereas it is usual to animate the world, such children in the extremes of uncertainty often go one step further by relinquishing their relationship to others and by focusing on things instead.

This tendency may become distorted into a narrow, anxious-minded, intense concern with how things work as interest in people and events is withdrawn. Characteristic preoccupation with the motion of things such as automobiles, airplanes, egg beaters, washing machines, pinwheels, or clouds and leaves seems to be replacement of interest in others and experiences. Regular, monotonous, repetitious absorption in his own acts and in things reduces his discomfort over uncertainty and unpredictability. Ritual and ceremony, important to every child, in these children becomes a compelling and undeviating necessity. A world of bizarre stability results. Fortunately, the incidence of such disorders is uncommon. But as a subject for study they reveal important aspects of emotional development which indicate that by forgoing a relationship to people, and by withdrawing from an encounter with events in an effort to reduce apprehensions, an isolated, impoverished condition is created in which the basic problems remain unaltered.

Most children are obviously curious. For their countless questions they also have their own explanations and reasons. The child is actually never without a catechism of his own making. To lack it would be to invite an ever-present uncertainty and bewilderment. The child harbors many contradictions not the least of which is in the development and expansion of his curiosity, asking questions and at the same time having an explanation for virtually everything. It is not natural for the young child to admit to not knowing or to having no explanation. Nevertheless, the eagerness to overcome ignorance is very strong and impels the child to learn quickly, and usually well. The two processes go on simultaneously. The weight of reality regularly reveals to the child that his answers are inadequate. The discrepancy between explanations of phenomena and reality gives rise to a dilemma. The child remains on its horns as he adheres to his old understanding and encounters reality to make new discoveries. It is as if two sets of accounts were being kept.

A system of thinking which explains all experience, which regards life as governed by the rules of a higher authority whose favor needs to be solicited, and in which logic and reason readily give way to the power of wishes and magic, constitutes what we recognize as religious belief. When practice or behavior is in accord with or is governed by what is believed, a religious life prevails. No people are without a religion, if by religion we mean a system of thinking that proceeds from a confession of impotence, as a means to influence and control the environment, through which the oppression of man's helplessness and uncertainty may be compensated by an assertion of power. Religion is neither a mere dealing with crises nor a continuing system of moral reform. These elaborate and complex systems have as their principal aim a lifesaving purpose, and develop and promote the expectation that when life is apparently over, it will be continued. According to Malinowski and to most theories of early religion, death and its denial — immortality — have always formed the most poignant theme of man's forebodings, from which much, if not all, of his religious inspiration has been derived [10]. The concern with death is therefore central to religion. It is to be found in all forms of religion, from the most primitive to the most highly developed. They all hold this central issue in common. It is not remarkable, therefore, that "the horror of death is universal among mankind. It depends not so much on the pain that often accompanies dissolution as upon the mystery of it. . . . This horror has given rise to an obstinate disbelief in the necessity of death, and to attempts, in spite of experience of failure, to escape it. Even the most natural and inevitable decease is persistently ascribed to causes not beyond human control. . . . The picture thus presented of the desperate refusal of mankind to accept a cardinal condition of existence is one of the most pathetic in the history of the race" [8].

If it is shown that it is not possible to distinguish the normal child's views from adult ones on the subject that is central to all religion, death and its denial, then such conceptions and their attendant emotional conflicts and defenses reveal a durability which growth, emotional development, and time affect very little. Those inclined to hold that these beliefs will be relinquished in favor of scientific knowledge will be disappointed. Foremost among those who held out such hopes was Freud. At the conclusion of his essay "The Future of an Illusion," he argued that the supremacy of the intellect would someday rule over religious needs and make them give way to reason and logic. Ives Hendrick, the great contemporary American psychoanalyst, writes about this expectation by Freud that "the very man who had done most to demonstrate the irrational in human life showed that even his mind has its peculiar inconsistencies" [9]. Does not Freud's fondest hope — that reason would replace the irrational — in this one instance betray him as an analyst, when he accords so much strength or power to reason?

The immense and widespread knowledge which has been disseminated throughout the world has done much to dispel ignorance. Man's attitude toward death, however, is not simply due to a lack of knowledge. The strength of the resistance is drawn from an early, deep persistent desire *not* to act in accordance with the available knowledge. It is a human need to maintain what has been correctly designated as an "obstinate disbelief and a refusal to accept a cardinal condition of existence" — namely, that death is final. Here the child does not differ from the adult. The child discovers death very early and he too shows his obstinate disbelief in what he knows. Where the end of life is concerned, there appears to be a universal characteristic, acquired in early childhood and persistent in most people throughout life — to disbelieve it. It is a demonstration that knowledge is tempered and even blunted when desire opposes it. In the conflict between the two, human history, from its most archaic time to the present, as well as the history of the individual from his earliest childhood to maturity, gives continued evidence that wishing or desiring often contradicts and prevails over learning and knowing. The struggle is timeless and indicates that no solution will be found that will permanently alter it. Regardless of what vicissitudes the instincts may be put through, their aim, gratification, does not change. And as a result knowledge or reason will be thwarted, defied, or denied.

The sincere devout piety and religious orthodoxy in the

lives of many great scientists is often puzzling to encounter. They appear to have devoted their lives unstintingly to the pursuit of their rational goals. It is at times disconcerting to find them highly religious. The two streams of the course of their lives seem apparently to be opposed to each other. If we credit them with a personal fear of failure, dying, and death, the contradiction may be in a large measure simply resolved. Perhaps, therefore, only our heroes, rather than our geniuses, triumph in this conflict. The hero has found his expression in a pursuit more important or an ideal greater than himself and he has thus transcended fears we commonly harbor. Paradoxically, he gains immortality by forfeiting his life; his ends are met through the means.

It is the conventional view that the child does not know about death. This seems to be as true of culturally archaic peoples as of modern society. Death as a subject for discussion is commonly treated by adults as if it were a prohibited issue where children are concerned. Children may play death games endlessly (they often use the same theme, e.g., in Warsaw, Berlin, the Kalahari, the "wild" West) so long as no one takes that play seriously. When taken as a matter for sober consideration, evasiveness is clearly evident on the part both of the adult and of the child. Adults themselves are reluctant to acknowledge, as we have noted, the inevitable fate which waits us all, and hence are the least likely source of information. Moreover, there are often concerted efforts to deny the child an awareness of death. The inevitable discovery of death then becomes a private individual experience of great magnitude. What such a discovery means is not conveyed to young children either as a body of dogma or as a natural phenomenon, nor is what to do about it once the revelation occurs. The attempted solution to the problems the discovery raises is universal in the sense that children everywhere seem to find remarkably similar solutions.

The serious significance of death is no more wasted on

the child than it is spared the adult. The child typically applies it not only to himself but also to others, and particularly to those upon whom he has learned to depend. Fears of the loss of an important person like a parent and the dread of abandonment arise demonstrably in young children, as I have shown elsewhere [13, 14].

A more trying burden is added to the child's existence when his fears and fantasies carry him on to the inevitable realization that the end of his existence as well as the existence of those who care for him may occur at some unpredictable time or in some unforeseen way. These somber actualities weigh heavily enough to have a compelling emotional effect. When it is remembered that this process goes on in the early phases of development, its significance is all the more profound. As one would expect, far from adding to the stability of the child's world, this insight has quite the opposite effect.

Ordinarily very young children make discoveries about death. They have plentiful opportunities from which to draw such information. They stand often as a mute witness when the successful hunt calls its fruits to their attention. A trip to the market or the barnyard has a similar connotation. The more clearly the child comprehends that life is followed by death, the greater is the demonstration of the uncertainty of the future. As a result, through these everyday experiences in addition to the growing realization of his utter dependence upon others some kind of social harmony is made imperative. Thus a further repression of destructive and aggressive impulses becomes a safeguard or offers a refuge. And an adaptation to social conditions which promotes the child's development is thus augmented.

Conflicts and reactions to unpleasant experiences, unwelcome ideas, or untoward thoughts are met too frequently to require proof. Long before the child has discovered death, he has acquired some experiences with frustration, the failure of fulfillment of many of his wants, and some practice at compromise with his demands. Confronted now with this fresh assault on his security, he refines a system of defenses which he has continued to perfect from those which were born of the loss complex and the dread of abandonment. This elaborate web of self-protective emotional devices is not only directed toward the grim realities, but also against the conflicts which they arouse within himself. In this way, I suggest, the need for self-preservation is converted further into a powerful social force which promotes and generates change and adaptation.

There seems little doubt that the young child learns rapidly that death means the absence of life, that life comes to an end. Despite this recognition of reality there is no pragmatic or philosophic acceptance. On the contrary, a rich variety of psychological defenses that the child has not only in readiness, but has to some degree perfected, is brought to bear on this problem. These include two rapidly developing orders of psychological processes: first, those which serve to modify or distort perception of an intolerable objective reality — in this case, the discovery of death; and second, those which will effect an alteration in subjective experience in order to overcome helplessness and a sense of loss through fantasies of omnipotence and invulnerability. Many of these defenses stem from a denial of the reality. Denial and negation are always to the fore of this problem, not only in the very young but throughout life — in the belief that death is not the end of life. The refusal to accept the finality that the dead are irretrievable bears out that the existing paradox of rejecting what is acknowledged is a manifestation of negation. Men are unwilling and hence unable to accept the fact that the dead are forever gone. The belief that the dead will return is born of the wish.

If we recognize that seeing is an especially important function to a particular child, being dead comes to mean not to see, yet the dead to such a child are conceived as seeing again. They can watch over and observe. Rather than having limits to their vision as they do during life, the dead acquire infinite powers of observation. For another child, being dead may be characterized as being motionless. Such a child believes the dead to be free, mobile — in fact whatever limitations in mobility the particular child may have experienced are believed not to affect the dead. The dead may move anywhere. The same reversal may apply to all or any functions. Being dead, instead of representing a giving up of functions and processes, comes to mean just the opposite. Powers previously limited are extended without boundaries.

In 1940, Sylvia Anthony's book *The Child's Discovery of Death* [1] appeared. Here is one of the rare studies of the subject. She found that school-age children thought readily of death. It appeared in their fantasies as well as in their play and it arose in response to suggestions of grief and fear, loss and separation. Death was commonly associated with ideas of retaliation and reparation. P. Schilder and G. Wechsler in 1934 had made a preliminary study. "The Attitude of Children Towards Death" [15]. Their work was done through family questionnaires. They concluded that a thorough study done directly with children was necessary. Anthony's book confirmed their findings.

No further clinical study of children concerning their attitudes toward death was reported until 1948. In a classroom setting, Nagy [11] put questions to a group of children aged approximately four to ten years, and encouraged them to make drawings and tell stories, to elicit their views on death. Although she provided little new information in her report, she succeeded in showing that the subject of death was a very important one even to the youngest child that she observed. Her conclusions were a reaffirmation of the work by Schilder and Wechsler and by Anthony.

During the next two decades, neither a critical review nor

a deeper study of the subject was attempted. It is the purpose here to demonstrate not only that death is a matter of deep consideration to the very young child, as has been indicated by others, but also that his thoughts of dying are commonplace. They serve as important determinants in his emotional development. I shall show, moreover, that his behavior is influenced by such thoughts, which are decisive in respect to some of his lifelong beliefs.

The selection of children for my study was based on rather simple requirements: (1) that the children be at least three years old and less than five; (2) that they be capable of revealing in a play session some organized thinking which could be expressed both verbally and through their play; (3) that they come from protected environments in the sense that they would be urban (rural life is more directly exposed to birth, death, life), and have well-educated parents without any formal church affiliation.

The children were all of at least average intelligence. They were free from any unusual circumstances such as serious separations, serious illnesses or mishaps, to themselves, siblings, or parents. They were not regularly indoctrinated in a set of religious beliefs. The children were carefully attended by their parents and the home situations by reasonable standards would be considered stable. Except for the birth of a younger child, there had been no significant major events in relation to the principal people involved. All the children had a history of good physical health and no unusual or conspicuous emotional problems. They were observed during play in a series of appointments in a standardized child therapy room — equipped with a one-way mirror; conversation with the child was recorded through hidden microphones. The number of visits was determined by the accessibility of their fantasy play, which was to reveal unmistakably some of their central ideas about death, dying, or being dead. Three to five individual periods of play were required for each child.

Four examples follow which illustrate significant aspects of how young children cope with their knowledge of death. I had not previously seen the children. They were brought to me by a parent who was interested in the study. It was considered important to verify in advance that no more than cursory attention had been paid to the subject of death by the family, although this proved to be hardly necessary. The parents were sophisticated adults and had themselves had direct experience with the problem of a death, either professionally or personally. They were without exception reluctant to discuss the subject of death or dying with the child beyond offering him some reassurance on the infrequent occasion of a question from a child. Parents thought the children were too young to have much said to them of an expository nature. Even a precocious two-and-a-half-year-old was considered too immature to share in a discursive exercise, particularly on the subject of dying or death.

The aim was to provide a situation in which the child would play alone with the investigator. When the subject of death came up spontaneously, it would be explored as far as the child would permit, within a limited period of time and within the limits of anxiety that the investigator judged the child could comfortably tolerate. The aim was to demonstrate that the subject of death had been given considerable attention by the child and that it had produced an effect. For purposes of the study, it was important to show that the subject was readily accessible in any child and that ample thought had been given by the child to a subject on which he had not been indoctrinated. Extracts of transcripts of these play sessions are included in the appendixes at the end of this chapter.

Child A was a boy three and a half years old. In the past six to eight months he had asked his parents spontaneously when he would die or they would die. Following reassurance that this was some time distant, he was heard to mutter to himself that he wouldn't die. During this period the maternal grandfather died. He was not well known to the child. The grandfather had lived in a distant city, and the child had seen him only on several occasions. In the two weeks that followed the grandfather's death there appeared to be no recognizable signs of a reaction, although the parents had expected that there might be one, since they themselves were disturbed by the event. Shortly thereafter, however, the child awoke over a series of nights with nightmares (meaning fears without any specific content). He would delay going to sleep each night. After some questioning it was evident that he had equated going to sleep with dying. (Could someone have said to him that grandfather had gone to sleep?) His questions were: "What clothes did grandfather wear when he went away?" "Does it hurt to die?" He said that he himself was afraid to die. I shall not attempt to describe all that went on during the child's visits but will include all that was relevant to the problems we are concerned with.

The child picked up a small man doll and spontaneously put him under a truck. When I asked what was happening, the reply was, "The man will die." In response to the inquiry as to what then happens, he replied, "When people die they go under." This line of inquiry was short. The play shifted to killing the object the doll represented. "Then it will go away." Another variation occurred while he was playing in the sink with water and dolls — a member of the family goes down the drain and drowns. "When people are dead do they go down the sewer?" was his question. When death occurs to some object in an episode of play, that toy is actively used and is viable soon after in a later sequence of play. A series of illnesses occur to the doll; infection and vomiting end in death. Deaths come from poisonous gas fumes. They also occur from being painfully killed after fighting against being hospitalized. These deaths occur regularly regardless of the individual's wishes or the will of the victim.

The association of being gone with death evokes anxiety expressed as fears of being left. The child immediately wanted to know his parents' whereabouts during this visit.

Injuries which may cause death, especially from a "hard fall," are dramatized by play with toys or the child actually taking the role of the victim. Each time, people return from the dead; I suggested that they may not, or then that they cannot, and the child insisted the opposite. To support his case he said that he saw a dead cat in a sewer and later it was not dead. Death in all instances is brought about by anything but natural events. Other causes of death are attacks by fierce animals, going out of the house without boots, being exposed to the elements, and swimming over one's head. If it is a child who dies, it continues to grow. The dead may get hungry and they must eat. Excremental functions continue after death. The child plays this out with toy bears he has shot, killed, and buried. They then continue their vital functions. They can also walk about. Some objects may remain motionless and not eat or speak but they are the ones whom the child wants to deprive of functions. Death is reversible. Life is a set of functions which one performs and which one may be deprived of. It is "death" to lose functions, but the functions are restored as before or even bigger than during life.

Child B was a girl four years and four months old. Within the year her paternal grandmother had died of chronic heart disease, a broken hip, and old age. The child needed repeated assurance after the grandmother's death that broken bones did not always mean death. When she was two she was first fearful about fish dying. When she saw them being caught by her father during the following summer, however, there were no further comments about the fish. She helped to catch a few fish and by the time she was four was considered by the parents to be an accomplished fisherman.

References to being run over by a car or to broken bones, to fears of the dark, and death associated with sleep were characteristic expressions of anxiety in the year following the grandmother's death, although questions about death actually preceded the event.

The child's play was about children being lost, frightened, and even killed. All of this was going on in and about a doll's house. The subject of being dead and what happens to people who die focused on going to a graveyard in a box. After a while the dead come out of the box. The dead person does not remain there. While focused on killing animals, the play was restricted only to those to be eaten. Those that are not eaten may die and they come back to life. Animals may go to a hospital when ill and may die, but the expressed belief is that good animals or "nice ones" come back. Dead animals can take medicine and be restored. This was played out in considerable detail. The child played that she was good after pretending to be dead, which is a clear implication that she will return from the dead. Play that ended with breaking the doll's legs was concluded with no wish to talk of it further. Play about broken bones occurred occasionally, followed by shrieks asking for medicine to prevent death. The child admitted that this was frightening and wished not to continue with this fragment of play. The belief is clear in respect to the return to life; particularly if one is good, it is believed that dying may be warded off or the effects of dying may be reversed. The anxiety about dying is thus reduced or modified.

Child C was a boy three years and eight months old. While driving home with his parents one day, he witnessed a cat in its death struggles. The child's immediate fears were for his own cat. "What happens to cats and where do they go when they die?'' were his repeated questions. A few weeks later there was talk in the house about Mozart. The child later asked who Mozart was. On learning that the composer was dead, the child provided a long list of people, asking whether they were dead or alive. He repeatedly asked, ''Where do dead people go?'' The grave as a hole in the ground held his interest. He did not express fears for himself, but he began to speak of his worry that his sister might die. He became a little anxious about her when she had a mild illness at the time. There is no doubt that there are many mixed motives in this concern, but regardless of what other conflicts there may be, the one about death is clear. There was frequent talk about dying during this time. When one is grown-up or when one is old, what happens if parents die — to the child, that is? There appears to be an invariably strong association between being dead and gone or going away, and being left.

This boy's play is particularly concerned with an animal that he shot, killed, and then took to a graveyard and buried. He did not know what happened after this until he thought of the animal being hungry. It could not come back, but it could eat earth. A variety of other creatures and objects were killed and buried, were hungry and ate. They could also talk although dead. The emphasis was placed on the sick and the old who die, people and animals alike. He himself would not want to die. If he had to die, he would ''go,'' but only with his mother and father, but he had to be sure, however, to come back. He knows that if people die they stay away, but he himself will return.

Child D was a four-year-old boy whose grandfather had died during the previous year in a distant city. The death actually occurred on the child's third birthday. He was told that the grandfather had died of old age. The boy immediately wanted assurance that his mother and father were not very old. He told them that he himself did not want to be

any older. For weeks afterward he repeatedly insisted that
his grandfather was not dead. Then a contemporary of his
father died of a heart attack. The boy insisted on knowing
exactly where the heart was and the details of the attack.
He was openly concerned with death and how often it comes
unexpectedly. He repeated his assertion that when he died
he did not want to be buried in the ground but wanted to be
buried above ground. His play emphasized dolls who became ill and had nothing further happen to them. Planes
would crash with no effect on the passengers. Operations
on tonsils, being boiled in a tub or being burned, led to no
harm. He does not want to talk about people being killed. It
is, he admits, too sad. Sometimes people are killed with a
knife; however, if you take the knife out they live again. He
once saw a dead bee, but he knew that it could come alive
and that was why he did not bury it. "People get buried
because they are no good." He will have to die and his
father will die. He knows that this will happen. Sometimes,
he hates his mother and he wants her to die.

Countless examples can be found readily if one listens
carefully to children and collects their accounts. Thoughts
which children express without any organized play session
and which can be casually collected include the following:
"Before you are born, you're dead, then you get born and
you live again till you're very old, then you die and maybe
you become just a little thing and then you start all over
again"; or, "I'll live to be more than a hundred, because
people I heard of live sometimes to be very old. I heard of a
woman who lived to be a hundred and three. When I'm a
hundred and three they'll find some way to make people live
forever." These and similar reflections are readily available to whoever cares to explore them.

The young child's discovery of death is a great personal
and private experience. The importance of a significant discovery often lies in what inventions it gives rise to. The
conflicts which are aroused by the knowledge, the fears, and

the recognition that life comes to an end bring out the child's entire store of psychological defenses. The old mental mechanisms which have developed from earlier conflicts over separation and the dread of abandonment receive an impetus to contend with newer problems.

The examples cited show that at a very early age well-developed mental faculties are functioning to defend oneself against the realization that life may end. An elaborate system of psychological defenses may be observed. At this period of life the logic used is implicit. A paradox such as "when the dead are hungry they eat," or "those who are killed return to life," needs no further explanation so far as the child is concerned. Wishes are not often distinguished from the facts; realities are altered to suit the wishes when questions about death arise. Magical thinking or homeopathic magic is an active process in young children and is seen when sleep and death appear to the child to be similar and then are accepted as the same. Magical ideas of contiguity are also common — for example, the fact that what is not wanted is disposed of through drains serves the child who is playing at the sink with the concept that unwanted and dead children and people may be discarded in sewers. Fears of death, like other concerns of the child, are in part mastered by repetitive play, as when planes are smashed and cars are wrecked over and over while harm to passengers is denied. The denial of the obvious may be so strong in a child that it leads at times to the complete negation that anything of consequence has taken place. It must be borne in mind that children, like prehistoric or contemporary or any people, who employ magical thinking neither subject it to analysis nor concern themselves with the abstract principles involved. Sir James George Frazer wrote in *The Golden Bough* (1947) about the magician, "he reasons just as he digests his food in complete ignorance of the intellectual and physiological processes which are essential to the one operation and the other" [2a].

Dying is recognized by the child as an arrest of his vital functions. The child determines the living functions as those which he regards as essential to himself. The organs of locomotion and motor activity, of perception, of the alimentary, excretory, and respiratory functions, and the genital organs are vital to the child. When death is signified as a loss of any or all of these critical organs or processes, the child's reaction is to make use unwittingly of the many available psychological defenses. Death is reconstituted to become a liberation rather than its opposite. What limitations life may have imposed are transcended in death.

The child regards death as not due to natural causes but as a result of strife, defiance of authority and retaliation, hostility and the wish to satisfy aggressive, destructive and sexual impulses. In sum, death is the outcome of certain relations between people. Morality is introduced very early by the child in the belief that the bad die before the good. The good are rewarded by a return from the dead. The bad remain dead. Wishes play an important role, as in the case of the boy who mutters to himself that he will not die but who becomes very solicitous about his sister when she has a trivial illness. His concern is that she may die.

The serious significance of death is not lost on the child. He knows that death is inevitable. The examples cited above reveal that elaborate defenses which have been aroused by the knowledge and fear of death are brought into effect. They represent an extension of earlier fears, the dread of abandonment or separation. These conflicts are not entirely allayed in childhood. They are only partially resolved, to a greater or lesser degree, because man is a social creature who exists only in the company of others, on some of whom he is intimately dependent, and who he knows will sooner or later leave him. He neither accepts final separation from those he loves nor his own inevitable end. His refusal to accept the human condition fires his conflicts and summons all his ingenuity to contend with those issues which begin very early in life. Taken in its totality, the reaction to the discovery of death, which defines fate as the uncertainty it is, leads both the child and the man into initiating an active civilizing process. He begins to propitiate and conciliate those who are superior, who are believed to direct and influence the course of events and his life. There is a powerful incentive to emulate these beings, to want the valued qualities which he has attributed to them. Thus defined, the child has fashioned a religion that he practices. The institutional aspects follow later in life.

Does the child's discovery of death lead him to recognize it as the extinction and finality of life? The foregoing data suggest that very young children seem to learn that life ends. They apply this information to themselves. To expect that the child would entertain adult conceptions of dying or death would not only be unreasonable but naïve. The facts of death like the facts of life, however, are to the child heavily embossed with every conscious and unconscious emotion at his disposal. These psychological vicissitudes do not serve the ends of reality, but rather quite opposite ends. The incentive to repress the real significance of dying may be judged from the powerful mental mechanisms which are brought into function in order to transcend death. What is remarkable is not that children arrive at adult views of the cessation of life, but rather how tenaciously throughout life adults hold to the child's beliefs and how readily they revert to them. The clinical facts show that the child's views of dying and death are inseparable from the psychological defenses against the reality of death. They form a hard matrix of beliefs which is shaped early and deep in emotional life. It appears not to alter throughout life. The concept of death fused with its amalgam of defenses is established as a core, around which a knowledge of the facts of life is wrapped. The knowledge will vary considerably in people and in different societies and cultures, but neither the core nor the defenses differ in any appreciable way. The core seems to be irreducible and unaltered. Although intellectual development modifies reliance on the more primordial defenses of childhood, it does not replace them. This is nowhere better illustrated than in times of crisis and especially in threats to life, when intellectual concepts and thoroughly substantiated facts are often relinquished and the elemental emotional mechanisms of childhood are brought into play.

Both child and man constantly and restlessly strive to overcome their limitations. If in so doing they destroy others, they are only following the path of all living matter, whose goal is to remain alive. There is no purposeless aim at destruction of others or oneself; on the contrary, there are the most elaborate structures, both internal and social, against destroying oneself and others. In his effort to solve the problems of life — and among the principal ones is death — man has erected elaborate institutions both within himself and with his fellows. Societies come into conflict with each other and man is inevitably drawn into their defense. Some of his institutions become dangerous to other people. The solution to the problem which this poses is not to get rid of man, as many imply, but to eliminate those of his works which are menacing. It is misleading to think that if you scratch a man you will find an ape. You find a man who will defend himself and his faith, which is but the affirmation of what he believes.

I have attempted here to present some aspects of an immediate and universal life problem. It may be studied simply, under clearly defined conditions which may be reproduced easily anywhere.

The thought of dying is an unforgettable experience. It occurs much earlier in life than is generally believed. It reveals itself to be among the powerful engines of change in man's development, gives rise to his religious beliefs, and advances his civilizing process.

The engine of change works in large measure in relation to the limitations that life imposes. The limitations, as I have shown, whether in the young child or in the adult, are perceived as anathema. What we learn is how early in life the conflict has its onset. The task, therefore, is to transcend one's bounds. What is to be observed is that the instincts of self-preservation manifest themselves psychologically earlier than has been supposed. In previous chapters, I attempted to show how the condition of ignominy was of necessity converted into a belief in distinction or being chosen, and that the threat of loss was made over into restitution. The realization of death produces a parallel effect. A transformation begins to take place which persists throughout life. Its ends are to defy an intolerable reality.

It has been correctly assumed that instincts of self-preservation must be present in early life. This remained to be demonstrated. Freud, as might have been expected, anticipated this in his 1914 paper "On Narcissism" [5]. He wrote that his concept of narcissism received reinforcement "from the observations we make of primitive peoples and children. In the former we find characteristics . . . [of] an overestimation of the power of wishes and mental processes, the 'omnipotence of thoughts,' a belief in the magical virtue of words, and a method of dealing with the outer world — the art of magic . . . In the child of our own day, whose development is much more obscure to us, we expect a perfectly analogous attitude towards the external world." At that time, he had little direct data either on primitives or on little children. His remarks, although more anticipatory than based on fact, are no less correct. He speculated that what threatens the self would be countered by the narcissism of the individual, and thereby a balance would be struck, an equilibrium established (homeostasis). He knew that difficulties hampered a direct study of narcissism, and felt that the principal means of access to an understanding of this central process would probably remain in the analysis of paraphrenics [schizophrenia], which would give us insight into the psychology of the Ego. At that time, nearly fifty years ago, the intensive research into young children was not anticipated.

Some of the young child's cardinal characteristics — his belief in the omnipotence of wishes and the power of magic; his imperishable egocentricity; his sense of helplessness coupled with a dependence upon others in authority whose favor he must solicit in coping with the loss complex and the dread of abandonment — play a critical part in the development and exercise of highly complex and essential mental mechanisms of defense. The child has a deep and pervasive concern with causality, in which the factors of change, of accident, and of caprice are suspended in favor of a closed determinism. The emergent momentous discovery of death strengthens and profoundly and permanently influences and governs the child's conduct. The chief ingredient of the child's cardinal characteristics, his belief in magic, are compounded into a religiosity. While the variations in religious expression are dictated in large measure by time, geography, local physical conditions, particular cultural levels and social circumstance, the principles show no alteration. From this view, the socialized, institutional, and formed aspects of religion of later life appear to be an evolved system of governing beliefs which rests upon a deeply rooted foundation that is fashioned in the early years. Actually, religious beliefs develop not so much by way of indoctrination as by the inevitable, specific, emotional conflicts of early childhood. Indeed, it is difficult to imagine how even a child subject to the most irreligious indoctrination would escape them. Religiosity thus plays a fundamental role in human experience. The significant, essential, and primary basis of religious belief is thus established far in advance of the final edifice, which, without it, would never have either its remarkable durability or its universality.

I have tried to show that the painful facts that people die, that limitations of one's powers exist, that life itself has limits and is uncertain in its duration, are all evident to the very young child. It appears that these threats to life and this recognition of reality are joined by the development of narcissism. The more closely death is encountered or limits to one's powers confronted, either early in life or as its end approaches, the more narcissism is relied upon. Narcissism is in fact an engine to recover, restore, and even to extend one's powers; to make restitution for loss; to transcend life by immortality. May narcissism then not be a principle of development — a *narcissine* principle — that has its origins in the psychology of childhood? Draconian in its persistence, it is this aspect of our own childhood psychology which constantly, although not exclusively, governs our contention with our awareness of our own inevitable but unpredictable end.

APPENDIX I

The two conditions of life a young child learns are that he has limitations and that he will die. These discoveries that each child makes for himself are abhorrent to him. In recent decades, since the child has been the object of direct psychological study, it has been found that at a very early age he knows his own fate and understands it to be true for others as well, but also he has erected emotional defenses against what he has learned.

These great discoveries, which have a lifelong effect, are at the root of melancholic discontent. It is these discoveries, moreover, that give rise to specific fears of being abandoned and isolated. The child's knowledge of what he has learned remains a permanent source of disquiet about reality; nothing is durable, and what is highly prized may be no exception to the rule. Hence, the disturbing import of possessing limitations, and of the certainty of dying at some unpredictable time, compels the development of elaborate defenses against a fate that cannot be escaped. The child does not rely solely upon himself, however. He turns to those upon whom he depends and who care for him. But the mere fact that he is in their charge is not enough to make him feel secure. Their fate, identical with his, must be altered. Therefore, he invests them with all the magical powers and privileges that he has taken upon himself. When he solicits their favor, they may be powerful enough to sway fate in his behalf. He expects little from a fate that is not cajoled into being kind. Self-inspired, unconsciously the child fashions a set of beliefs that counter all the disquieting details that he has acquired about living and dying.

The reactions which develop to mitigate fate are not confined to childhood. Only an uninformed view of psychological development would consider that the child's greatest discoveries, having had their impact in infancy and childhood, remain principally as recollections of events; that once having had an enormous influence, they are then carried into adult life only as memories. Since no period in life is free from losing what is valued, the past is thus constantly being renewed and linked to the present. The anticipation of what losses may come ties the past and the present to the future. In later development, the more intellectual and derived values, that is, those of high purpose and principle, the altruistic and philosophical ones and the cardinal virtues, are *parvenus,* elevated late to a high station but precariously placed. In a crisis, they are quickly deposed to give way to the older, more firmly established values of childhood. Thus in each encounter with a limitation, with every curtailment of a function, a failure or a loss, it is the inability rather than the unwillingness to accept them that is plain. When there is uncertainty of fulfillment, or a discrepancy between desire and desert, and when life itself is endangered, intellectual and logical reasoning are not left to hold the field alone. (This is not to say that reality is excluded, but that the use of fantasy is coupled with it rather than relinquished in the face of reality.) High-wrought emotional processes aim at undoing all dangerous and repugnant losses and limitations. Operating toward these ends as an engine of change is restitution.

Each phase of life has its characteristic means of finding or fashioning restitution for the limitations and losses that are encountered during it. Even so, the earlier methods of young childhood are not discarded for newly acquired methods of later periods. It is as though there were an old pharmacopoeia at hand in which the recipes never suffered deletions. However much the new remedies improved over the old, both are retained and used.

Efforts at restitution take place at all times. There are conditions throughout life that challenge the self-preserving instincts and the self-serving aims. Both the instincts and the aims may be satisfied only by favoring oneself. Between the demands of narcissism and the dictates of reality, conflicts arise. It is the human condition to rediscover this paradox throughout life. In the conflict between narcissism and reality, necessity requires that narcissism be put first.

"Actually we can never give up anything; we only exchange one thing for another, what appears to be a renunciation is really the formation of a substitute or surrogate."[1] These remarks by Freud first appeared in 1908, in a short paper, after he had included them in a lecture the year before. They may be found, slightly modified, in several of

[1] S. Freud: Creative Writers and Day Dreaming. In *The Complete Psychological Works of Sigmund Freud*, Standard Edition (London: Hogarth Press, 1959), IX, 145.

his later writings and also in some of his personal corre-
spondence. They were not elaborated upon. The context in
which these comments were written is the attachment to
what is pleasurable and thus valued, fears of loss, and transience as an experience leading to sorrow. Freud did not
incorporate his observations into his conceptual structure
or explanation of narcissism. But it is narcissism which his
observations concern.

The most skeptical observer would agree with the neglected fact that narcissism is a stable lifesaving process
which holds the seeds of discontent as well as those of restitution. The idea that discontent in the mental life of children
is no more than the frustration of their simple wishes neg-
lects the fact that it is their utter dependence upon those
who care for them, their lack of skill and mastery, their
feeble influence upon the environment, the experience that
their wishes are not always fulfilled and that they can lose
what they value, that leave them fully aware of their plight.
The child must confront these facts of life and find reality-
eroding narcissism. Reality compels discontent. A solution
is found to the conflict.

However, the discontent which reality compels is mitigated through the use of negation, an important mechanism. Negation allows intellectual acknowledgment of a
hostile reality, which it dismisses at the same time as emotionally unacceptable.[2] The fact that this mechanism is
present in the three-year-old child has been overlooked.
Negation is found to intervene on behalf of narcissism in
order to spare the child the oppressiveness of a too burdensome reality. Negation, which is part of the process of repression, is a defense used to resist the sense and the fact of
limitations on the self that reality imposes. The child is no
more willing than the adult to accept his limitations or to
accept his end. When reality confronts narcissism, adult

[2] S. Freud: Negations. In *The Complete Psychological Works of Sigmund Freud,* Standard Edition (London: Hogarth Press, 1961), XIX, 236.

defenses are not to be distinguished from those of the child. Freud reported them fifty years ago in his treatment of the concept of narcissism. He did not, however, indicate the tenacity or the durability of these defenses, nor that they served a basic need in the elaborate process of restitution for the limitations and losses experienced and anticipated in life. It is still customary to relegate these mechanisms to children, so-called primitive peoples, and to those adults who are childlike or "primitive." Freud wrote: "In the latter [referring to children and primitives] we find characteristics which if they occurred singly, might be put down to megalomania: an overestimation of the power of their wishes and mental acts, the 'omnipotence of thought,' a belief in the thaumaturgic force of words, and a technique for dealing with the external world — 'magic' — which appears to be a logical application of these grandiose premises. In the children of today, whose development is much more obscure to us, we expect to find an exactly analogous attitude towards the external world." [3]

The psychological development of children is not now as obscure as it was half a century ago. As Freud surmised it would be, the child's world of magic has been fully acknowledged. It is known to persist in the child for an indefinite period and it is also, in some uncertain measure, present in the adult. The general assumption, in the past and also currently, has been that magical thinking rests upon the use of fallacious premises. In addition, it has been assumed that enlightened intelligence replaces the world of magic. The latter assumption is founded upon the premise that reason is more appealing than unreason and that, true to the beliefs of John Locke, where reason is offered, the irrational yields. Common experience shows that reason does appeal within limits as a means of adapting to reality. However,

[3] S. Freud: On Narcissism. In *The Complete Psychological Works of Sigmund Freud,* Standard Edition (London: Hogarth Press, 1957), XIV, 82–102.

when reality contains danger or uncertainty that reason cannot penetrate, another system of thinking is manifested. It is the oldest one, magic.

When narcissism is menaced, reason seems to have little effect, it is the world of magic that is relied upon. There is no time in life when the archaic system of magical thinking may not be invoked. Striving to extend one's limits, to fulfill ideals, to recoup losses of self-esteem, of functions, and of valued objects, to reduce anxiety about an uncertain future and even to evade one's death,[4] will not be satisfied by appeals to reason. The rational system of thinking will inevitably reach its bounds in failing to provide gratification that is sought for wishes that narcissism requires. The result is that the archaic system is never altogether relinquished, regardless of one's level of intelligence and reason, because the demands of the wishes are far beyond what may be rationally satisfied by reason or rationally justified.

Freud's monumental work, "The Psychopathology of Everyday Life,"[5] reveals that it should be possible, at least theoretically, to demonstrate the processes of the mind in its smallest details. The work is so thorough that little has been added to it by other authors since its first

[4] The supposition of a death instinct, to which Freud (see his "The Ego and the Id" in *The Complete Psychological Works of Sigmund Freud,* Standard Edition [London: Hogarth Press, 1961], XIX, 3–66) gave credence, although stating categorically that it was not a psychological phenomenon, led him into fruitless speculation and drew others into endless controversy for decades. The continuing speculation no longer interests most psychoanalysts but it seems to retain polemical viability in some academic circles. (See N. Brown's *Life Against Death* [New York: Random House, 1959], pp. 87–134.) Confusing speculation with clinical findings leads to overlooking that the notions about a death instinct are being associated with self-destructive acts and behavior arising as specific conflicts connected with unbearable destructive wishes toward a valued object which are instead directed toward oneself. Others since Freud are responsible for the continued confusion by failing to note his comment that if such instincts are present they are "mute."

[5] S. Freud: The Psychopathology of Everyday Life. In *The Complete Psychological Works of Sigmund Freud,* Standard Edition (London: Hogarth Press, 1960), VI.

appearance in 1901. It was not within the scope of Freud's work to include the psychopathology of everyday magic, that is, the expression of the archaic system of thinking in daily existence. He made many references to it throughout his voluminous work, but he did not place everyday magic with everyday psychopathology.

It may be argued that the two are not often distinguishable. This, while correct, is the best reason to attempt defining the distinction. So little study has been done on this aspect of everyday life that there is no significant psychoanalytic literature to cite. For reasons that seem indeterminate, the daily use of magical thinking in support of narcissism throughout life has not been studied much by psychoanalysts. It is paradoxical that a science attentive to unconscious motivation and to the irrational in man should have neglected definitive studies of the archaic system of thinking in everyday life. Studies of this subject have been carried out principally in relation to the most serious emotional disorders, the psychoses, and to a far lesser degree in relation to the thinking of young children. Perhaps the explanation for this lack may be in the restricted view of narcissism that has prevailed.

Narcissism, to judge from the extensive writings upon the subject, is regarded primarily as a condition of childhood that needs to be converted from one of egoism and egocentricity, characterizing early development, to one of object relations, in which narcissism is relinquished for the love or for the sake of another and valued person. Or it is considered in its disorders, as displayed in the psychoses and neuroses. Freud explained that "certain special difficulties seem to me to lie in the way of a direct study of narcissism. Our chief means of access to it will probably remain the analysis of the paraphrenias [psychoses, especially the schizophrenias]." In the same paper he states that hypochondria and the "behavior of human beings in love, with its manifold differentiation in man and woman,"

offer ways of studying narcissism.[6] Freud had not anticipated that the direct study of children would provide one of
the most profitable sources for the study of narcissism. But
the question that Freud poses, What brings narcissism into
being?, goes begging.[7]

Freud takes off from the point that narcissism exists and
he goes on to considerations of its vicissitudes. But the way
in which the feeling of self-regard, that is, narcissism,
evolves is not extensively discussed except as "a measure
of the ego," to use his phrase. " . . . what various components go to make up that measure is irrelevant," he adds;
"everything we possess or achieve, every remnant of the
primitive feeling of omnipotence that experience has cor-
roborated helps to exalt self-regard." He admits the
importance of the subject and the difficulty of surveying it.
He attributes the development of the ego to a departure
from primary narcissism which leads to a vigorous attempt
to recover it. For ego development to take place, some of
the instinctual aims are deflected and recovery of what has
been sacrificed by the way of instinctual satisfaction is attempted. "This departure is brought about by means of
displacement of libido to an ego-ideal imposed from without, while gratification is derived from the attainment of
this ideal," [6] he wrote. "Self-regard is in part primary —
the residue of childish narcissism [primary narcissism];
another part arises out of such omnipotence as experience
corroborates (the fulfillment of the ego-ideal) whilst a third
part proceeds from the gratification of object libido" [6].

The achievement of object relations is a process of de-

---

[6] S. Freud: On Narcissism. In *The Complete Psychological Works of
Sigmund Freud,* Standard Edition (London: Hogarth Press, 1957) XIV,
82–102.

[7] Reference here is to secondary narcissism. Primary narcissism forms
one of the hypotheses of the libido theory. It is deduced rather than observed and is perhaps best indicated by the autoerotic and the instinctual
processes, in contrast to secondary narcissism, which develops as a part
of the ego.

parture from concern solely with primary needs, in which they are given up and invested in the need for another person. The human condition is that instinctual needs (as they are expressed in primary narcissism) are not self-sustaining. Contrary to Freud, human survival does not rest solely upon the primordial instincts; it rests also upon another person (or persons) upon whom one has come to depend. Ego development is thus defined; survival is thus insured. Therefore, survival depends upon departure from the primary state.

It was Freud's observation that "normal adults show that their former megalomania has been subdued and that their mental characteristics from which we inferred their narcissism have vanished"[6], that is, undergo repression. These characteristics that Freud refers to return readily and with viability in the course of everyday psychopathology. Magical thinking does not seem to be remote when, in the dream, all the characteristics of our former megalomania are often present. Our movement from the world of reality to the one of magic is commonplace. We are never entirely in the one or the other at any given time. Rather, we are chiefly in the one while not having given up the other. The extent to which we live in a world of magic can, as yet, only be surmised.

APPENDIX II

Case A:
A boy, 3 years 6 months old. The action takes place in a doll house which is furnished with the usual household goods. A family of dolls (mother, father, brother, sister, and baby). First the dolls are being knocked from the chairs.

A: They fall down and get hurt.

Dr.: How?

A : From falling down.

Dr. : What now?

A : To the hospital.

Dr. : Then what?

A : Get shot with a needle.

Dr. : But he doesn't want it.

A : That's what he's going to get.

An interval now. The play continues with shifting the dolls to a sink, with running water. The child indicates that the dolls are frightened.

Dr. : They are scared?

A : Put him in there and he'll die.

Dr. : Will he?

A : Yup.

Dr. : Then what?

A : No more. He'll be all gone. He died. He goes down the pipe.

Dr. : Not really.

A : Yup. Down the sewer. He gets died. The pipe and the sewer is where he goes down. (*He eats candy and then says*) They have to have some food.

Dr. : But they're dead.

A : They have to eat.

Dr. : Food for the dead ones?

A : Yes, they're hungry. (*He puts another doll down the drain.*) They're all dead. They come back.

Dr. : If you're dead, don't you stay dead?

A : No, you grow again. You don't stay dead.

A : I shoot that (*rubber toy bear*) dead. The bear went down the sink. He's gone.

Dr. : When it's dead it's gone?

A : I shoot him again.

Dr.: But he's dead.

A: Yes, I'm going to eat him for supper. Then he'll be gone. (*Runs water over the toy bear.*)

Dr.: What are you doing now?

A: He's drinking it (*the bear*).

Dr.: I thought he was dead.

A: He can drink now.

Dr.: Can dead bears drink?

A: Yes.

Dr.: They can? (*The bear is filled with water again.*)

A: I'll drink out of the bear.

Dr: Then what?

A: I'll grow to be a bear.

Dr.: You'll do what?

A: I'll grow to be a bear.

Dr.: Is that what happens?

A: Yes.

Dr.: Suppose you eat a chicken?

A: Yup. (*Drinks from the bear again.*) He's walking in a pond (*refers to the bear on the edge of the sink*).

Dr.: You said he was dead.

A: He can still walk.

Dr.: Really? Can dead people walk?

A: Yup.

Dr.: Oh! I thought dead bears couldn't walk.

A: Yes they can. They can eat.

Dr.: They can walk and eat? Anything else?

A: No.

Dr.: Can they talk?

A: I'm going to turn the water off.

On another occasion the action takes place between a group of toy soldiers and a plane.

A: The soldiers get hit with a plane. He's dead.

Dr.: You killed him?

A: Yes.

Dr.: What happens?

A: He goes bye-bye.

Dr.: Now you are hitting that man.

A: I'll get him down here (*the drain*).

Dr.: Down there?

A: Yes, down in the sewer.

Dr.: Is that where dead people go?

A: Dead things get in sewers.

Dr.: They don't want to go there.

A: Yes, they do. They're already in.

Dr.: Well —

A: He comes to get him out. (*Ambulance comes to the sink.*)

Dr.: To take him out?

A: No, we'll take him to the hospital.

Dr.: Isn't he dead?

A: He's still dead in the sewer. Now he's going to throw up in the sewer.

Dr.: Maybe he doesn't want to be in the sewer.

A: He's going to scream.

Dr.: He's dead.

A: He doesn't want to go to the hospital. He's going to have to get shot with a needle.

Dr.: He doesn't want that.

A: But he is. Two men are going to take him. He's going to get gasoline in his mouth.

Dr.: He doesn't want it.

A: He'll get it.

Dr.: What happens if you put gasoline in his mouth?

A: What?

Dr.: What happens?

A: He dies.

Dr.: If he dies?

A: They're all gone.

Dr.: Will he stay gone?

A: Yes. If he's gone he can't come home. (*He puts doll once more in drain.*)

Dr.: You're putting them all in the sewer. Are they dead or alive now?

A: Alive.

Dr.: Alive?

A: They are all in the sewer again.

Dr.: But then they're dead.

A: They can be alive again.

Dr.: Dead people can be alive again?

A: They're wet. I put gasoline on them.

Dr.: That's enough, isn't it?

A: No. I want more. He's left behind (*designating a doll*).

Dr.: Why is he left behind?

A: He did something.

Dr.: What?

A: Nothing!

Dr.: He did do something?

The play with dolls goes back to the sink again.

A: He went over his head. Too deep. He has to be over his head.

Dr.: You're going to put him in over his head?

A: Yes.

Dr.: Why?

A: Well, I like to be mean to him.

DR.: He says, "Don't be mean to me."

A: I'm going to be.

DR.: He says, "Don't."

A: I'm going to be.

DR.: You're going to be mean anyway?

A: Yes.

DR.: Really?

A: He's going to be killed.

DR.: He says, "Don't kill me."

A: He is.

DR.: He says, "Please don't."

A: Going to put water on him. Going to put gasoline on him.

DR.: Then what?

A: Nothing.

DR.: Nothing?

A: He's down the pipe. He's killed and gone.

DR.: You brought him out.

A: He's back.

DR.: He was dead.

A: Yup, but he's back.

Another interval. He picks up a dog.

A: The dog is going to have a shot.

DR.: What's wrong?

A: He has a temperature. See, the man is in the sewer and I'm taking him out.

DR.: Wasn't he dead?

A: Not now. He's looking in the pipe.

DR.: What for?

A: To see if dogs and cats are in the sewer.

Dr.: How do they get there?

A: People put them in the sewer.

APPENDIX III

Case B:
A girl, 4 years 4 months old. On this occasion the action takes place around the doll's house. There is a mother, a father, a little girl, and a baby boy.

B: The lights are out. It's dark.

Dr.: If the lights are out?

B: The kids get scared.

Dr.: What is there to be scared about?

B: They would get lost.

Dr.: Anything else?

B: They could get killed.

Dr.: In the dark?

B: They might have an accident. They couldn't see where to go. Not know where they're walking.

Dr.: They might get killed if they couldn't see where they're going?

B: Well. They might walk into the woods by mistake. I'm pretending they're in the woods.

Dr.: And if they get killed?

B: They die.

Dr.: Then?

B: They go in the graveyard.

Dr.: Have you seen a graveyard?

B: I once saw someone get buried.

Dr.: Did you really see it?

B: Well — No.

Dr.: What happens when people are buried?

B: I don't know. I saw my great-grandma killed.

Dr.: You saw your great-grandma killed?

B: She got too big and too old.

Dr.: When they get too old they die?

B: Yes. My mother told me people die. They get buried. Before they get buried they just get in a box and they put them in a truck.

Dr.: Then?

B: (*Silence*) I wish you would say the words. What I was trying to think of.

Dr.: What words?

B: They have all kinds of boxes.

Dr.: For different people?

B: Big sizes.

Dr.: Then after the people are in the boxes and buried?

B: They come out. Somebody digs the dirt off them.

Dr.: They can't do it themselves?

B: No. They take the box out. I'm thinking where they go.

Dr.: Where dead people go?

B: In the woods.

Dr.: They go in the woods? Do they do anything?

B: How can they do anything when they're dead? In the box.

On another occasion in the playroom she picked up a rifle saying, "I'm going to play with a gun and shoot."

Dr.: What?

B: I'm going to shoot animals. I'll keep them and save them and eat them. (*Shoots animals.*)

Dr.: Which animals will you shoot?

B: Just the ones to eat. I don't shoot the elephant (*a rubber toy*). I wouldn't kill him. We'd save him for a pet.

Dr.: What happens to animals that die?

B: They don't get buried.

Dr.: What else?

B: They go to animal doctors and get fixed.

Dr.: After they die?

B: Yes.

Dr.: They don't stay dead?

B: No.

Dr.: Maybe you are mistaken.

B: Only if they get dead. They go to the animal hospital and they get fixed.

Dr.: Does it happen to people too?

B: No.

Dr.: People stay dead but animals don't?

B: Because animals are more nice.

Dr.: And animals only stay dead if you eat them?

B: I'm going to shoot myself.

Dr.: Kill yourself? Don't do that.

B: Yes. I'm dead.

Dr.: Now what will happen?

B: I'm going to get buried.

Dr.: Can't we take you to a hospital?

B: Yes. O.K. Now you fix me.

The play shifts to dolls. One is dead, taken to a doctor, and given medicine.

Dr.: Can dead people eat medicine?

B: Yeah. They swallow it.

Dr.: I thought they couldn't eat when they're dead.

B: They can. Give her more medicine. (*The doll is given
    medicine.*)

B: She isn't dead any more.

Dr.:   Is she alive?

B: Yes.

Dr.:   Just as she was before?

B: Yes.

*On another occasion the child began with the following
statement:*

B: Remember the day I shooted myself? Let's do it again.

Dr.:   You're going to shoot yourself? What will happen?

B: Nothing. I get shot in the arm. I don't fall dead. Only if
    I get shot in the eye.

Dr.:   Then you're not dead because of the arm shot.

B: You fall dead if you get shot here.

Dr.:   Where?

B: Because that's the heart. Right here.

Dr.:   If you get shot in the heart, do you get killed?

B: Yes, if you get shot in the head you could get dead.

Dr.:   But I could take pills so I won't get dead.

The play then shifts to puppets.

B: Get the right medicine. I believe I have a broken bone.

Dr.:   How did you get it?

B: Because I fell out of a plane.

APPENDIX IV

Case C:
A boy, 3 years 3 months old. The setting is a tabletop with a

small family of dolls (mother, father, boy, girl, and baby) rubber elephant, bear, and tiger.

C: Let's run a truck over him (*the bear*). O.K. Let's put him in a graveyard.

Dr.: He doesn't want to have it happen.

C: I'm going to put him in the graveyard.

Dr.: Maybe —

C: I'm going to put him there. He can talk and eat dirt sometimes.

Dr.: What else?

C: Let's shoot him again.

Dr.: I thought he was dead.

C: I just wanted to wound him, so he's going to be more killed.

Dr.: But he is dead?

C: I'm going to kill him once more.

Dr.: What happens?

C: He will have to lie down in the graveyard. He's dead. When they get very old they die.
Cats die when they get too old.

The play shifts now to a toy rubber tiger.

C: He is going to growl and bite.

Dr.: Who?

C: It bites different kinds of animals.

Dr.: You don't want to get bitten?

C: Sometimes my sister does.

Dr.: She bites you?

C: She tries. But I kick my foot. I want to shoot another animal. (*He takes a gun and fires away and then says*) Smoke came out of the gun.

Dr.: What happened?

C: I burned him. I'm going to shoot his head.

Dr.: I'll watch you do it.

C: I'm going to make a bigger hole. Maybe I can smoke him up. Now he's just got dead. They have to go to the graveyard.

Dr.: I wouldn't want to stay.

C: I'd be sorry not to see my house. My mother and daddy would come with me to the graveyard.

Dr.: What if they did not?

C: Then I wouldn't go. When grown-ups die, they die. People who die have to stay there.

Dr.: Well, what happens?

C: They can eat inch worms. Can I make a big lobster? (*He begins to work with clay, and I help him to fashion a lobster. After we have completed this he says*) He's going to bite.

Dr.: What will he do?

C: Let's take his mouth off.

Dr.: What for?

C: So he won't bite.
(*He then picks up a rifle and shoots the house.*) Should I kill the house?
(*The lobster bites the boy and then the boy turns and says*) I'm going to make him flat as a pancake. (*With that he destroys the lobster.*)

APPENDIX V

Case D:
A 4-year-old boy. The action takes place in the kitchen of the doll house. D says that the mother is washing the dishes.

Dr.: Why is she washing them?

D: To get the germs off.

Dr.: What are germs?

D: They make people sick.

Dr.: Did you ever hear of anyone being sick?

D: No. They take medicine and it makes them better.

Action shifts to an airplane that he flies to Chicago. He puts the family of dolls in the plane. All fly off. Suddenly the plane crashes.

Dr.: What happens?

D: It ran out of gas.

Dr.: And the people inside?

D: They have to go to the doctor.

The plane flies once more, crashes again, and burns.

D: He's going to check the gas.

Dr.: What about the people?

D: They have to run. Nobody gets hurt.

Action returns to the doll house kitchen now. The mother is cooking dinner.

D: Baby is sick and he needs medicine. (*While he is saying this, D eats candy and drops one on the floor. He says*) Are there germs on the floor?

Dr.: Some.

D: I hate them. (*But he eats the candy he dropped.*)

The action shifts to shooting rifles at the dolls.

Dr.: What happened?

D: The baby gets killed. He won't live forever.

Dʀ.: Why not?

D: You're just not alive any more.

The action goes back to the doll house. He fills a tub with water for the baby to bathe.

D: I'm going to fill it with hot water.

Dʀ.: Hot?

D: It's going to be very hot. Roasting hot. He's going to get a roasting bath. The baby has to get it. He's burned. Now I'm going to shoot the baby.

Dʀ.: What will happen?

D: (*Will not answer.*)

Dʀ.: You don't want to say.

D: I don't like to talk about it. It's too sad. (*Suddenly*) Oh, they're still alive.

Dʀ.: What's going on?

D: If you killed them with a knife and you take the knife out then they're still alive.

The action changes to filling a plane with passengers. The plane crashes. Before it falls to the ground the doors open and all the people fall out.

Dʀ.: You know that if people fell out they could get hurt.

D: No. I don't know that.

Dʀ.: What do you think happens?

D: You bury them.

He plays again with a plane roaring about the room, crashes it. The pilot is not hurt at all. He then goes to the blackboard and draws a "wrecked-up house."

D: It has ghosts.

Dʀ.: What are they?

D: They scare people. But there is no such thing my father says. (*He draws a small figure who he says has run away scared.*)

The play shifts to a rifle. He shoots animals — elephant, bear, tiger — and kills them.

D: They get buried.
Last night I found a dead bee.

Dr.: Did it look dead?

D: He got killed. Someone stepped on him and it got dead.

Dr.: Dead like people are dead?

D: They're dead but they're not like dead people. Nothing like dead people.

Dr.: Is there a difference?

D: People are dead and bees are dead. But they're put in the ground and they're no good. People.

Dr.: Are no good?

D: After a long time he'll get alive (*the bee*). But not a person. I don't want to talk about it.

Dr.: Why?

D: Because I have two grandfathers alive.

Dr.: Two?

D: One.

Dr.: What happened to one?

D: He died a long time ago. A hundred years ago.

Dr.: Will you live long too?

D: A hundred years.

Dr.: Then what?

D: I'll die perhaps.

Dr.: All people die.

D: Yes. I will have to.

Dr.: That is sad.

D: I have to anyway.

DR.: You have to?

D: Sure. My father is going to die. That is sad.

DR.: Why is he?

D: Never mind.

DR.: You don't want to talk about it.

D: I want to see my mother now.

DR.: I'll take you to her.

D: I know where dead people are. In cemeteries. My old grandfather is dead. He can't get out.

DR.: You mean where he is buried.

D: He can't get out. Never.

REFERENCES

1. Anthony, Sylvia: *The Child's Discovery of Death: A Study of Child Psychology* (London: Kegan Paul, 1940; New York: Harcourt, Brace, 1940).

2. Eliade, Mircea: *Myths, Dreams and Mysteries* (London: Harvill Press, 1960), p. 227.

2a. Frazer, James George: *The Golden Bough: A Study in Magic and Religion* (New York: The Macmillan Co., 1947), p. 11.

3. Freud, S.: Analysis of a Phobia in a Five Year Old Boy (Little Hans). In *The Complete Psychological Works of Sigmund Freud,* Standard Edition (London: Hogarth Press, 1955), X, 101–149.

4. ———. Leonardo da Vinci and a memory of his childhood. In *ibid.* (1957), XI, 78–79.

5. ———. On Narcissism: An Introduction. In *Collected Papers* (London: Hogarth Press, 1948), IV, 32–39.

6. ———. The Sexual Theories of Children. In *The Complete Psychological Works of Sigmund Freud,* Standard Edition (London: Hogarth Press, 1954), IX, 205–209.

7. Hastings, James (Ed.): *Encyclopedia of Religion and Ethics* (New York: Charles Scribner's Sons, 1911; Edinburgh: T. & T. Clark), III, 520.

8. *Ibid.* (1912), IV, 411.

9. Hendrick, Ives: *Facts and Theories of Psychoanalysis,* 3rd. ed. (New York: Alfred A. Knopf, 1960), p. 309.

10. Malinowski, Bronislaw: *Magic, Science, and Religion* (New York: Doubleday Anchor Press, 1948), pp. 7, 15, 47.

11. Nagy, Maria: The Child's Theories Concerning Death. *J. Genet. Psychol.,* 73 (1948), 3, 4, 26, 27.

12. Piaget, Jean: *The Child's Conception of Physical Causality* (London: Kegan Paul, 1930), pp. 241, 258.

13. Rochlin, Gregory: The Loss Complex: A contribution to the Etiology of Depression. *J. Amer. Psychoanal. Ass.,* 7 (1959), 299–316.

14. ———. The Dread of Abandonment: A contribution to the Etiology of the Loss Complex and to Depression. In *The Psychoanalytic Study of the Child* (New York: International Universities Press, 1961), XVI, 451–470.

15. Schilder, Paul, and David Wechsler: The Attitude of Children Towards Death. *J. Genet. Psychol.,* 45 (1935), 406.

4

LOSS AND RESTITUTION

There are few experiences in life which are of greater emotional significance than the personal losses which occur and the attempts that are made for their restitution. Losses test our measure of achievement. Our degree of mastery over our instincts, the quality of our personal relationships with others, our adaptation to the world of reality, and the extent of our individual autonomy are revealed in a lifelong chain. The cycle of loss and restitution begins in early infancy and extends to the end of life [12]. Losses throughout life tend to be regarded as inevitable but adventitious, painful, and primarily detrimental to well-being. The saddening aftermath of loss which results from the effects of personal deprivation has obscured the fact that losses, real and otherwise, by serving as catalysts of change and forcing substitution and sublimation, play a critical role in psychic development, and especially in that most exalted of human qualities, creativity.

Loss and restitution have been the subject of long controversy among psychoanalysts. It is not my intention to contribute to an argument so much as to attempt to resolve a problem.

Many psychoanalysts have asserted that loss and restitution begin at birth. Such views became current when Freud first advanced his assumptions about the psychology of infancy in 1911 when he wrote of the infant that its "state of equilibrium was originally disturbed by the peremptory demands of inner needs . . . that whatever was thought of (desired) was simply imagined in an hallucinatory form . . . this attempt at satisfaction by means of hallucination was abandoned only in consequence of the absence of the expected gratification, because of the disappointment experienced'' [6]. Freud pointed out that the pleasure principle, a classic principle of mental functioning, was no longer unique because a new principle of mental functioning was introduced: ''. . . what was conceived of was no longer that which was pleasant but that which was real even if it should be unpleasant.'' The existence of the reality principle, Freud wrote, proves that a momentous development has taken place in the child's mind. Its importance is, first, that the child forms a conception of the real circumstances in the outer world; and second, that he exerts himself to alter them. Freud's later work, and that of others following his theory, has led to great advances in the understanding of human psychology which are based primarily upon the clinical evidence of unconscious wish fulfillment. Wish fulfillment is central, therefore, in our present psychoanalytic understanding of man.

Sprinkled throughout Freud's voluminous works are countless references to the role and function of unconscious wishes. Some of these references are made as theoretical points in ''Beyond the Pleasure Principle,'' ''Instincts and Their Vicissitudes,'' in portions of ''The Interpretation of Dreams,'' ''Metapsychological Supplement to the Theory of Dreams,'' ''The Future of an Illusion,'' and ''The Ego and the Id.'' Other references are more clinical: those in ''Mourning and Melancholia,'' ''On Dreams,'' ''Group Psychology,'' ''The Case of Shreber,'' to name a few of the principal ones. The unifying theme to which I wish to call attention and which draws these works together in terms of unconscious wishes is expressed by Freud when he says: ''Really we never can relinquish anything; we only exchange one thing for something else. When we appear to

give something up, all we really do is to adopt a substitute"
[3]. In the myriad complexities which are encompassed by
the process Freud describes in these two sentences, the
principle of his statement is largely lost sight of. Freud
himself did not neglect the significance of his statement and
he seldom failed to be guided by it, as is illustrated by his
frequent references to the tenacity with which significant or
valued relationships are held. Nevertheless, he did not fully
exploit the importance of the process of relinquishment and
substitution. Those who have followed Freud's work in this
particular area have dealt only with fragments of it. Thus
we find that the deeply emotional experiences of deprivation and loss are treated as though they were entities in
themselves — as though there were a psychology of loss, of
deprivation or frustration, or one of security and trust, or
one of infantile helplessness and another of restitution, although the last, unlike the others, has never been conceptually developed to a significant degree.

A great deal of modern psychology is based upon efforts
to explain the infant's primary emotional state. In these
investigations the chief emphasis has been placed upon the
child's helplessness. There is some risk in taking such a
concept literally. To do so assumes that the infant sees himself as an impartial observer might: weak, puny, and unable
to care for himself — as if the infant were making an objective appraisal of his actual situation or were making an
ego-developed judgment. Although there is no supporting
clinical evidence that such views are held by infants, a psychology of infancy has been constructed which presupposes
such grounds. Another concept is that an infant's sense of
security, more romantically expressed in metaphor as
"basic trust," endows the infant with the powers of judgment about others that he is alleged to possess about himself. There is also a similar but reversed view of infancy
which may have a bearing on the notions expressed by
many psychoanalysts who, concerning themselves with the

phenomenology of early psychic development, view regressive behavior in adults as representing a literal return to infancy. That is, they see infancy as a social condition in which value judgments of others, which are indistinguishable in many ways from adult ones, are readily made by the infant. This is best illustrated by the writings of Melanie Klein and her followers, who have introduced into the mental life of the infant such speculative ideas as "good" and "bad" objects (meaning the persons who care for the child, usually the mother, over whom the child moralizes). Such ideas which enjoy a certain popularity and influence with some of the present generation of psychoanalysts, tend to preempt the notion of development itself. Indeed, an entire, developed psychology of infancy was put forth as characteristic of the early months of life.

In the last twenty-five years, however, a shift has taken place in the psychoanalytic psychology of childhood, and particularly of infancy. Meticulous attention has been paid to factors which had previously not been stressed. Notably, the profound effect of the environment has been emphasized. Nevertheless, the infant's psychology, during this shift, has been viewed in essentially the same way as before. Earlier, the infant was thought to possess a sophisticated mental life, with defined conflicting attitudes about his parents and their relationship with each other, and with a somewhat objective view of himself. These views have been only slightly modified. The former hypothetical period of infantile psychological development was extended from the first few months of life to most of the first year, and the infant was regarded as having the same conflicts as those of a much older child, only expressed in infantile terms. To support such views of infantile psychology, the psychoanalysts who hold them are obliged to compress psychological development into the earliest months of life. The clinical facts do not sustain the speculation that the psychology of the infant is elaborated within the first year of life and in relation to the infant's naturally limited development and experience during that time.

Probably the most important developmental step that takes place in early psychological life is the infant's relation to another person, that is, to one who is associated with gratification and the relief of discomfort. If, as is conceivable, the infant hallucinates or in a crude way dreams satisfactions as a relief from discomfort, his hunger, for example, will not be met by a fantasy feeding; the discomfort quickly supersedes any hallucinatory effort to dispel it. Perhaps the earliest needs are momentarily gratified through some fragment of a dream of pleausre, but the dream quickly gives way to being comforted by the one who takes care of the infant. How long human life proceeds without awareness of the need for another person is a matter of conjecture. The time is probably very short. The simplest care of an infant introduces the indispensability of another person. The experience of being cared for becomes rapidly commingled with gratification or pleasure and the relief of tension. Only under these circumstances are the primary conditions of the child's and every adult's life established. These primary conditions, or principles of mental functioning, are: (1) the universal pleasure principle, by which emotional life is governed, and (2) the reality principle, or seeing reality as it is. In addition, there is (3) the principle which modifies reality to serve the ends of pleasure or gratification.

We are thus in the unique position that the fundamental principles which govern our mental life are directly associated with and depend upon a relationship with another person. These basic principles of mental functioning cannot be achieved by an individual alone. An appraisal of weakness, a judgment of good and evil, a sense of trust, are all later developments which depend first upon the firm foundation of the basic principles by which a measure of constancy is achieved through a relationship with one who provides care.

It is not surprising, then, to find at the core of a child's emotional development a striving for relief from the experiences of frustration and deprivation. Compensation is sought for what may be currently withheld. As renunciation or repression of the instincts takes place, a demand for gratification grows. These dynamic conflicts represent another fundamental axiom: that it appears to be alien to human nature to accept a lack of fulfillment. What is felt to be wanting, or wished for, or otherwise of value that has been forgone or lost is being perpetually sought and is constantly in the process of being restored. Restoration may be accomplished in fact or in fantasy, by symbol or by substitute, consciously or unwittingly. The purpose is to make up and restore what was sacrificed in order that the balance may be set right again.

During the process of restoration the two very important and essential functions of reality are in operation. First, reality is perceived through a lack of fulfillment. This is best demonstrated by the fact that life provides a constant reminder that satisfaction is in jeopardy. Longed-for wishes are often not met and self-esteem is regularly compromised as reality renders its verdict. Second, the wish and the need to alter reality in the persistent pursuit of satisfaction are compelling. Thus the second principle of mental functioning (which Freud defined as the formation of a conception of reality) not only accomplishes an appraisal of the conditions of life but, in so doing, compels realization that fulfillment is transient. The more clearly reality is perceived, the more uncertainties there are to be discovered. As though to contradict the lucidity of the perceptions according to the second or reality principle, the third principle mentioned above alters reality and modifies it to bring reality more in accord with our wishes.

Who has not failed to wish to influence and even to change a displeasing outcome? A farmer whose crop is dying for lack of rain will pray for it and inveigh against Nature. He is in no way significantly different from his neolithic ancestor in his feeling or in what and whom he calls upon to alter reality. The child, too small to reach what he wants, is no more active in the practice of these principles than the aged man who discovers that he is too feeble to climb his favorite hill and longs for strength that he will never again possess. The burdens of reality are too heavy to support for long without wishing for them to be lightened. The durability and universality of the myth of paradise amply prove this point. To limit a view of paradise to the conventional beliefs of its existence in the hereafter is too narrow. The common and plentiful daydreams and fantasies of a better life to come tomorrow, like those of immortality, are not fashioned at the end of life, but throughout it.

The formation of a concept of the real world, while it leads to dissatisfactions on the one hand, on the other hand compels exertions to change. This lifelong activity is central to psychological development. Much attention has been paid to the pain which losses or failures produce, but their obverse — the restitution and creativity they generated — has been accorded too little notice. When losses occur, it is generally believed that a balance is restored by the final acceptance of reality. Insufficient attention has been given to the judgment of reality that impels men to attempt to alter it. Both the reality principle and the principle which modifies reality to the ends of pleasure are indispensable.

The mentally disordered exert themselves to alter reality no more than those who are not. They merely do so in a pathological fashion. Disappointments, frustrations, displeasures, or a lack of gratification are never really accepted. It is important to note what substitutes, alternatives, and exchanges they invariably put into operation.

The infant has but limited emotional means at his disposal to spend on recouping his losses or disappointments and frustrations. He has only limited and rudimentary ways in which restitution can be made. As development and maturation take place a richer variety of responses and pathways to satisfaction becomes available. They become additions to the infantile forms which they often appear to have replaced, but under the burden of a significant loss, regressions to the earliest forms are frequently noted.

Most mental institutions can furnish examples of people who have maintained themselves most of their lives but who have then relinquished their previous mode of behavior for regressive forms of infantile satisfactions. Lest it be supposed that this applies only to the mentally ill, the same process may be commonly observed in the mourners at the time of death of a personally important person. The mourner's normal patterns of feeding habits, for example, frequently alters, perhaps in the direction of disgust with food and no desire to eat, or a sudden capricious taste that perhaps the dead person enjoyed; or perhaps a voracious appetite may develop. On closer examination, it will be noted that these variations of habitual modes of behavior stem from much earlier periods in life, wherein important experiences in relation to another person — frustration, anger, disappointment, and even pleasure — were often reflected in reactions to feeding or food. There are also social as well as individual forms of eating related to death, such as *post mortem* feasts, testimonials, and even Communion, all expressing the belief that a loss may be rectified through eating, whether it be the Blessed Wafer or the totem animal.

A loss, a deprivation, or a disappointment to be reconciled does not necessarily involve a relation to another person. The same process, that is, the striving to alter reality, takes place when the loss refers to a satisfying image of oneself that is forgone. Daily losses from the vicissitudes of life, contrary to conventional belief, are probably not simply accepted. Compensation is made for them. Functions previously well performed, if impaired and not carried out, lead to a sense of dissatisfaction. These everyday occurrences lead to some wish or some ambition or perhaps some act which will attempt to restore the previous balance.

When a sense of well-being is lost through illness or infirmity, restitution is often made through fantasy of achievements which will be forthcoming with recovery. Meanwhile, excessive needs and even demands for nursing care are common. For example, a vigorous, handsome, athletic young woman who prided herself on her skill fell from a horse. The accident humiliated her. She was momentarily stunned and severely bruised but not seriously injured. She was taken to a hospital where doctors seemed to her to be too busy to be concerned with her. She complained that the seriousness of her condition was unrecognized. She demanded more nursing care than was warranted. Her self-concern increased as she blamed and devalued herself. The lack of attention demeaned her as though there had been no accident, but rather a test of her worth. She attempted to make up for her loss of face and poor self-image by increasing demands for attention to restore her self-esteem. To her, *being cared for meant to be valued.* As a small child she had found that her mother was solicitous only when she was ill. At those times she believed her mother cared for her, but the rest of the time she believed her mother was negligent. When she received the care that she wanted from the nurses, her self-esteem was restored and she made a quick and uneventful recovery. Her regression to childhood behavior was brief. The process of making restitution followed her loss of self-esteem.

There are significant manifestations of the process of loss and restitution to be noted in the everyday activity of young children. Observe a little boy's first haircut. It is often followed by his wish to keep the shorn hair. There is no doubt that to have a part of oneself cut off has a symbolic castration meaning. Moreover, the wish to save the cuttings or put them back is to want to restore what has been removed. Such a child may often either not want his fingernails pared or, if they are cut, will want to eat or save them, just as his nose pickings are not to be thrown away.

Another example of the same process may be noted in a three-year-old boy who became extremely constipated when he felt threatened by an elective minor surgical procedure for his foot. He literally refused to part with his stools. Cajoling, threats, warnings of dire consequences by his parents were of no avail. When he was assured that he would have stools as long as he lived, he stopped his struggle against his feared loss; he relinquished his miserliness when he understood that the supply of what he valued and hoarded would never give out and that whatever he lost would be constantly replaced.

In the daily life of a young child countless losses occur; although they may be minor, the child responds as if they were major. The coming and going of important people, the loss of or separation from a favorite toy or blanket, the loss of parts of oneself as shown above, the lack of satisfaction with what one has in contrast to what one wants, are a few common instances, repeated myriads of times, in which restoration takes place for the losses encountered. They provide the child with a slowly growing, reluctantly acquired tolerance.

A fantasy about loss may play a governing role in some of our attitudes. For example, a young doctor, reflecting on his student days, was reminded that when he was studying anatomy the cadaver was in shreds and tatters at the end of the course. His associated thoughts expressed his resolve never to will his corpse to a medical school; nor would he consider giving his eyes to an eye bank after his death. He then realized that he did not wish to feel that he had lost such important possessions as his body or his eyes. His further associated thoughts were that he might want them afterward. He vehemently denied a belief in resurrection, yet his behavior contradicted him. He could not tolerate an uncompensated loss, and he therefore hoped he would escape death in an afterlife in which he would use all parts of his body. This man had had no religious training and thought of himself as an avowed atheist.

Fantasies such as the young physician reported, which become convictions and govern behavior, date from a period in life that is ruled by the same principles that influence the child who abhors giving up his excrement because it is part of himself. These ideas may be and often are consciously denied, but they appear to be present and to persist in the unconscious. They do not give way readily to rational thought, logical reasoning, experience, or even, as we have seen, to professional training. The young doctor's belief in a resurrection is related not so much to theological argument as to his fears of loss without compensation.

The denial of reality, the negation of a loss, fantasies of loss without recompense, or the turning from despair to elation are common signs which signify that an anxious process to settle accounts with oneself is in full operation. Such reactions find their most important expression in the alteration of reality. On countless occasions, many of which in themselves may seem trivial, they indicate that escape from the burden of a sense of loss is imperative. It appears, therefore, that acceptance of a loss in emotional life is but a philosophic and academic concept. It is probably neither a clinical fact nor a human characteristic.

The experience of loss or the sense of it, whether it occurs in fact or fantasy, is an engine of change. The reactions vary from psychosis to sublimation. Edmund Wilson in *Axel's Castle* wrote of Marcel Proust that "following his beloved mother's death, he was obliged to find something to take her place and for the first time set himself seriously to work'' [14]. The product of Proust's loss and of these labors was *Remembrance of Things Past* which transformed him from a Parisian literary dilettante to an artist of note. There is no doubt that other factors played a role. Loss to Proust was the significant element that led him to his preoccupation with time and people that were lost. In seeking to retrieve them he became a major literary figure [11].

The way in which a loss effects a change may be fleeting, entirely unwitting, unconscious, and imperceptible. For example, a middle-aged man long since removed from his childhood home learned of his aged father's death. The old man had been infirm, and his death was realistically anticipated. The son regretted his father's death. The mourning period was brief and uneventful. Some months later the son became aware of a persistent cough which he attributed to his excessive smoking. Within a short time after its onset it seemed to have a nagging familiarity which he could not identify. A few weeks later he suddenly recognized the cough as though it were a name he had wanted to remember and which had continued to escape him. The cough had an identity that he had taken unto himself. The son was not aware of that, however, until the day he realized that the cough was his father's hacking cigarette cough, which he had known well as a child. In a short time the cough ceased and did not return. During this brief interval the man had walked about and coughed with his father's voice. The two went together.

A consideration of the problems involved in loss and restitution rests substantially on the psychodynamics of self-esteem. Self-esteem, unlike many other qualities, is perishable. It is easily lost and difficult to recapture. It is indispensable but unstable, readily affected by a variety of influences; care must be taken to insure its preservation. Its loss must be redeemed. A forfeited, damaged, or decreased self-esteem is an unacceptable condition. Whatever lowers it needs to be worked off. To preserve it also requires effort. Thus the condition of self-esteem is not permanently achieved; it requires constant attention for its maintenance.

Self-esteem not only plays a role in the clinical aspects of personal inner life but it plays a powerful part in the affairs of men. This is readily evident in religious tradition. Worthiness or the lack of it is always present in relation to the object of worship. The Stone Age people of the African veld, those at the foot of the Andes or in the Australian desert who practice ancestor worship, are no less eager to prove their worth than modern man in his most sophisticated state. Since it was the gods, the demigods, or the civilizing heroes who, it is generally believed, created the world, it is their favor that must be courted.

They have not only created but have ordained and prescribed an order that is to be observed. Their behavior is exemplary and acts as a model for all eternity. The object of worship is invested with an extraordinary importance; hence it may be believed to embody one's origins, like a sacred animal or ancestors; or it may be viewed as a model of behavior, like the Buddha; or it may be a governing power like Allah or a judge of the future like God. These qualities may be distributed among diverse objects of worship or rendered to one alone, depending on a variety of influential cultural or social factors. Those who pay divine honors derive some significant measure of self-esteem from such acts. Moreover, a sustained sense of worthiness or self-esteem cannot be supported by any one set of acts or rites but must be constantly renewed. One does not worship once.

All who worship strive to escape the suffering of existence. They long to be rewarded and thus to find a blissful relief in life after death. A full sense of worthiness and self-esteem in the worshiper is only approximated. He cannot expect to become his own god. However, through a careful observance of religious duties or principles, especially through the renunciation of instincts and the practice of kindliness and charity, or ritual purity, or a variety of other self-abnegations, he can raise his self-esteem to the point where he feels that the favor of the gods is obtained. Daily life constantly puts him in arrears. He must repeatedly review his unworthiness, and through religious observances he attempts to restore himself in his god's eyes. All religions promise salvation and with it a release both from suffering and from a lower self-esteem. Characteristically, what has been forgone will be restored. For loss there will be restitution, sometimes for a chosen people, or through the achievement of elevated aspirations to Nirvana. The Tamil poets of India suggested that through mutual love between God and the petitioner worthiness will be joined with divine grace. Self-esteem will thus be permanently achieved. In the afterlife, prayers, ritual, self-abasement will be unnecessary because worthiness will no longer be in doubt. The relief offered by a predictable existence in a definite future in which there is no transience establishes permanently self-fulfillment and self-esteem.

Reality obliges us to constantly feel our limitations. The conflicts which it arouses are among the oldest that we experience and those which we continually struggle against. There are countless experiences which strain and temper our self-esteem. The constant variations in our moods, the fleeting despair and elation which are commonplace in our daily life, are probably due to such encounters of self-esteem with reality. Whether they arise from external reality or from the reality of our inner life, they convey a sense of our limits. The sense of limitations may come through frustration or disappointment in a real experience, or through fantasy and dreams that are often no less pointed.

The process of extending one's limits is nowhere better illustrated than in man's perpetual myth-making. Mircea Eliade correctly views myth-making as an element of all civilization or culture. We need but to recall, he writes, that our modern literature is replete with the primordial strug-

gle between good and evil, hero and villain, a world of strife
and a land of paradise. Eliade describes myth-making as a
characteristic pattern of human behavior. As a compara-
tive religionist, he shows man's eternal and nostalgic
striving for renewal, for a world to be remade, to be reborn
— "created afresh." The granting of privilege where laws
are abolished and where time stands still, he emphasizes, is
among the chief functions of myths.

This description of most familiar myths does not indicate
their function, but rather the qualities which myths possess.
Moreover, their ubiquity adds to their timelessness and
durability. They are also of such remarkable sameness
throughout the world that they are truly universal. To understand their place in psychology, their function, like the
motives that go into making myths, needs to be distinguished from other aspects of myths.

The motives for myth-making and the function of myths
are in such close harmony that it would be artifical to attempt a sharp separation. The human psychological condition regularly reveals in its conflicts that throughout life
uncertainty remains, risk exists, and unpredictability in
human relationships and events persists. These facts of life
are learned remarkably early. The wisdom accumulated
with years confirms these truths. Wishes to the contrary
arise equally early and remain as a solid core in the matrix
of personality. The need to fulfill wishes is as formidable as
the events and conditions which thwart them. Fantasy formation and its communal form, myth-making, are best
understood as functions aimed at the needs of wish fulfillment. The content of myths draws from wishes often expressed as fantasies. Some of the sources may be unconscious. The motive for myth-making, in part, is a form of
the need of a defense against the limitations that living
imposes.

Myths have one basic principle. They must suspend the
laws of reality (or, as Eliade states, abolish them). A myth

must enable its believer to have faith that his own wishes may be fulfilled. The ends gained by abrogating the laws of reality are to govern, suborn, or influence reality, so that myths will show that limitations may be transcended and that there are no bounds, and that laws are no longer subject to caprice but instead to wishes. Myths, therefore, are part of the elaborate means developed to serve the ends of our wish fulfillment.

Old myths are retold or rewritten, and new ones may change the characters and the scenes. The themes do not alter. The fascination with a historical past which gathers a mythical quality is constantly being expressed when each child presses his wish to be told where he came from. Although it may satisfy his sexual curiosity, the young child also wants to hear of his continuity with the past. How he was once a part of his parents and how he belongs to a family are essential to him. He longs to hear of a timeless past with family heroes, of vicissitudes overcome and of adversity thwarted. The nostalgia which Eliade [2] finds everywhere for a good, perfect, happy past is evident in every child's wish to reflect on a retrospective history of a harmonious past that has been lost but that may be retrieved.

The elders of each generation help actively to perpetuate the memory of the ''good old days.'' They long not so much for the way things really were, as for the way they wish things had been, the way that would have come nearest to their wish. A lost past in the retelling is better than it ever was. Recalling the past, like foretelling the future, obliterates the pain of the present grind of existence. Both are efforts to escape the threat of disintegration of the present, that is, the hazard of living which leads to death. Both courses, through the past and into the future, omit the present. They are woven into a fabric of immortality, another and a future life, or a refashioned life in the past that overcame adversity. Self-esteem is restored and the suffering of the present is relieved by a promise.

Myths themselves describe a lost paradise and the paths which lead to its rediscovery. These tales speak of a life that is rewarding in that the limitations of the human condition are transcended. Eliade [2] writes that although Christianity may be ruled by the nostalgia for paradise, it is only the mystics who in part obtain the restoration of that state. Friendship with animals (like that of St. Francis of Assisi), ascent to Heaven and meeting with God, and longing for paradise are attested at every level of religious life. The same situation obtains in archaic religions.

Myths and fantastic wishes for resurrection are not confined either to religious practices or to childhood. A common fantasy that reappears throughout life, in classical and popular literature, is to be present at one's own funeral. Accompanying it is the unconscious sadistic pleasure of observing the survivors' grief which has been evoked by one's death. This fantasy also recaptures one's lost life by experiencing the loss through identification with the mourners. The limitations of life are thus surpassed. Such a triumph over limitations leads to a feeling of freedom, a liberation from the binding restrictions of life and to the accretion of powers.

Perhaps the most famous exemplifier of these conflicts is President Lincoln. His tense and anxious wife was made very uncomfortable by his telling her of his dreams and his depressing fantasies of his death by an assassin. He often read aloud parts from his favorite play, *Macbeth.* According to some sources [8], the lines "Duncan is in his grave . . . nothing can touch him further," seemed to preoccupy him. President Kennedy, it is said, distressed his friends with details of how he wanted his funeral conducted. He too, like Lincoln before him, expressed his fantasies of his death through violence. King Henry IV in Shakespeare's

play says of these conflicts and preoccupations, "Uneasy
lies the head that wears a crown" [13]. The heads of state
seem to know well the envy that their position fosters.

The restriction of powers by authority and by one's own
limitations is learned very early by a child through his
daily experiences. With each level of achievement, obtained
as he grows and finds a degree of mastery over his narrow
existence, he makes a model for overcoming his limitations.
The model is shaped in two ways: first, by the child's drive
to master and perfect his functions; and second, by dreams,
fantasy, and a belief in magic where his abilities fail him.
Thus the struggle for liberation and freedom — meaning
growth, development, and independence with an accession
of powers through which the former may be assured — is
every child's wish as he suffers from his dependence and
apprehensions. What is more, a prototype for adult life is
fashioned.

Our entire history shows that there can be no contentment with our limits. A restless exertion for liberation from
whatever we feel circumscribes us compels us to surpass
ourselves. It seems, therefore, that our striving to satisfy
our unfulfilled wishes is an inherent expression of our attempts to extend ourselves and in accord with our needs,
real or imagined, to be restored. What we lose in the desires
that are not met we want to regain. In other words, restitution is the gain in our effort to exceed our limits. For the
adult, as for the child, both mastery and myth promote the
ends of restitution, instead of (as Eliade claims) satisfying
a longing for a paradisal existence where the aims are
solely to elude earthly laws. The function of myths of
paradise is identical with that of magic: the extension of
limits without boundaries and of desires without disappointment.

The great religions of the world as well as the most
archaic ones are directed toward fulfilling man's hope.
Without this promise they would be but a bag of tricks

similar to those of simple magic in giving the illusion of
defiance of some natural laws but otherwise having no significance. Throughout life a reliance on magic, even among
the most sagacious of us, is considerably greater than is
generally acknowledged. The inadvertent little rituals
which are observed in daily life seemingly are meaningless
except for the hope that by their performance a possibly
doubtful outcome may be influenced. The open declaration
that an expressed wish may not be realized, whereas if it is
held privately it may be fulfilled, is a frequent expression of
the story of Cinderella. A fragment of prayer muttered
under the breath or the carrying of a charm or amulet are
commonplace magical practices. These daily observances
and expressions of a belief in magic appear to have but a
single purpose, which is to exert influence, extend powers,
and through them to enhance independence and reduce
apprehensions.

No religion fails to rely on magical beliefs and through
them to help realize its aims, which are to relieve the
burdensome present for a better future. Eliade writes: "It is
important not to forget that, at every level of culture and in
spite of their [widely] different historical and religious
contexts, the symoblism of the 'flight' invariably expresses
the abolition of a human condition, transcendence and freedom" [2]. He cites a Buddhist text, the Brahmanic and
Mithraic rituals, the myth of the Nativity, as all centered
around a heavenly ascension, pointing toward the world of
the gods. They assure us of a privileged condition after
death. The beliefs of the North American Huron Indians,
South Sea Melanesians, or the African Pygmies are not
significantly different in this respect. Eliade goes on to
state that neither the origin of religion nor the most ancient
beliefs of mankind are related to this subject, and attempts
at explaining the "germinal" phases of religion in these
terms would be useless. By this he means that an effort to
find the origins of such beliefs would be fruitless. If, how-

ever, Eliade's work is interpreted in a context of motivation and aims, he has made a significant contribution, albeit unwittingly, to an understanding of the origins of religious belief.

Man needs to overcome the daily burdens of his life, but in order to do so he requires an increase in his powers. This resource he confers on his gods, who are infallible and omnipotent. In the life to come these qualities will be forthcoming in some measure, as if death will enable man to become one of God's subordinates, embodying His characteristics. The parallel to the child's view of his parents and the wish to identify with the quailities attributed to them is striking. The childhood conception of what death leads to is similar. The preschool child has among his beliefs the fantasy that death is both a liberation and an enhancement of powers, a freedom from encumbrances which in life are confining. What was lacking in life is compensated for after it. Death is conceived of as a regeneration. It is an enhancement and a restoration, so that nothing is lost and much is gained by death. These are the beliefs which develop in early childhood, and later are added to and supported by formed religious beliefs and community practices (see Chapter 3).

In the struggle for freedom from his limitations, and while attributing a large measure of them to his personal circumstances, the child, like the man, denounces himself. He thus builds up dissatisfaction with himself and thus forces the realization that he can never be completely satisfied with himself. He is impelled to drive toward a restoration of what he believes he has lost or forgone, or wished for but did not have. His needs therefore oblige him to alter reality, and thereby to make restitution. His aim is not simply to gratify his desires but also, and equally important in later childhood and throughout adult life, to restore his self-esteem. Self-esteem is an emergent developing phenomenon. A dissatisfied infant would hardly consider nonfulfillment of his needs as meaning that he was unworthy. Deprivation and its dissatisfactions have their effect on him as a loss of pleasure. In a remarkably short time, however, by the age of three or four years, as his regard for others increases, the self-critical faculty begins to develop. The desired powers are vested in others. The child naturally aspires to the qualities of the people upon whom he knows he depends for his satisfactions, as well as to those powers which he believes may insure his safety and well-being. These qualities and powers, when his, he feels will be the means to independence.

Freud refers to this process, particularly in early development, as pointing to the conclusion that the character is a repository of "past object choices" [5]. In this way significant people become part of the character of the child through his identification with them. Identification has its role in overcoming the child's sense of helplessness, dependence, and limitations. As the admired and feared qualities of these adults become part of the child's character, the ego ideal is formed. The distance between what is wished for and what may be found satisfying increases. A gap is left. There remains the striving to fill it. The wish to serve and satisfy the demands of a superego, as Freud wrote about it, is "the struggle which once raged in the deepest strata of the mind and was not brought to an end by rapid sublimation and identification . . . [and which] is now carried on in the higher region" [5]. The development of these higher functions curbs the instincts. A reaction takes place, however, against this restriction which leads to the sublimation of gratifications, so that the disturbed balance of wishes to satisfactions gained may thus be righted. It appears, therefore, that at each level of psychic development something of pleasure is relinquished and then through restitution is regained. Thus an enormous impetus to extend one's limits is supplied by what is relinquished. The reactions to the experience of loss, such as regret, disappointment, anger, a sense of deprivation, and a legion of others equally common and often more severe, obscure the fact that loss invokes dynamic changes.

The effort to regain something pleasurable that is gone or a valued object one has lost, or to reinstate a tarnished self-esteem, makes possible a rich variety of substitute gratifica-itons. The yield of such efforts is dictated by whether the aims are childish or adult. If the experience of loss merely leads to attempts at simple restoration, little psychological change, no dynamic development, and meagerness of adaptability result. Their ready acceptance of a facsimile, and even insistence upon sameness, expresses the characteristic conservatism of very young children, who regard adaptability, accommodation, and change as more threatening than desirable. Variety and novelty are acquired tastes. They come only with development and experience. The commonly observed repetitiveness that young children enjoy in their diet, in the routines of their care, in the play that they initiate, their resistance to change and their inherent opposition to innovation, show their conservatism.[1] What is new requires adaptation. What is old repeats the familiar. The young child is no adventurer. As though to subvert the child's efforts to keep the world still, his growth and development in a constantly changing environment promote an expanding desire for gratification. Yesterday's pleasures become today's limitations. Thus, for the young child, both his inner immediate world and his external one is characterized by flux.

The child's unrequited wishes are more pressing as his world increases its demands upon him. He will dare, in response to the pressure, what he may have formerly feared. He dreams of change, not because of the gratification he finds but because of the dissatisfaction that remains.

[1] The "repetition compulsion" serves the aims being considered here. It will be referred to later in respect to its function in the process of mastery.

Discontent is thus a source of appetite. The child sets aside, as it were, his earlier ways, that is, the comforts of his routines. He cannot be said to give them up. Under alien conditions which may arouse his anxiety, he tends to revert to his old habits. The return of the old routines of behavior gives him a comforting familiarity in a situation that may be utterly foreign and often alarming. It is an error to believe that these old set ways are actually relinquished. They are repressed. The old ones are not discarded; they are stored and are to be taken up when an old comfort is useful to relieve the concern over a new experience.

Fortunately, most people can welcome change, although they may resist giving up the old and tried. Everyday life shows us how poor and deprived is the man who simply tries to restore what he has lost. By repetition he attempts to gratify his infantile aims. He cannot adapt and therefore cannot sublimate or find enjoyment in variety. He will neither accommodate to novelty nor take delight in Spencer's "ever whirling wheels of change."

Impoverishment reaches its extreme form in the "autistic" child. He resists changes in the environment as well as those he discerns in himself. He regards his growth and development, over which he has no control, with the same alarm and rage as he does events and circumstances about him that are not subject to his will. He strains to hold his world together through repetitiveness in his thoughts, speech, and acts. While these severe compulsions hold an exclusive and intrinsic meaning for himself, they are carried out with a devotion that permits little or no intrusion. They thus serve as a barrier between himself and the world outside. He adheres to them as though they would constitute stability, arrest diversity, give everything a durability that does not exist and perhaps a hoped-for permanence that would require no further conformity or reconciliation with reality.

Similar characteristics are to be observed in some small

measure in all children. They are usually transient phenomena. These qualities, we recognize, perform an important function. When they persist, lose their transient nature
to become more fixed, we observe that in the child as well as
in the adult a pinched existence results. We may learn from
a study of these qualities, prevalent in all children, that the
goals of childhood offer no ring of changes. The goals of
childhood actually provide, contrary to conventional views,
only a narrow base for satisfaction. This in no way suggests that the goals therefore lack importance, but it does
indicate that adherence to them can hardly be enriching.

The narrow-based satisfactions of infancy and childhood
progressively fail to meet the expanding needs of the
child's growth and development. The gratification that
falls short of fulfilling the child's wishes in his maturing
system, he feels as a loss. He betrays his increased self-
interest in his selfishness during the oedipal period. He is
not able to realize the gratification that he wants. The increase in his narcissism is therefore not only inevitable: it
is also characteristic of the child. There are precedents in
the past for the reaction. When the child suffers a disappointment, narcissism increases. Many psychoanalysts
have observed this reaction and they tend to regard it as the
child's attempt to compensate himself for a loss. It has
often been asserted by Freud and by many others that a
self-withdrawal, that is, giving up of the disappointing or
lost object, takes place when a failure in a relationship occurs; in other words, when an important person is lost or a
relationship forgone in fact, or is in fantasy relinquished, a
compensating self-contained reaction is the result.

Recent studies, Modell's (on chronically psychotic
adults) [10] and my own (on children and adults) [12]
show that Freud's is an incomplete statement. Regardless
of the extreme isolation which may develop, a relationship
to previously important people that appears to have been
given up altogether still exists. The bizarre hallucinations

of chronically psychotic adults, when carefully studied for their content, reveal that the hallucinated voices are those of parents or parental figures; a child who seems incapable of a relationship and who appears indifferent to everyone is deeply attached to a fur coat, which is taken as a substitute for his mother at a time when she is not available to him [10]. He continues his attachment to it, more certain of the object which represents his mother than he is of her. He cannot tolerate his mother's absence.

Children who are orphaned, young children who, after their parents' divorce, rarely or in some instances never see the absent parent again, or young children who suffer the death of a parent have, among many reactions in common, one in particular. For years afterward, they find themselves searching strange faces. They hope to find a sign of recognition which will restore the lost one. The search for a lost parent and fantasies about the eventual reunion are common. The restitution of someone loved and believed lost is a timeless theme. It continues to appear in countless folk tales, dramas, and novels, and in real life also. For example a young gifted musician who enjoyed his work was nevertheless unhappy to be playing with a resident orchestra that was rarely on tour. He wanted to visit new places he had never seen before. He knew that if he became a member of an important orchestra, there would be many engagements away from the home city and he would be happier because he could satisfy his craving. With this in mind, he improved his performance so that in a relatively short time he was in demand as an accomplished musician. He joined an orchestra that traveled frequently. As soon as it was convenient, when he arrived in another city, he walked the streets for hours. He looked intently at men. He searched for men who he thought would be approximately his father's age, hoping to find a face with some resemblance to his own. Perhaps, he thought, he could thus identify his father whom he had not

seen since he was a child of four years. The father divorced
the mother when the musician was a small child. For a few
years the absent father sent money to the mother and the boy.
Then he no longer sent money, nor was there any further
communication with him. He had simply abandoned them.
It was not known whether he was dead. The boy seemed not
to stop wondering what had become of his father. Throughout his adolescence he continued to feel puzzled. He answered his questions by taking the resolution to find his
father. He believed that when he discovered him, the mere
recognition would restore them to each other. The happy
reunion would be mutually shared. He continued his search
in the streets for years. At times he was quite well aware of
what his aims were. On other occasions, they were expressed as an irresistible wish to go to another city, to
walk about and see the sights.

Another example is that of a man who learned that one of
his best friends, while in another city, had died suddenly. No
illness had preceded the death. The body was cremated. A
brief memorial service a few days later concluded the episode. It was as though the friend had suddenly vanished.
Years before, the two friends had met by accident on a
street in the same distant city where the death occurred.
The unexpected meeting was an occasion to celebrate. Many
years after his friend's death, the man occasionally visited
the city on business and walked about in the vicinity of the
accidental meeting that had taken place a decade before. He
was often aware of a sense of excited expectation. After
this had occurred a few times, it became clear that his
reaction was in response to the fantasy of wishing that his
friend might appear. Perhaps there would again be an accidental meeting. He would for a moment look about the
street as though to make certain that he would not fail to
see his friend. It was as though there had been no death.

It might be argued that these experiences are simply
understandable wishes that we would all naturally want ful-

filled. There is nothing remarkable in the musician who wishes he had a father or the man who wishes his friend would return. In each instance, however, there is more than an expression of wishes: there is the *expectation* of restitution for what is gone. Moreover, each of these men knows well that his wishes are not to be satisfied. Yet the anticipation, in these two cases, meaning the need to make restitution, if only in fantasy, is evident and persistent. Such experiences indicate that important relations are never completely given up. The fantasy of restitution expresses the need.

We have many traditional ways of not giving up those whom we love and value. Naming a child after someone valued, searching for family resemblances in the new generation, and establishing kinship with particular people that excludes others are but a few of the instances of this active renewing process which show that it is not within human ability to disengage ourselves entirely from a significant relationship. The importance of our relationships to us is further emphasized by the fact that even though we may unconsciously heighten the identification with someone whom we have loved and lost, and may increase our narcissism in some instances even to seriously psychotic proportions, we still find that we are searching for an object outside ourselves in the effort to complete the task of restitution for what we have lost.

If we give our attention to a child's play, he will reveal in it that he has invested the inanimate objects of his play with magical qualities. The articles that have become significant to him are as inseparable from him as were the important people they may represent. When a young child has suffered the loss of an important person, and often when a human substitute fails him, as occasionally happens, the child's attention becomes fixed on the inanimate objects that he can possess, control, and influence with aims similar to those that were previously directed at an important adult. Studies in grief, mourning, and depression point to restitution as a continuing process. The lasting effect of the loss will vary considerably with the phase of psychological development in which a significant person was lost. The child cannot seek restitution along the same paths as the adult, but the latter, who will not fail to draw on his earlier experiences, undergoes a similar process.

At what period the process of restitution emerges from its infantile forms has been a matter of speculation. In the earliest years of life, when attachment to the nurturing person is deep, self-interest is greatest. A substitution for such a person is easily made. As interest in others develops and deepens, the substitution of one person for another is correspondingly more difficult to achieve. The degree of self-interest by which the child is ruled determines the critical difference in the kind of relationship he can make. In other words, an intimate concern with another person correspondingly reduces the readiness to accept a substitute for that person. With development, some self-interest gives way to the interests that serve another. Our own pleasure in part derives from gratifying another whose value to us has been established. The opposite of an exclusive relationship that is valued, promiscuity, may illustrate the point. Promiscuity, by its definition, denies the distinction between one person and another. All have equal value. In practice, this means no one has any particular or special significance. Both partners in such an encounter have tacitly agreed that neither has importance for the other. Don Juan's reputation epitomizes a contempt for the value of another under the guise of acts that would give it the lie. Don Juan serves himself. It stands for his effort to raise his own esteem, about which he has little conviction.

Conversely, truly placing a value on another person gives him this unmistakable distinction. A replacement of him is correspondingly difficult to accept. A part of the self, that is one's self-interest, is transferred to another person and invested in his qualities that are valued. With the loss of that person the part of the self given over to him is gone. Such a loss lowers self-esteem. This marked change that diminishes our worthiness is oppressive.

All people appear to be concerned with their worth. Our sense of worth is not a stable value. It is fluid, subject to circumstance, and it is revealed as fragile. A conventional view about the sense of our own worth directs attention primarily to the role events play. Undoubtedly, events are important, but they are just as often secondary to inner experiences. This is particularly true when, in the privacy of our feelings, we experience with intensity and with recognition that our sense of worthiness rather than circumstance may often rule behavior. Jacques Barzun wrote recently: "Psychoanalysis has taught even the common man that he is in some ways an impostor; he has spied on himself and discovered reason for distrust and disgust; in all honesty he cannot turn in a good report" [1].

The question of our worth is raised early in life. It continues without a final answer until we die. This means that self-esteem is a continuing problem. Establishing our worth to ourselves is an activity that is constantly being renewed and revised. An example of a question of worth in one who had spied on himself and who had discovered reasons for not turning in a good report is afforded by a three-year-old boy. During the last trimester of his mother's second pregnancy, Jason, who during the first two and a half years of his life was an easy, amenable child, rapidly changed. He began whimpering and was more dependent upon his mother than he had been since he was two. In the months that followed his baby brother's birth, Jason reverted in his toilet training and on several occasions he bit his new brother. Being a very bright and socially precocious child, Jason enjoyed going to nursery school for a few hours each day. He was a physically well, active, alert, imaginative child. His teachers enjoyed him and he played happily with the other children. But in the few months following his brother's arrival, he became very aggressive toward children and attacked them, which he had not done before. He stubbornly repeated biting them. It was necessary to remove him from school. He had become menacing and provoking. His behavior at home was what it was at school. He bit his brother. The two could not be left alone together.

A study of Jason confirmed that he was a healthy, intelligent, and friendly child. He was curious and adventuresome. A brief series of diagnostic sessions revealed that in addition to his interest in mobile toys such as trucks and planes, he paid attention to a family of dolls that he included in his play. When it came to playing with the doll baby he pretended to be a doctor. He used toy instruments such as a stethoscope to apply to the doll's chest. And he often used a ridiculously designed microscope and otoscope, that neither he nor any other child could assign to any function, to attack the baby. The chief areas of the body which received his attention were the mouth and the buttocks. Jason assaulted the doll in both places. The play concluded with discarding the "baby." The baby "cried" often and made "messes" in his pants, according to Jason. It was true about his brother. Although it was equally true that Jason was "messing" his pants, he did not allude to it. Jason carried out other assaults on the "baby." He played that he shot and killed him; he put a fragment of clay on various parts of the doll's body, called it a frog, and gave the excuse that it had to be killed. He then threw away the frog. The most important conclusion to the play was riddance of the "baby." He left no doubt that he wanted to be rid of the intruder at home. Yet Jason was perpetrating at home the same acts he was asserting justified sending the "baby" away. He had, in addition, been sent away himself from school for biting. He wanted his brother discarded. Did not his own acts raise the same question? Was not the crying and soiling baby, in Jason's opinion, worthless? Was Jason any better when he was doing the same thing? Perhaps he was worse in biting because it earned him punishment. He was soliciting his parents' opinion of himself through his regressive behavior. He also passed his own judgment on his brother — a no less harsh judgment, however, than on himself.

If we questioned our worth only when we were very young like Jason, the burden would be considerably lighter than it is later in development when self-critical faculties are matured. Jason, as any child, judges himself first by his behavior and not by his motives despite the fact that it is his motivation which determines what he will feel about himself, that is, his worth. He makes it plain, regardless of what justification he may find for his acts, that while in his opinion his brother is worthless, he at the same time confesses his own lack of value. This is not so much a judgment as it is what he believes is his parents' view. In other words, this is not so much self-criticism as it is the criticism made by others. They are the figures in authority whose criticism he will later make into his own and which will become a part of himself. Meanwhile, we may observe the fusion made, of being aggressive toward another, hating him and having destructive wishes, with being worthless. The relation that is established between lowered self-esteem and aggression will be contained in the opinion Jason will tend to form about himself.

A young mother of three children was very troubled over what she believed to be serious limitations she was imposing upon her children on account of some of her own difficulties. She "can see that [she] might be happier, enjoy things, feel that [she] was making free choices in [her] life and for [her] children and that all this was an advantage to them and to [herself]. If only [she] were not so harsh upon the children and less harsh upon [herself]." She is very self-critical, being severely strict. Worthiness seems often to come up in her mind. She questions herself and concludes she does not like her own replies. They are devaluing.

She feels a sense of apprehension which she knows is not dictated by the situation. It is her "notion that it serves some purpose." It satisfies something so effectively that she often repeats to herself, "Don't forget to be afraid!" "It is somehow safer to be afraid, and [she] must feel scared at all costs." These are not reasoned words. They express her dilemma. The irrational wish is "I want to hurt myself, limit myself, be immature, do as I wish, take no responsibilities." "It makes me bitter and unhappy to be this way but I need the criticism and the harshness to deal with such wishes and impulses."

It was no difficult problem to help this woman to recognize that she was guilty and anxious, that her distress was directly related to her excessive self-criticism, and that she was unable to relinquish it. "It is a system that I protect myself with." It would not be humane or correct to dismiss what she presented as symptoms of obsessional neurosis. It is the correct diagnosis. It illumines little, however, to neglect that this young mother is obsessed with her worth, that is her lack of it. It would be no greater service to reduce her difficulties to penis envy, although it is present to an intense degree.

She is a hard-working, intelligent scientist. She is committed deeply to her three children, who are well, clever, attractive, and in no evident difficulty. She is also greatly interested in her profession. She is doing only a minimal amount of work until the youngest child is well established in school. Then she plans to resume her career.

What is most important for our consideration is this woman's burden that she dares not give up. She needs it. Without its restraining effect, she would be tyrannical in her demands and aggressiveness. She fears they would have no bounds. She has a view of herself that she is mean, angry, hateful, jealous, disappointed, and that she is worth little consideration. She acknowledges but she cannot accept that these are her qualities. Her fear is that in spite of her generosity and self-sacrifice, the inner shoddiness will show itself. She will be exposed. She must protect herself against that happening. A further loss of self-esteem would become deeply depressing.

The effort to prove her worth drives this mother to near exhaustion. Her purpose is to restore self-esteem, yet she cannot relinquish aggressiveness, which she believes demeans her, adds to her guilt, and impairs her sense of worth. She longs to be kind, warm, and more free. She does not fulfill her ego ideal but instead she feels that she must obey a harsh, cruel conscience whose decrees she feels tyrannize her. Obedience to the tyrant does not make her worthy — it serves no ends of restitution. To rebel would simply add to guilt. She feels she is a victim who is determined not to succumb to despair.

The child Jason directs his conflicts outward. He holds another to account for his difficulties. He must then contend with the fears that are the result of the hostility that he believes is directed to him. The others, not he, are dangerous and destructive. He ascribes his impulses to them. They are at the same time those upon whom he depends, whom he fears to lose, and who may abandon him. We have seen that Jason has exonerated himself by blaming others for his misfortune of having a brother. The burden of self-accusations and loss of self-esteem exists, but it is attributable to the others; he is but their victim, unloved and hence of dubious value.

The young mother, however, has taken the criticism into herself. Jason's despots are external, whereas she tyrannizes over herself. In obedience to the demands she makes of herself, her sense of worthiness hinges on whether she can fulfill them. A failure to comply with the demands of her conscience makes a loss of self-esteem severe.

Both she and Jason are alike in that each suffers from rage, jealousy, and the personal conviction of being in danger of not being wanted, that is, of being of questionable value. These reactions and their corresponding fantasies of losses in self-esteem are part of the everyday attitudes of childhood. They demand some restitution. For this there are a larger store of fantasies to draw upon. The burdens of the child's life are lightened through wishes, beliefs, and fantasies of the reverse of whatever is oppressive. Freud wrote in *An Outline of Psychoanalysis* [7] that the weak and immature child's ego is permanently damaged by the strain of the child's efforts to ward off the dangers peculiar to childhood; moreover, the child pays for the security of his parents' protection by the fear of losing their care and love. Thus, whatever tends to disrupt the relationship of parent and child represents an exposure to risk and reinforces a sense of helplessness that needs to be warded off. Such strain comes not only from dangers from without but also from inevitable inner impulses of frustration, hostility, and self-devaluing fantasies.

If a little brother who is regarded as an intruder, envied, and at times hated should become sick and even die, the young child believes that his own hostility may have had some vital part in the unfortunate outcome. The child's fantasies of magic, his belief in the power of wishes, and the press of active jealousy convince him that he has played a role in the sequence of events. The child will also regret his involvement; he will want to undo what is done. Two inseparable fears develop and are joined: a fear of loss and of death or abandonment.

It has been generally thought that mourning over the loss of something we have become attached to or loved finally spends itself, and that substitutes are found after what has been lost is finally renounced. We are then free to replace what was lost with fresh or even more valuable objects. Freud was the first to write about this as a psychoanalytic concept in 1913 and again in 1915 in a more specific way in his famous work, "Mourning and Melancholia" [4]. In this paper the psychodynamics of grief, mourning, and pathological melancholia were established. A voluminous literature on this subject, on which all modern concepts of normal grief and pathological depression are based, has developed over the past fifty years. But still unanswered is the one open question which Freud raised initially: Why is it that our detachment from loved objects should be so painful?

Loss is a continuous process. That it goes on when a loss has in fact occurred is well known; but that it goes on long in advance of an actual loss and in anticipation of it rather than just *post facto* has not generally been recognized. The experience of losing someone personally important has been throughout life repeated in fantasy countless times, and just as often the lost person has been restored again. The instances are boundless which may be drawn, for example, from fantasies about a trivial illness whose outcome in advance may not be certain, or tardily kept appointments where the delay in the one who is expected seems unwarranted, or a trifling period of absence. All become experiences in life in which the process of loss and restitution is distressingly and endlessly repetitious. It may be provoked by reality perhaps, but the process takes place essentially in disturbing fantasies which tend to be quickly repressed. They form the prototype for the more realistic events which sooner or later inevitably occur.

The young child whose mother goes off on even a brief errand will wonder when she will return and the separation be ended. The separation arouses uncertainty and questions in the child. They are largely dictated by what he believes would occur to him if he were to be absent. He has learned that dangers exist for him. It is natural for a child to believe that those hazards to which he is subject would befall his mother, just as he is convinced that what happens to others may be his fate. This dependence in children creates a distressing condition.

A. A. Milne has made these conflicts into a classic poem, "Disobedience," in which "James James Morrison Morrison (Commonly known as Jim)" warns his mother not to disobey: "You-must-never-go-down-to-the-end-of-the-town-if-you-don't-go-down-with-ME!" [9] Countless experiences have schooled the child that life is precariously balanced. The fears that catastrophes may cause an unwarranted delay are fantasies which do not develop in adult life but rather, like many others, are carried on from an earlier period. They may not be entirely conscious; they may be subject to repression and they may be influenced in their expression by the mechanism of denial. All may be acting together or in part to relieve anxiety. The mother's return dispels the fears of loss; the interval of fantasied grief is ended and the pleasure of recovery from the fears takes place as restitution occurs. Similar experiences are repeated countless times throughout life.

The process of disengagement from someone loved and dead or someone who represents what is valued begins with a reaction that is directed toward the outside world, which is now believed to be impoverished. At the time this chapter was being written, the President of the United States had just been assassinated. The immediate public reactions were disbelief and denial, followed by the shock of recognition of the truth, and grief and anger. The streets were filled with weeping people who felt personally outraged. Expressions of anger were heard everywhere — against the assassin, against those responsible for guarding the President from such a wanton act. Angry remarks were directed against the dead President himself, who deprived the country of what he represented by his own lack of precaution.

A few hours after the assassin had been apprehended, he too was murdered. His killer claimed motives of rage and

revenge on behalf of the President's widow. The familiar
faultfinding for the death was present in the mourning.
Influential public figures blamed themselves for not having
dissuaded the President from making his last public appearance. The President was accused of being careless with
his priceless life and at the same time extolled for his
courage. Prayers were said by millions of people in joint
memorial services as they turned to their religious beliefs
in the face of the tragedy. A sense of unreality and disbelief
coexisted with the intense grief. The elaborate and solemn
religious death rites overshadowed the secular burial ceremonies.

A new President was immediately installed. Even as he
assumed the duties of the man he had just succeeded, he was
careful not to intrude himself too quickly. Everyone understood that the government would continue uninterruptedly;
the strictly administrative functions would be performed.
The more personal aspects of leadership were kept from
public view. The new President offered himself in restitution for the loss. The process was not obvious lest it violate
the sensibilities of a people experiencing a loss and not
willing or able to give up or detach themselves quickly in
order to accept a substitute. The new President's adequacy
for the high office was immediately questioned, not simply
as a physical or administrative reality but because restitution was emotionally rejected in the crisis. Disbelief or
denial of the reality was still operative. At the same time,
because he was regarded as a figure freshly in the place of
the dead one, the new President's policies were evaluated in
terms of the extent to which they would expand and continue those of his predecessor. The new President's first
speech said that *this* was precisely what he would try to
do.

The high drama of that tragedy raises the question: Why
is it painful to detach oneself from what has gone or someone who is lost or dead? The answer is to be found, perhaps,

in the fact that to do so means to give up the demands for imperishable relationships, to acknowledge the transience of all things without resort to denial and without a counter-belief in immortality, to renounce expectations of wishing to alter reality and hence to give up wish fulfillment. For example, a colleague on hearing the shocking news said aloud immediately with the firmness of conviction; "The President has been assassinated but he has not been killed." The rationalization that this statement embodies also reveals an assumption that the President was still alive. Such reactions cannot be relinquished without implying an acceptance of the finality of loss and of death. Neither is negotiable in human relations. Along with our acute awareness and repeated experiences that date from our childhood knowledge of the transience of what we most cherish, our defenses derive from what we also know: namely, that when faced with the finality of loss, we expect restitution to take place. The third principle of mental functioning will prevail and exert itself to alter reality. "No instinct we possess is ready for a belief in death" [7]. We have a great deal which prepares us against our ultimate fate.

Elaborate emotional defenses are mobilized to alter reality and to mitigate the confrontation with threats to life out of the need to preserve valued objects and to sustain life. Out of these human needs and the emotional defenses arising from them comes the repression of instincts. As man's religious and social history and his individual development show, his aggressive instincts, while renounced, are not relinquished, and his sexual instincts, although inhibited, are not given up. In order to become a social animal, however, such alterations are necessary. Repression not only functions so that the individual child will contain his deepest instinctual wishes and his unresolved conflicts; it also serves at the same time to make secure social relationships. When the repressive emotional forces fail in their aims, psychological disorders and hence a disturbed rela-

tionship with others occur, as is well known. Nevertheless, it
has been suggested, often somewhat naïvely, philosophically
and in the abstract, that inhibitions resulting from repression have impeded man's development. Often it has been
proposed that if he were free of them, many personal and
social problems would be solved. Similar theories, in a variety of forms, have been repeatedly propounded since
Freud's empirical discoveries about the unconscious. There
is neither a society of men nor an example of a child's development which, carefully studied, would support these
speculative ideas. It is correct, in the case of certain individuals in whom everyday psychopathology has gone to the extremes of disorder, that repression plays a major part in the
evolution of the particular neurosis concerned. Repression
in turn may seriously affect social relationships. In principle, however, repression plays a critical role in the formation of character. Invariably, it has a governing effect on
relationships with others, but this is no valid argument in
favor of no repression; nor, to judge from the examples of
behavior without repression, does it support the theory
that to live without repression is a better way to live.

Emotional defenses are constantly called upon to mitigate harassment from conflicts. We have called attention to
Hendrick's observation as a clinical fact that the experience
of hostility and its associated anxiety is far less intense
when it is referred to as stemming from another person
than when it is perceived as one's own primary impulse or
intention. A return of what has been repressed is often
threatening. A further observation is to be made, that the
experience of frustration, hatred, and sadistic wishes and
fantasies, when perceived as having its origin within ourselves, threatens the continuity of any relationship. Such
feelings, when perceived as originating from within, risk
bringing about a return of aggressive, destructive ideas in
their most primitive forms, such as early infantile oral and
anal wishes with cannibalistic desires, fantasies of mutila-

tions, murderous intentions, and wishes for tyrannical license — ideas that are incompatible with either forming or
maintaining a relationship. A rising anxiety is associated
with these asocial intentions. They create fears that they
will break out of control. When directed specifically toward
someone valued and important, the hostility gives way to
fear of bringing about one's own isolation. The intensity of
the anxiety associated with such inner experience is not
diminished by denial alone, but relies heavily on projection
for its alleviation. Examples are plentiful in the rages and
tantrums of young children with their rueful accusations of
others and an insistence on their own innocence even while
they are exhibiting their rage at a provocation. The
child will not view himself as the source of destructive
wishes. The dangers of doing so are too great, not simply
because of fears of retaliation which are prevalent, but because it would lead to an acknowledgment that he may be
responsible for his own losses. Therefore, the child adopts
the ready solution of accusing others. Although the fear of
danger is not diminished when the sources of it are external-
ized, one is then at least able and may attempt to assert one's
own innocence and avoid self-blame. The following example
of projection in an adult illustrates these characteristics,
which exist in all people, carried to the extremes of neurotic
psychopathology.

A young, successful teacher, who was generally regarded
by his colleagues and students as lenient and conscientious,
feared that his real feelings would escape his control. He
had always privately assumed that the kindliness and devotion to students and the willingness to work which he
closely observed in others was a mask. Behind the façade
that everyone maintained he was certain that "people are
really mean, cruel and selfish; they are dangerous sadists,
in fact monsters." He offered many examples of behavior
which indicated that people were hypocritical and vile. "So
long as everyone is bad underneath, I know there is much to

fear. The only reason I do things I am supposed to do is by fearing the consequences to be suffered in not doing them. It is necessary to be afraid of everyone, but especially those in authority, to follow along with what is wanted and to be told what to do. I want them to sit on me. If I was not so scared of them, that is, what they might do to me, I would hurt them. They keep me civilized. Otherwise, if I was not controlled by my fears of them, I would kick them in the teeth, torture them with pleasure and watch them squirm. I'd care for no one. I would do just as I pleased. I'd go berserk satisfying only myself. I'd get in a plane and leave my family; wife and children would starve and I'd be on a beach enjoying myself. It could happen if I was not controlled by someone. It makes me mad. I want my father to be dogmatic and have him tell me what to do. It makes me feel safe; otherwise I get afraid of what I want to do. Many times as a boy, I would just argue with my father so that he would get after me. He was right but I would take the opposite view to get him to say he was sure he was right. It would control me. So long as I know how terrible everyone else is it means that I am under control. I am not so bad then. I want no personal responsibility. If I get too bad I want to be able to kill myself. When I think I want my father to die, I think I have a time bomb I can set off in myself. I have a mole in my mouth. If I bite into it and make it bleed, maybe it is a cancer mole, and I'll die from it. I could get the mole removed but I want it there for this purpose.''

These are private experiences that extend back into early childhood. This man recalls that as a small boy he rehearsed endlessly to himself exactly what it was that his parents would disapprove in his behavior. He would then, after having fantasies of a sadistic and destructive nature about each member of the family and often about his friends, make certain that he did not carry out what would not be condoned. He was not manifestly deterred by guilt, but by his fears of what his parents would do to him. Both parents were kind, indulgent people; never given to scenes, they rarely punished him and never severely. The origin of this teacher's sadistic character is not important here. But the fact that he could not tolerate his own violent wishes and hostility, and projected his own impulses onto others and particularly upon those who were closest and in authority, is significant.

It is always more effective to blame the devil than to hold oneself to account. There are countless instances in history which affirm this kind of behavior: the witch hunt, the search for heretics, the chase after the unbeliever, the reigns of tyrants, despots, and demagogues, are typical in their pursuit of victims they require as objects to blame. Powerful defenses will be elaborated and can be depended upon to mitigate the burden of responsibility for one's own losses. Otherwise, restitution for these losses would be far more difficult. The fury the child fails to express toward the mother who has been sick, the father who has deserted, or the grandmother who has died, frequently finds its voice by attributing the causes for these happenings to events which entirely exonerate him, the child, or indirectly blame some trivial failure in himself. The hostility felt at having been left or deprived of the important person is not acknowledged. It remains unconscious and endlessly produces guilt.

Guilt is an oppressive conflict. It compels relief.

The guilt that is derived from repressed hostility directed at a valued object often finds expression in devotion to a person whom one would otherwise wish to destroy or see become the focus of vilification. The same guilt may also find expression in moral rectitude, in devotion to a person or even a cause that one would not be altogether in sympathy with, or even perhaps have nothing to do with ordinarily. In other words, anger, hostility, and destructiveness produce a gap between oneself and what is valued which the complex process of restitution serves to close. The insupportable burdens of guilt become lightened through the wishes to undo the evil. Religious beliefs, fantasies of renouncing the instincts, deeds of sacrifice, are all proffered as compensations for unconscious and conscious prohibited and asocial impulses and acts. Such impulses and acts occur throughout life. The striving for restitution in relation to those impulses and acts is not confined to any period of psychological development but is continuously expressed. These recurring reactions are not basically cultural; they merely find different expressions in different societies and cultures.

REFERENCES

1. Barzun, Jacques: Meditations on the Literature of Spying, *Amer. Scholar,* Spring, 1965, 177.
2. Eliade, Mircea: *Myths, Dreams and Mysteries* (London: Harvill Press, 1960), pp. 27–31, 33, 43, 47–49.
3. Freud, Sigmund: The Relation of the Poet to Day-Dreaming (1908). In *Collected Papers* (London: Hogarth Press, 1948), IV, 175.
4. ———. Mourning and Melancholia. In *ibid.* (1925), IV, 243.
5. ———. *The Ego and the Id* (London: Hogarth Press, 1947), pp. 36, 53.
6. ———. Formulations Regarding Two Principles in Mental Functioning [1911]. In *Collected Papers* (London: Hogarth Press, 1948), IV, 14.
7. ———. *An Outline of Psychoanalysis* (New York: W. W. Norton, 1949), p. 112.
8. Lewis, Lloyd: *Myths After Lincoln* (New York: Reader's Press Club, 1941), pp. 295–296.
9. Milne, A. A.: *When We Were Very Young,* 170th reprinting (New York: E. P. Dutton Co., 1935; London: Methuen & Co., Ltd. [copyright, C. R. Milne]), pp. 30–33.
10. Modell, A. A.: The Theoretical Implications of Hallucinatory Experiences in Schizophrenia. *J. Amer. Psychoanal. Ass.,* 6 (1958), p. 450.

11. Proust, Marcel: *Pleasures and Days,* Introduction by F. A. Dupee (New York: Doubleday, 1957), pp. vii, viii.

12. Rochlin, Gregory: The Loss Complex: A Contribution to the Etiology of Depression. *J. Amer. Psychoanal.,* 7 (1959), 315.

13. Shakespeare, William: *King Henry IV,* Part II, Act III, Sc. 1, line 31.

14. Wilson, Edmund: *Axel's Castle,* Scribner Library edition (New York: Charles Scribner's Sons, 1959), p. 184.

5
CREATIVITY

The creativity generated by the need for restitution is enormous. Simply to contemplate its magnitude is to appreciate what a virtually endless fund of activity stems from the experience of loss or the fear of it. It is characteristic of all human beings to attempt to recoup their losses in order to restore an inner balance which has been upset. The resources which are called upon to achieve this aim do so through the creative process. We will show that creativity as a process is a means through which restitution is achieved for the losses that we experience either in fact or in fantasy.

Perhaps the greatest and most continuous source of restitution is the dream. The dream attempts to restore through the unconscious what has not been satisfied in waking life. This regularly recurrent phenomenon is the most typical means through which we may all find our wishes gratified or recapture what was lost. This applies also to the fantasy and the daydream. Given that the dream's aim is to fulfill wishes, why should this be so indispensable a function? We are obliged to acknowledge once more that we never accept or relinquish an unrequited wish as such, but continue to press for it despite whatever verdict reality may render. The daily or regular recourse to sleep, and hence to dreams, beyond the physical restoration it provides indicates that the demand for fulfillment persists when reality cannot satisfy it and that this is accomplished through the dream. Perhaps the daydream or fantasy serves more immediate ends, whereas the dream during sleep is limited neither by time nor place as a daydream or fantasy tends to be. The day's residues are woven into the fabric of the dream, but the dream has virtually a lifetime of experience and unrequited wishes to draw upon and to attempt to satisfy. It scarcely needs saying that wish fulfillment in dreams means not merely a gratification of the simple daily demands for the resolution of some passing frustration, but rather their inclusion in the deeper unconscious wishes, which are persistent.

It is of special importance, therefore, to investigate the persistent need to restore to oneself that which has been forgone, sacrificed, or lost in thwarted wishes or postponed needs. All the elements characteristic of the dream, particularly of its latent aspects, when disentangled, reveal wishes that are to be fulfilled. The wishes are not always current ones; frequently they are wishes of the past which appear to have been given up or repressed [17]. In effect, the reality principle, which has been evolved with difficulty during waking life, and which has put aside pleasure, must be reversed in the dream if the dream is to accomplish its purpose. It is in the dream that the reality principle gives way to the pleasure principle; the engine of change operates to transform losses into gains. This is not to say that all wishes have the aim of transforming losses into gains, but rather that the aim cannot be realized without them. The dream, in its wish-fulfilling function, makes restitution. We are here referring to the latent aspects of the dream and not simply to what is manifest. The dream, therefore, is an essential part of the lifelong cycle of loss and restitution. Nowhere in life may discontents, deprivations, or limitations be transcended as they are in dreams. A significant mental activity which serves to restore a balance or to resolve a conflict which arises from loss is in its most specific sense a creative function.

Fulfilling wishes is at the root of dreaming. The vast literature in psychoanalysis on dreams, beginning with Freud's major scientific classic, "The Interpretation of Dreams," offers ample evidence that the dream is an activity expressing unconscious wishes and strivings for their satisfaction. This requires no confirmation here.

A fantasy may serve the same purpose as a dream; no less, however, than a psychotic hallucination. It follows, therefore, that the significant difference between the two lies *not* in their aim but in their relation to reality. The following example illustrates an unconscious loss, a fantasy of restitution, and a highly sublimated activity that serves a creative function. Restitution is found.

A healthy young jet pilot had suffered in childhood from an impairment. It was gradually corrected. Largely through his own determined efforts, by late adolescence the last signs of his difficulty had been eradicated. He was left, however, with the disquieting conviction that the attention he required as a child and as a growing boy was due to his "deficiency." Within the family, his impairment was designated by the term "deficiency." He was, he believed, "cared about or for [his] 'deficiency.' "

This young man was capable at school and he rapidly was able to distinguish himself as an athlete. No trace remained of his "deficiency." Yet privately he felt that the "deficiency" was still driving him hard. He knew that the impairment had long since ceased to exist. An extremely competent young man, he was eminently suited to his ambition to be a jet pilot. He succeeded without difficulty in becoming a flyer.

Flying a jet plane "became a way to reassure myself there was no 'deficiency.' " He had repeated the following details on other occasions. This is an uninterrupted account of himself:

"I could prove it to myself that flying is a tremendous way to express yourself. There is then no 'deficiency.'

Through your own will, through your own control, you feel your power in a plane. You express your will in all directions, in all dimensions. You find that you satisfy yourself by winning your own approval, respect, and recognition by what you can do. Everything works perfectly, the smooth control of the plane. It will do whatever you decide; the control surfaces, the control systems, instruments, engines are all working for you. You have the pleasure of your skill and knowledge that you can make it all work for you. It is gratifying to see it turned tangibly into a performance that you can feel good about yourself. It is a special thing that you do — it is not just acrobatics, it's precision, planning, the timing that you have calculated out. You can't just take one of those things out and fly it around like a toy. You come in on a fix and you know you are right, what you planned comes out. I recall once I was out at midnight high above the clouds, totally alone, the stars, the dim lights of the instruments, cross-checked coming in on position and except for the occasional weather report I was all alone. And I knew I was secure and right, the goal felt achieved, it was a feeling of independence, although temporary. I'll grant you it was a structured brief time, precarious but it was mine. I felt something came of it. You overcome dangers, threats; any real errors in plans or conditions or instruments and you can kill yourself. You ask, Can you handle what you will encounter? Can you meet what could happen? Knowing and seeing the dangers and overcoming them — you feel capable. The 'deficiency'? I now don't have it. Why repeat the flights? They are a pleasure. Once achieved, who wants to give up a pleasure!''

It would indeed be an oversimplification and reductionist to interpret this young man's experience strictly in terms of libido theory. His phallic representation of his flying is plain, as is his concern with castration. It indicates his unvoiced but nonetheless implied oedipal strivings. To suggest that he demonstrates only sublimation does not credit him with the high degree of ego function that he expresses through work, skill, and mastery. Since much of what he relates is fantasy, it is tempting to discount the significance of his act and to suggest that he gave evidence of merely an effort to overcome the effect of an old yet unconsciously present infirmity.

I would not suggest that every pilot who takes a plane off is being creative, any more than whoever lifts a crayon is an artist. Many pilots are but bus drivers. A definition by Albert Camus seems most appropriate. ''The true artist is halfway between his imaginings and his acts. It is he who is 'capable of.' He might be what he describes, live what he writes. The act by itself would limit him, he would be the man who has done something.'' It is not the act alone that gives the pilot in our example importance, but the fact that he has gone beyond it, to do ''something'' creative [3].

As the excerpts of ordinary child's play recorded at the end of Chapter 3 show, the imaginative play each child constructs includes figures that are of special importance to him. The ordeals that the characters encounter are undone. Losses are recouped; life is restored. When the common themes of loss appear in play, restitution in some form also appears.

A child's play, indistinguishable in many ways from dreaming, shows condensation of ideas, contradictions, distortions of reason and reality, various levels of emotional involvement, the use of daily experiences, symbols, a return of repressed wishes, and the exercise of censoring. These are only some of the most common elements of mental activity that a child uses in a wholly unself-conscious fashion. The elements do not all appear at any one time, nor all of them in any one child.

The problems the child attempts to solve, however, are beyond the one intimately bound to pleasure [5]. His play reveals situations in which loss and restitution occur. What is done is undone. Altering the outcome in favor of wishes

is such a common occurrence in child's play that it makes
one wonder whether children's creative activity comprises
much else, outside the cycle of loss and restitution. Perhaps
it is an activity that is more prevalent in adults than has
been realized.

In childhood during play, as throughout life during sleep,
daily life is reworked, that is, reexperienced. Under conditions of sleep, however, and with the aid of the mechanism
of condensation and symbolic representation, common daily
experiences are altered, fragmented, distorted, and resyn-
thesized. Of the residues of experience which appear in
dreams, reveries, and fantasies, some are unconscious,
others are silently stated, and some are acted upon. All this
is a creative effort. It would be a weak argument to re-
strict creativity only to artists, writers, inventors, or composers. Children are none of these, yet they too are characteristically creative. That their productions seldom have
permanence or a market value does not gainsay their
creativity. The common denominator which artists share
with children and with everyone else is that through the
creative process something is being restored or realized.
The creative process makes restitution possible.

If we regard as creative only those activities whose
products society thinks valuable or admirable, we shall
limit our understanding of the creative process. Being creative does not seem to be an exclusive gift of the talented. It
belongs to the many rather than the few. That fact does not
reduce its importance. We expect studies of creativity to
deal with ordinary men, or at least those who do not produce "Great" art, but we do not get this. The discussion
wanders back to great artists or at least good ones. The
interest in motivation, and particularly in the creative
process in great artists, writers, composers, has widened
considerably since Freud made the first of such studies fifty
years ago, "Leonardo da Vinci and a Memory of His Childhood." Many artists, since Freud's imaginative effort, have

become the object of searching investigations of creativity.

But as creativity cannot be separated from personal life and conflicts, there has developed the belief that creativity arises out of particular emotional disturbances. This in itself is not a new idea. It has a degree of common currency which has been supported by artists themselves, who have honestly believed it to be true. The creative process by its very complexity encourages a mystique to surround it. Many of the world's geniuses, such as Leonardo da Vinci, Van Gogh, Beethoven, Balzac, Proust, and others, are cited as examples of people whose sufferings and conflicts and even madness support the hypothesis which ascribes creativity to neurosis, illness, and even infirmity. Instead of demonstrating the existence of extraordinary faculties in creative people, these searches for common factors of psychic life which produce great creative works have revealed that great artists and other geniuses have emotional disorders and neuroses of the most prosaic variety. The ordinariness of their conflicts, which are far from unique, shows them to be indistinguishable from the conflicts commonly found in most people.

If we should ask whether there is substantial indication that particular disorders tend to beget creativity and are characteristic of great artists, inventors, or composers the answer would be negative. There have been far too many madmen who have had similar disorders and who have left no great creations as a lasting mark on the world. It seems more likely that the great works of certain mentally disturbed artists were the products of geniuses who were creative in spite of their madness rather than because of it.

It appears that all creative work, whether in the arts or crafts or sciences or in countless other occupations, often less distinguished or dramatic, makes use of particular cognitive and sensory-motor functions. It could hardly be otherwise. To ascribe works of creativity to neurosis or conflict is but to point to the nature of man and beg the question. To propose that they represent an acquired skill, even if of an exceptional quality, is to stress behaviorism, to exclude deep personal motivation. It is insufficient to ascribe creativity to a particular culture, time, or place since no people has failed to produce creative works. Arthur Koestler, himself a creative person, has recently offered a seriously considered theory of the act of creation: that creativity is in large measure derived associative thinking [14]. This has been proposed by many before him. Has he overlooked that all people throughout their lives make constant use of associative thinking processes? It is but another way of affirming that in everyone there exists some irrationality and that sometimes it is useful in everyday living. The scientific basis for this evidence is among Freud's permanent contributions: that man has an unconscious and that it frequently governs his behavior. The question that remains is, When are these processes operative or useful in solving a problem in a novel way or in producing an original work?

It is important to note that Koestler, unlike any other writer on creativity, and this includes the vast number of those who are engaged in research on the subject, suggests that "self-transcending emotions . . . transformed 'magic' into 'science.'" He also writes that unconscious prerational magical thinking enters into the creative act and into the beliefs or superstitions of the scientist. These are ideas that Lawrence Kubie has written about at length. Koestler, like other writers, misses the importance of these concepts that he touches upon [15]. Their significance escapes him when he reduces them to an act of peaceful catharsis. He sees the self-transcending emotions as an effect but not as a cause or a motive [14]. Koestler argues that art and discovery draw on unconscious sources. He suggests that this means, therefore, that in all creative activity there is a regression to ontogenetically and phylogenetically earlier

levels as an escape from the restraints of the conscious
mind. Psychoanalysts have known and written about this
extensively. But, like Koestler, they have not dealt with
restraints that may motivate creativity. There has been no
suggestion that there may be a common conflict which creativity attempts to solve. Self-transcending emotions appear
to be indistinguishable from what was in an earlier day
called self-expression. But what need there might be for
either self-expression or self-transcending emotions other
than catharsis has not been brought into view. It is no
more illuminating to argue that neurosis distorts or prevents creativity, because this argument too rests on an
assumption that creativity derives from some level of consciousness which in itself is a source of creativity that may
become distorted by the effects of a neurosis. Is neurosis an
essential ingredient of creativity? So far as we know,
neurotic conflict is present in all men and psychosis in
some; creativity appears not to be a product of either. May
it not be the product of a particular conflict which might be
just as common to the mad as to the neurotic?

One such supposition is offered by Phyllis Greenacre.
Her views require careful examining because they tend to
exert a wide influence upon many who have an interest in
the psychology of creativity. It is also necessary, in order
to understand Greenacre's opinions, to place them in a historical context of the opinions of others from whose views
hers cannot be distinguished. She suggests that the Oedipus
complex or, in her words, "the family romance constella-
tion" has "an intrinsically strong place in their [the
artists'] psychology and probably in that of the creative
person in any field" [11]. She speculates further in the
same paper that "creative gifts exist in fantasy in infancy
as some exquisite cognitive sensitivity" that later expresses itself as a "love affair with the world, an obligatory
condition in the development of great talent or genius"

[11]. She believes that the artistic product is created to be offered universally as a love gift to some fantasy of a collective audience.

Greenacre's theory of the childhood of the artist is a clear application of Freud's early theories on anal sadism and Karl Abraham's theory that the infant has a "second anal phase," in which the baby's stool is symbolic to him of a sacrifice or gift of his valued excrement to his mother. Going on to a later period of infantile development, Greenacre suggests that artists as a group retain to an inordinate degree oedipal conflicts which "have not been adequately resolved," and states that "their ensuing hostility is of an intense quality," which she defines as "fierceness of expanding development." She asserts that "creative work" is therefore "an expression of the intensified development of various phases of early psychic life," referring especially to the anal-sadistic period. In talented people, she believes there is "a sense of pressure, some compelling need for seeking harmony . . . an obligatory creative pressure."

Her conjectures lead her to the supposition that the intense conflicts, especially the oedipal ones, under conditions of "frustration and disappointment in the personal object" will bring forth creativity. She surmises, for example, that if the potentially gifted infant (and it is difficult to know how such judgments are made), who has a greater than average sensitivity to sensory stimulation to begin with, receives reinforcement in his oral and anal periods, it will lead to the sublimation of sadistic wishes, characteristic of these phases, and to a high degree of inventiveness. Such deterministic views as Greenacre's reduce the role that chance or external conditions, let alone choice of occupation, may play in the formation of character. Moreover, to accept her premise would lead to only one conclusion: that one's destiny is fixed in the earliest phases of psychic life and that, like a character from a Greek tragedy, one can only follow where the finger of fate points.

Greenacre's views with their emphasis on the psychology of early infancy define adult life in its differentiated forms in terms of the conflicts and behavior of infancy.

Infantile anal erotism finds expression throughout later life in some individuals, particularly those who seem not to have relinquished their earliest attitudes toward anal functions. They continue to enjoy their overevaluation of their feces. To follow Greenacre's reasoning, a directly derived form of this perversion is to be observed in the artist who enjoys pigments as he originally did his feces, takes pleasure in their manipulation as babies do, and by the application of a certain talent presents the new product, his art, to "an audience or a recipient" as he once did his feces to his mother. A psychoanalytic study of an artist may reveal that his psychological development had taken such a course but he could hardly be characterized as typical without assuming that all artists tend to be fundamentally more alike than different.

A study of Greenacre's recent work compels the conclusion that her view of the psychological development of infants ascribes more and more content, and hence conflicts, to the earliest months of life, with the result that maturation is correspondingly compressed into a smaller space of time. She has not placed the oedipus complex in an earlier period, but it appears that she has crowded into the first two years of life much that belongs in early childhood rather than in early infancy.[1]

There appears to be a common inclination, among those who accord a foreshortened maturity to the ego, to correspondingly regard the effect and hence the significance of the role of reality as reduced in later periods of development. The tendency leads to increasing emphasis upon determinism. Greenacre's views seem to conform closely to those put forth by the late Melanie Klein, whose specula-

[1] Direct experience in studying young children would not support the precocity of infant ego that Greenacre suggests.

tions about the early psychic life of infants were not based upon clinical evidence. The repeated criticism of her assumptions by Anna Freud, Edward Bibring, Ives Hendrick, Lawrence Kubie, and many other less distinguished psychoanalysts apparently had no discernible effect upon her ideas, which remained fundamentally unaltered, as have those of her followers in their recent publications. The critics would find much in Greenacre's views on creativity that would be compatible with Kleinian conceptions of infant psychology, which assert it to be virtually independent of the total process of growth and of environmental influence. Environment merely functions, according to such views, as only a reinforcement of innate qualities [2].

There are few subjects in psychology in recent years that have received more attention from both the scientists and the simply curious than creativity. Virtually no principle of psychology has not been applied. Yet it continues to remain an elusive subject, just as those who are known to be creative escape a stereotype. It would not be either profitable or appropriate to review such diversified writings here. A great many of them, however, have been excellently reported by M. I. Stein and S. J. Heinze [19]. Their review and others show that the research efforts directed toward testing, measuring, and experimenting with creative people reveal certain qualities of creativity. The results are often interesting but they cannot be said to be typical or predictable, or to uncover more than some fragments of unconscious motivation.

One line of argument is that the creative person is one who in some manner, thought to be accidental, has retained his capacity to use his preconscious functions more freely than others who may potentially be equally gifted. While the creative process may depend heavily on the production of free associations and an unencumbered alliance between the preconscious and the unconscious, these seem but the instruments through which the creative operation is achieved, and are not the operation itself. The recent theories of Koestler [14] were well formulated by Kubie in 1958 [15]. Kubie cites as an example a playwright whose works portray a theme important to himself: a father's struggle to mask his destructive homosexual impulses toward his son. But the play does not resolve the artist's neurosis. Creativity, Kubie attempts to show, is not a self-healing process. He gives examples from many other art forms that are no more therapeutic than playwriting. Then he points out that the creative effort, of itself, does not solve problems. He regards the creative process as ''the capacity to find new and unexpected connections, to happen on America as we seek new routes to India, to find new relationships in time and space and thus new meanings'' [15]. While the creative process may indeed not solve problems, Kubie's definition nevertheless suggests that creativity may be the means through which part and perhaps all of a problem may find a solution. How this may take place remains elusive. The neurotic and the creative process are not as easily separated structurally and compartmentalized as Kubie seems to believe.

Probably more than others, Kubie has suggested that creativity is related to certain explicit particular personal problems of the artist. But what the nature of the problems may be that creativity may solve has not been defined by him; nor is it clear what problems promote creativity. He leads us to conclude from his argument that creativity and neurosis coexist. Some individuals he shows us are so thoroughly ruled by neurosis that their ability to be creative is sharply curtailed. He raises a question, however, that neither he nor anyone else deals with: How is it that as a common sight some people, clearly and severely hampered by a florid neurosis, are highly creative? Would they be more creative were they less neurotic? The nearest we can come to an answer to this question, based on our current clinical experience, is that some creativity must have been clearly evidenced before treatment. Creativity often resumes after treatment and it may increase. It has not been my experience, nor has any been reported, to my knowledge, that creativity began only *after* treatment for the neurosis. These questions in the main are unanswered. They represent another interesting problem that only a further study of creativity may help to solve.

Artists or writers have no unique emotional conflicts. Their personal problems are as mundane as those which trouble the rest of us. A professional painter or writer whose work is original may indeed portray some of his private self in his work. Writers may not reveal more of themselves than other artists, but what they show is more readily accessible to psychological analysis than the work of composers or painters. (Those who are essentially copyists or imitators, whose style is difficult to distinguish from another artist's or who have little style of their own, will naturally be more obscure as people. They represent a separate and interesting problem, one that is related to the psychology of the impostor. It is a problem that is not appropriate for study here.)

Painters show us that they take bits and pieces of their experience and relationships, personally meaningful, and use them in their productions. The artist takes his own experience and couples it with the mastery of a technique. Art is a presentation of the two together. Many vain efforts have been made to separate them in attempting to understand creativity. There is a tendency in the search for motives of the artist to give insufficient attention to the technique he has employed, as though it had not intervened between his motives and his works. (Some modern works of art suggest that the artist has dissociated himself from his past experience. This in itself expresses a particular kind of presentation of himself that would limit a study of the artist from his works. Mark Tobey and Julius Bissier, for example, are well-known artists to whom this would apply.)

Only an individual study of an artist makes it possible to trace him out from a particular canvas to some of his motives. A study of his representative work may reveal certain characteristics, in form, style, subject, and perhaps a variety of other qualities. His motives may be suggested, but it is doubtful that the creative process will be demonstrated or that his actual motivations can be defined from a scrutiny of his works.

A successful and well-known painter needed treatment for symptoms that were limiting his taking trips away from the city where he lived. When he attempted any such excursion, severe phobias and somatic reactions took place. They made him sufficiently uncomfortable that he finally made no further efforts to leave the city. His neurotic difficulties gave no indication that they interfered with his work. The analysis proceeded uneventfully and resulted in the patient's finding a freedom he had not previously enjoyed. The treatment could not be said to have made any changes in the artist's painting.

The artist, on one occasion, reported that he had about completed a new portrait. It was of a withdrawn, frigid woman. She was stark, rigid, and remote — very much like his mother he thought. She was not actually like his mother in appearance, but what he called her "essence" evoked the feelings he used to have about his mother. The painting itself did not betray any resemblance to his mother. The portrait was of special interest because it had two images of the subject. One was reflected in a mirror. In contrast to the direct portrait, the one in the reflection was a warmer and more voluptuous rendition. He accounted for the difference in the two by saying that the direct image, which portrayed the woman's distance and her coldness, was how he felt she was, and the reflected image was how he wished she was. He was acutely aware that he often felt just this way about his mother. The colors he used expressed the same theme. There were colors that he felt showed her coldness, or at least were suitable to indicate the way she seemed to him. The other colors stood for warmth. The direct image was well defined, the reflected one was more suggestive.

The designs in the background of the painting, the choice of objects in the foreground, beyond adding to the organization of the work, the balance of objects and spatial relationships and the weight of masses, also represented some personal elements related to childhood. The foreground showed the subject somewhat obscured by objects. The woman was standing behind them. To the artist they showed, as he meant them to, how inaccessible his mother had been to him. But there was no hint to the observer that the composition contained these important personal signs. There were many. They were articles that came from the artist's remote past. Putting them into his paintings was his way of keeping things from that period for himself. The painting itself was regarded as beautifully executed, representative of the artist's best work. When Proust accomplishes the same aims in his famous *Remembrance of Things Past,* his purpose is plain. The painter we have been discussing has the same wish but his work is purposely obscure. It might be argued that this is due to the painter's choice. Actually, this is not the case; he wanted to in part achieve what he reported. He wished to remember things from his past, but though it is obvious to him how he accomplished it, the observer is not privy to what has taken place.

Attempts at discerning this man's motives from his manifest productions, in the absence of his latent material, would not be likely to succeed. In such a search, there is a conventional tendency to regard a painting as though it were a product of the unconscious and outside the influence of the conscious ego. Insufficient attention is paid to the technique that has interposed itself to cover the artist's nakedness. It is doubtful, despite how subjective this artist's paintings are, that his motivations would be uncovered or that his conflicts would be exposed. There is no doubt that some productions, as some dreams, have more obvious meanings than others. Both may lend themselves to easy interpretation, but this is no assurance that a correct conclusion will be reached from the manifest material of either.

Perhaps literature should be sharply distinguished from music and painting. Literary works lend themselves more readily to an interpretation of sources than the others. The writer presents himself in a language that is readily understood. What he thinks, what he wishes to say, often coupled with documents of childhood and with adult artifacts, are all often of a piece. The painter or the composer, no less than the writer, wishes to be understood. But the means through which he must make his communication rests heavily upon a technique that often requires to be translated into thought. The result is not often satisfactory. Bach's music may be easily identified: a mere snatch of his music when played makes itself immediately known. But Bach the man is unknown.

The author is a more exposed artist than the painter, the composer, or perhaps any other who makes a profession of being creative. Who would doubt, in Melville's *Moby Dick*, Faulkner's "The Bear," or Conrad's *Lord Jim*, that the chief character attempts to resolve problems of self-esteem? The well-documented lives of these authors reliably support the opinion that self-esteem was a serious personal dilemma for each of them.

It has often been suggested that the creative product itself may betray some of the underlying conflicts and some personal proclivities. It cannot, however, be relied upon to do so. There have been many attempts to use the product as a code to decipher the unconscious conflicts which motivated its creation or to reveal whether they were brought to resolution by the product. If Beethoven's *Ninth Symphony* expressed some personal problem of the composer, it cannot be discerned in his work, any more than a Rembrandt

portrait exposes the painter's inner life. Who would doubt
that each artist has his personal purposes? But the techniques of the medium he uses transform his motives into a
mode of expression which has intervened. May not the
mastery of skills or techniques be a part of the creative
process which helps to convert some motive into something
creative? For example, the composer does not really speak
his mind except through the techniques that he employs in
his art, which then stand between him and the listener. Nor
does the painter portray his unconscious except through the
use of his techniques. All artists have unconscious motives
for what they do. While some of these may be inferred, the
royal road to the artist's unconscious remains more in his
dreams than on his canvases. To inquire informally of the
artist what he had in mind, or of the creative scientist how
he happened on his discovery, is often to invite a fatuous
answer to an impertinent question.

Determinist and behaviorist explanations have greatly
influenced most psychoanalytic theories of creativity. Theorists often base their explanations on suppositions about
infantile behavior. They obscure the creative factor itself
by drawing analogies or by assuming that creativity wells
up from mental levels of consciousness. They cannot explain them, but they can show that they are subject to disorders or distortions of normal processes. Usually such
theorists proceed to reconstruct infantile life from data
gained from adults. Beginning with Freud, many have
found this a profitable procedure. It has led, however, in the
case of these theorists, to attempts to reduce complex or
highly derived adult behavior to the same simple antecedents. By this is meant explanations that reduce complex
adult conflicts to mere expressions of instinctual behavior,
or suggest that such behavior had directly intruded into
adult relations unchanged or unmodified from infancy. In
some people this occurs, but no general concept of creativ-

ity may be drawn on the basis of such pathological individuals.

An opposite trend among theorists is to seek adult disorders in childhood. This is the logical outcome of ascribing sophisticated mental mechanisms to infants and very young children. Just as there are those who would reduce adult behavior to infant psychology, there are others who would make adults of children. They explain the manifest behavior of young children in terms of the behavior of adults, as if human psychological development had been compressed into the first years of life. The most important result of these theories is that they unwittingly abrogate the laws of growth and development. It shows how distant such theories are from the readily available clinical facts.

Furthermore, these attempts at defining creativity as occurring in infantile periods of development tend to be regarded as factual, even though they are only constructions, and as constituting the psychology of the infant. Conversely, a large body of speculative notions formed through the psychoanalytic study of the child and the direct observational studies of infants by psychoanalysts are extrapolated to adult life. A common example of this exercise is the use made of studies of the anxiety reactions in young children at being separated from their mothers, or of adult experiences in the loss of a personally important object relationship. These two observations are put together and the conclusion drawn that the adult is experiencing separation anxiety as though his reaction were literally a piece of his infancy returned through regression. The psychoanalysis of creativity has fallen between two such inferences.

Creativity has long been known as a process involving some of the most profound human motivations. This is not to say that they are thus simply instinctual, but rather that they are *derived* from the vicissitudes of the instincts and are not the instincts themselves. Even when creativity is ascribed to temperamental responsiveness to one's environment and to its social demands, in which perceptions, fantasies, and skills are employed, creativity as a continuing mental activity has persistently eluded many writers. Some of the difficulties may be due in part to the proclivity to regard creativity in terms of its final product: a person is considered creative when he has produced a sculpture or a poem, or when he has invented the first pair of scissors or discovered the heretofore unknown and unsuspected relationship between gravity and electrical fields. These views of creativity often lead to a spurious question: When does creativity begin? They support a premise which is not based upon a complex variety of determinants, themselves dependent upon development and subject to the vicissitudes of accident, but instead rests upon a concept of reductionism that aims at establishing infantile antecedents, as though the solution would be found there. This, however, is a static concept of human behavior which, while attempting to use dynamic principles, encases them in a rigid determinism. Being born in a stable does not make one a donkey. The problem of creativity seems to lie elsewhere than has been suggested. Creativity is a special or particular mental activity. It remains to show what functions it performs, what conflicts it serves to resolve, and then to show that the products of such activity may be and often are of lasting value.

The most intolerable condition that seems to confront man is that of his own limitations, if one is to judge from the variety of his attempts to overcome them. A curtailment of his freedom or of himself as a physical being does not fail to mobilize him for a struggle to assert his liberty or to contrive compensations for whatever restrictions he may suffer. When his grasp is not equal to his reach he devises implements. And when he fears his life is going to be too short, which it always seems to be, he finds a way to extend it beyond death into immortality. Whatever view he may hold of the limitations that are man's lot, he never finds them acceptable, nor is he resigned to them. These remarks are not intended as either philosophical comments or abstractions. They refer to the pragmatic process which reveals itself at a very early age.

Losses and limitations that are experienced are not confined to literal privations. Wishes to receive preferential treatment, to be accorded distinction, to satisfy greed, or even to solve a problem may not be realized. Such desires when not gratified confirm a sense of limitations. They have their onset in earliest childhood.

The child's wishes always exceed his frailty or his weakness and helplessness. Ordinarily, his wishes are well in advance of his performance and his satisfactions. Thus every child is in constant debt to his own desires. His mental economy is constantly operating at a loss, and like any conscientious defaulter he is obliged to settle his accounts, even if by evasion. He does so by invention, that is, creativity. The effort to transcend limitations does not begin with some mature reckoning of his condition. It has its onset in very early life. The disparity between his wishes and his rewards is partially closed by the active fantasy life that is a part of every child's existence.

Commenting on the conditions of childhood, Freud wrote that "the loss of love, or failure, leave behind them a permanent injury to self-regard in the form of a narcissistic scar which . . . contributes more than anything to the sense of inferiority. The lessening of affection he receives, the increasing demands of education, hard work and occasional punishment . . . these show him at last the full extent to which he has been scorned" [10]. Here, clearly set forth, is the child's state. It is so evident that it requires no illustration. The child is in a constant position of indebtedness to his naturally excessive wishes and his greedy demands that circumstances alone cannot relieve. He has, however, but to turn to his inner sources — his fantasies, his play, and his dreams. There he is certain to find some fulfillment. If this were the case simply stated, would not the operations of inner life be sufficient? Would not restitution be amply made and indebtedness canceled?

Fulfillment lies in dreams and fantasies. But we also know that the restoration of losses, or attempts to heal narcissistic scars and to relieve the sense of inferiority, solely in dreams and fantasies means not altering reality so much as abandoning it, divorcing oneself from it and giving oneself up to the pleasure principle. When this course is taken to a significant degree, psychotic states prevail. The erotic relations to persons and things will be ruptured in reality and replaced by fantasy to the exclusion of the outer world. Then ''the over-estimation of the power of wishes and mental processes, the 'omnipotence of thoughts', a belief in the magical virtue of words, and a method of dealing with the outer world — the art of 'magic' — which appears to be a logical application of these grandiose premises'' [6] will be tenaciously held. This tack is a morbid course in adults.

Such beliefs are common in early childhood. The difference to be found between the adult and the child is that the child, even though actively concerned with these processes which are based on such extravagant premises, remains deeply attached to important figures and does not relinquish them, whereas the adult gives them up in reality. Furthermore, the child uses these attitudes of magic and dependence to influence those upon whom he relies; he will not disregard them nor isolate himself from them. Thus the young child tries to alter reality in relation to others.

A parallel may be drawn from the Bushman of the Kalahari Desert who carefully prepares his spear for hunt-

ing. His life depends upon its true flight. To insure its
accuracy he fashions it with great care as to balance,
weight, and other necessary requirements. When he is fin-
ished he rubs it with spittle and thus endows it with magical
properties. If he were asked why he does not have enough
faith in his magic alone, his answer would show his conster-
nation at such ignorance. Magic is to provide some assurance over the uncertainty that any throw of the spear
entails. It would not take the place of a correctly fashioned
implement. So the child does not replace his objects by
magic but wants to use it to minimize uncertainty in his
dealings with them and with reality.

Only a mad child or a crazed Bushman would want to rely
exclusively on magic and abandon reality.

Another aspect of a child's need to overcome his limitations, to relieve his sense of inadequacy and the anxiety
engendered through narcissistic wounds and his tenuous
self-regard, may be observed in what Hendrick [12] refers
to as the "need for mastery." As the child gains skills, he
begins to make active use of his sensorimotor and intellectual faculties to master his environment. The course is set
to bring increasingly under control an ever-larger segment
of the environment. There seems to be little doubt that
successful mastery earns satisfaction and reinforces a
cathexis to the organs used to these ends and that the aims
of the pleasure principle are to a certain degree met. It
would be too narrow a consideration of creativity not to
include this critically important process as the means by
which the hobbling of limitations is released and self-
regard elevated. It is thus also the means by which a sense
of loss may be restored. A skill that a young child has
acquired or learned produces an unmistakable pleasure
which is an incentive to put it to use and thus to bring
himself nearer to increasing his control over the uncertain
and therefore hostile environment.

These same patterns may be just as clearly demonstrated in later life. This should not suggest, however, that

the skills acquired throughout life are but repetitions of infantile needs conveyed into adult life. It appears that the root development of the need to master is extensive in the early years. The foundation for creativity is laid in early childhood and depends upon mastery, although the latter does not insure creativity. Without mastery, however, creativity does not come into being.

Hendrick in one of his later publications speaks of the "tools for effecting control of the outer world which we call work" [12], the precursors of which are partial ego functions. Hendrick is concerned in this paper with the difficult problem: What provides the energy and the need to exercise the physiological organs available for work and hence leads to the development of the integrated functions of the ego? Our concern here is not with Hendrick's answer but with the fact that the "skillful use of perceptual and motor techniques" aims at altering a piece of the environment or reality. In other words, what is desired in the first principle of mental functioning, the pleasure principle, is in part realized through mastery and is now to be further fulfilled by reconciling the first principle with the second or reality principle. Mastery is thus a critical part of the restorative or restitution process, and functions to overcome limitations. Internal restorative psychic operations (hallucination, fantasy, dream, or reverie) are also active in modifying or altering reality to gratify wishes. The external operations which culminate in mastery serve the same ends and may alter reality as well. There are thus two ways by which the principle of restitution is fulfilled. One is through mental phenomena operating in the service of the pleasure principle; the other, which extends the same principle into ego functions, is through that mental function which uses the acquisition of skills, perceptual, motor, and intellectual, in the service of mastering the environent in such a way that it is altered to gratify wishes and hence provide restitution for what was wanting. The driving force, as always, is a desired satisfaction which first must be perceived as lacking. The simplest illustration is that hunger is the incentive to get food.

Hendrick's thesis may be useful to show that the striving for mastery is part of the work of restitution that is carried out. Through it the child may recover from his losses, disappointments, and failures. Moreover, he often fashions the results so that they are bigger than life, of heroic proportions. Was there ever a hero or god on mortal scale? By definition he could not be so; "super-human" would lose its meaning.

For reasons that should now seem evident, the phenomena of creativity have not generally been dealt with as though they were subject to growth, change, and maturation. The significant modern psychological concepts which attempt to explain the process of creativity are psychoanalytic ones. These begin with Freud's concept about Leonardo da Vinci (in a letter in 1898 to his friend Fleiss) in which he noted that Leonardo was "the most famous left-handed individual who is not known to have had any love affairs." Nearly fifteen years later, in 1910, Freud published his well-known work on Leonardo. This short biographical work is an attempt to reconstruct some of Leonardo's childhood conflicts to show that they had an influence on his work and moreover that they appeared in his great art, unconsciously [9].

Granted that the work of an artist is derived in some part from fantasies, the supposition is that if they were uncovered, or analyzed, the artist's motives for his creation would be revealed and his works therefore better understood than they would be otherwise. Such studies have concerned themselves with the fantasies of childhood, which in some way occasionally become transformed into works of art. The process is ascribed to creativity, which may be enhanced or promoted or impaired according to certain psychologically dynamic events taking place. Leonardo's greatness is in part derived from his vast knowledge, which Freud assumed was based on an insatiable curiosity that had its origins in childhood.

There is a period, beginning at age three, that Freud calls one of "infantile sexual researches." This period of curiosity is not awakened spontaneously so much as it is aroused by the impression made by some important event — by the birth of a little brother or sister or by a fear based on external experiences in which the child perceives a threat to his selfish interests. The child's interest and curiosity lead him to the realization that oedipal wishes and begetting a child are beyond his abilities to realize. This in turn leads to abandoning the entire venture. Freud concludes that this first attempt at intellectual independence, of interest and curiosity which results in failure, appears to be of a lasting and deeply depressing kind. Furthermore, this thwarted attempt may serve as a prototype of brooding over, and doubting of, all later intellectual work that is directed toward the solution of problems. From the time of Freud's writing, the prevalence of such conflicts and their consequences have been confirmed by countless clinical examples.

There is, however, another series of conflicts which also confront the child during this same period and to which not enough attention has been given. These are fears of loss of important people, abandonment by them, and the horror of dying which were discussed in previous chapters. As in the case of thwarted attempts at intellectual independence, the child fashions a way out of his dilemma through restitution. We know that the passing of the oedipal period leads to the phase of latency in which sexual repression effects sublimation.

The fears of loss, the dread of abandonment, and the thought of dying are three major conflicts during the early years of life. The convictions upon which they are based are that relationships are tentative, that is, not permanent;

that stability is threatened, that is, by change (that which occurs within and that which occurs outside oneself); and that a deep and necessary dependence upon others exists. Each of these conflicts acts in concert with the other as the loss complex. It represents the course defined by the relationship between narcissism and object relations that is followed in the early developmental years. When the oedipal wishes finally compel repression, we may observe that the loss complex also invokes repression. These conflicts also lead to the sexual repression which occurs in latency. They are also responsible for the further development of the ego. This is the engine of change at work. Whereas the oedipus conflicts evoke libidinal repression, the loss complex and oedipal conflicts together bring about the elaboration of the ego's defenses.

When Freud called attention to the termination of infantile sexual researches, brought on by way of sexual repressions, he thought that there were three possible solutions open to the impetus of the child's curiosity. The first, he wrote, is fear of the outcome of sexuality, or inhibition, that is reinforced by the powerful effects of religious education and that leads to neurotic disorder; the second is intellectual development, which is often strong enough to resist sexual repression, with the two remaining in conflict, so that the intellectual goals, when eroticized, lead to pleasure mixed with anxiety; the third and least common is sublimation of the libido, which evades the fate of repression and leads to creativity.

The three possible solutions available to the child's curiosity focus exclusively upon the doomed oedipal relations. The child's oedipal wishes fail to be realized. Up to this point fulfillment was expected in relation to the parent. But with the recognition that it will not come about, the child's greatest libidinal experience fails. It turns into a colossal loss. Whatever the compensations may be, and to whatever degree repression may either succeed or be evaded through sublimation, the fact remains that the highest level of libidinal aspiration is thwarted and must be forgone. The element of object loss is introduced into and becomes a part of the child's greatest libidinal experience. With that the *loss complex* is firmly rooted; primarily it mobilized ego function. Whatever may have been the earlier experiences which made object loss an important consideration that the adaptive functions of the ego mitigated, in this period the loss complex that forms calls for a further maturation of ego functions that will carry the child into the next period of development.

Freud based his assumptions about the creative process entirely on the libido theory. His views on creativity have been continued by Felix Deutsch, Greenacre, Kris, and Kubie, the principal psychoanalytic writers on this subject. These writers leave little room for consideration of the development of creativity on any other than a libidinal basis, as a study of their work reveals. In the psychoanalytic framework, art is generally spoken of as being determined by the artist's own relationship to reality. Unable to come to terms with reality in his childhood development, the artist, through fantasy life, finds his way back to gratification in his work. The frustration of certain infantile needs compels the artist to create a world of gratification that he either previously had to forgo or wished he could have had and now finds in his artistic productions. This view is simply a restatement of Freud's concept that the libido, always requiring an outlet, in some people finds neurotic expression in art. These views, which rest on the libidinal component of creativity, regularly ignore creativity as an ego function. More than twenty years ago, Hendrick pointed out that psychoanalytic theorists had become enslaved by the libido theory, that they had failed to take advantage of the freedom offered them by Freud's "Beyond the Pleasure Principle," and that they remained confined by the "complicated traditions of sexual instinct theory" [13]. The same comments apply to the current psychoanalytic theories of creativity. Too little attention is given the role of the ego function in creativity.

Creativity is perhaps further clarified by taking aspects of Hendrick's work into account in addition to some of Freud's relatively neglected formulations. If we see that gaining supremacy over sensorimotor skills leads to a realization of the need for mastery, then creativity is but a further complex extension of a central process. Which of the skills — sensorimotor, intellectual, perceptual or all of them together or which combination — will become enhanced depends on many factors. From many clinical examples it is clear that whichever of the systems — sensorimotor or intellectual or perceptual — is most cathected (cathexis: a libidinal investment) will be a heavy determinant of the form creativity may take. What their developmental fate will be is dictated by the course which libidinal development follows. If we add the unpredictable role that circumstance plays, both effecting the evolving ego, we have some conception of the complexity of the developmental process. For example, a young child with a speech impediment was brought up by rigid, perfectionist parents. The father, constantly apprehensive of the future, put his principal efforts into planning against it. The mother, managerial and intolerant of frailties, reinforced the father's apprehensions. This fearful child, whose intellectual achievement was not highly prized, developed unusual control over sensorimotor functions. These values were unwittingly encouraged so that the child exercised inordinate self-control and managed to become a superb and precocious athlete, a gymnast. He could perform as if he were a member of a circus troupe, defying death, extending the limits of human endurance, and refining his self-control while refining his skills. Such an example serves to illustrate the enormous complexity of the creative process. Furthermore, it shows that the libidinal and ego functions operate in concert, the former through self-control and the latter through refinement of skill.

The observation that a child's play is creative, especially when not chiefly ruled by his sadistic wishes, needs no confirmation through psychological insight. But a consideration of what function it serves requires more than casual observation. When Freud and later Melanie Klein, particularly, brought child's play under the scrutiny of psychoanalysts it ended the idea that children's games were merely fun. It marked the beginning of the era when a child's play could no longer be taken to be meaningless. A child's play is a universal phenomenon; it knows no cultural or geographical bounds. (Reference is made here to children who have acquired enough basic skills and can direct their activities so that their play has a more than fragmentary configuration.) Small infants also play, but to what extent they are able to go beyond the rudimentary mastery of their sensorimotor skills is a matter of speculation.

In the young child, prior to the onset of latency with its repressive forces, when play becomes more formal and institutionalized, play expresses a child's inner life in a way that more nearly parallels the characteristics of the dream. It has at its foundations a wish-fulfilling aim, a manifest and latent content; it uses residues of the day's experience and is complete with symbols, condensations, fantasies, and memories. The entire experience is under the aegis of the pleasure principle and reveals a working-through of conflict in much the same way that a dream does. In play men fly at will, animals talk, the dead live, what has been lost may be restored, what has been a deprivation may be gratified; objects are accorded powers and influence and are commanded and identified with. When scrutinized in this way, play is revealed to be a means of restitution. The only limits to play are time and the influence of immediate reality.

The similarity to many of the elements of creativity in the artist is striking, with one great exception: the creativity of the artist has had one further major development; it has come under the aegis of the work principle, going beyond the aims of immediate pleasure to achieve gratification in accomplishment. This distinguishes it from the play of the child and the dilettante, both of which are under the aegis of the pleasure principle.

How the young child overcomes the profound effects of the discovery and horror of death is seen in his inventive or creative behavior. The child's beliefs have been dealt with in Chapter 3. The arrest of functions is death, but invariably the arrest is thought to be subject to reversal. Death is not final. Life may be extended. Its continuity is expressed by the child through those functions which are of special importance to him or in relation to the particular emphasis which his social group may support. The child will then express his beliefs in his everyday play. If visual experiences are of particular significance to the child, then the powers of sight are played out to be infinitely increased after death. If his society stresses that crime or evil will always be revealed, then the child will show in play that the dead know his most hidden misdeeds. Mobility is important to all children but is ordinarily somewhat restricted by the dictates of their care. Although the child recognizes that death is that condition which lacks movement, he develops in his play that the dead have no limitations. They can move freely. To be dead, when all is lost and life is gone, will lead to transformations. The most valued functions of life, it is believed, are restored but in larger than life-size proportions. Through feats of the imagination restitution is made in extravagant, heroic measures. The child at play practices religiosity. This process is not confined to childhood and so-called primitive peoples: wherever the paradise myth exists, this will be found.

Religion, one of the greatest inventions and institutions,

is constantly being fashioned to meet the needs of each new generation. It is another part of creativity that has its origins in early childhood. The transition from the childhood invention of religion to participation in its institutionalized forms is everywhere an easy one. A child does not remain an atheist for very long. He may in later life develop such beliefs, but the vast majority of human beings do not, and find them alien.

Constant fear and dread of loss is not acceptable to man and forces restitution, the route to which is creativity. It seems to matter little what is lost or forgone. The variety is infinite. It may be a deprivation of food, water, strength, important people, whatever is valued or is a source of pleasure or satisfaction, even life itself. None of these losses are acceptable. An old principle of living organisms again operates — the pleasure principle. The gratification of instincts, however deflected, whatever their vicissitudes, will always be served by it. The reality principle intervenes only to assure satisfaction with more certainty. Thus the ends of satisfaction, while thwarted or postponed or often modified, are achieved through a creative process. This process is only limited by the qualities of the dreamer. The rich fantasy life of the child, coupled with his emerging elaboration of dreams, and then his participation in formal religious beliefs indicates that the creative process is intimately linked with loss and restitution.

Viewed in this light, creativity is a means through which the oppressive grind of daily life may be mitigated and from which compensation for it is fashioned. Freud's words apply, "that really we never can relinquish anything; we can only exchange one thing for something else; when we appear to give up something all we really do is accept a substitute" [7]. This applies to the relentless pursuit of pleasure, to the process in which the play of the child gives way to the fantasies and daydreams of the adult. To this must be added "So past, present and future are threaded, as it were, on the string of the wish that runs through them all" [11]. This suggests that the wish contains man's aspirations as well as his disappointments. The engine of change that transforms wants to pleasure works also through creativity; restoration or restitution is always made possible by this faculty.

Artists further illustrate the point made by child's play. A work which faithfully reproduces nature and goes no further is not considered art. A nude is not a naked body. Symphonies are not the sounds of nature. Writing is not the spoken word set in print. Through his medium, the creative artist produces something which does not depict a natural state but which has synthesized reality and self-expression and created an illusion that is shared and satisfying. Myths, fairy tales, stories, may and often do succeed in producing the same effect. The reader or listener knows that they are not true to life. Their universality and durability do not depend on veracity or on any need to depict life as it is, because in fact they are more often than not illusions, like paintings, and are no more transcripts of life or actual events than great music is an arrangement of sounds in nature. In each instance, the artist has succeeded in producing an effect that is (to him) better than that encountered in life. The fact that the artist chooses materials from his own experience simply asserts that his sources are those upon which we all depend. No search into which pigments he uses or how he uses them or the subject he selects to paint will do more than reveal how similar his motives are to those of the rest of humanity. The artist's problems cannot be distinguished from the peasant's, and when they are of a particular severity, they probably prevent great work.

We have never seen the great works that might have been had the artists been different. Had Proust not lived pathologically in a cork-lined room, would his work have been greater? We will never know. If Van Gogh had been less mad, would he have been a better painter? This is idle speculation. There are countless other examples that could be cited. What is known of these men is that their personal problems were seriously pathological. That these problems would have a significant bearing on their work is to be expected. Whose personal problems do not have a bearing on what he does? But what the artists produced were not simply expressions of their everyday psychopathology. Such productions are probably rarely successful, to judge from the complaints of artists who deplore that their neurotic difficulties are interfering with their creative efforts. Uncovering the neurosis or the psychopathology of an individual who is engaged in creative work of itself has not led to an explanation of his choice of occupation or of his powers to carry it out. A series of the most skillfully executed psychoanalytic sessions carried on with a masterpiece, a painting, failed to show either why it was painted or why the individual was a painter. Freud's study of Leonardo da Vinci, while suggesting what may have been some of the artist's qualities, and perhaps some of his conflicts, obliged Freud to make pointed concluding remarks about this exercise in speculation. "The aim of our work has been to explain the inhibitions in Leonardo's sexual life and in his artistic activity," he wrote, and added: "We should be most glad to give an account of the way in which artistic activity derives from primal instincts of the mind if it were not just here that our capacities fail us" [9]. Freud's comments on his own work of imaginative reconstruction over half a century ago seem to have been prophetic about the efforts of those who have carefully followed him, except that they were unmindful of his caution.

Creativity, we have learned, is based upon the skillful use of illusions, particularly as they represent unfulfilled wishes that press for satisfaction. The products of such activity are varied in the extreme since the process is common to all. When its yield is meager it is because the materials that go into what is produced are poor. It is not that the creative process is uncommon, as has been conventionally held, but rather that abilities, needs, degree of mastery, and the role of circumstances are but the central variables which dictate what may come of the creative process. Less commonly, not because creativity is scarce but because geniuses are, creativity results in the highest art forms, novel inventions, or the shrewdest of contrivances.

The creative process thus seems to be part of the ordinary persistent striving for wish fulfillment. It is in the service of the attempt to produce satisfaction, not by offering immediate gratification — which the process of narcissism is more directly concerned with in order to carry out instinctual needs — but rather by offering a resolution to some hoped-for permanent condition. It represents the striving to overcome the sense of limitations, regardless of whether it stems from realistic experiences or from a lack of satisfaction in everyday life that the dream fails to fulfill. In this connection, perhaps all artists strive for a bit of immortality in their works. They hope their products — and thus they themselves — will live on and endure. Do not all who write address themselves to posterity rather than to an audience that is perishable? These appear to be the ends that creativity serves, analogous to the purpose of religion for most people: to overcome the limitations that life imposes.

The degree of success in overcoming discontent or the sense of limitations through religion and creativity is necessarily both uncertain and variable. The aim is to displace our wishes from the discontent with the present to a hope in the future. It often results in deploring the paradox that one does not live long enough to know he has been immortalized. Religious people also never live long enough to know with certainty whether they will go to heaven. We all recognize immortality as the greatest reward bestowed upon artists and heroes. They are the people who are not lost to posterity. As for the rest of us, we must make our way and hope that our conventional religiosity and creativity will provide us with some fragment of immortality, and in that way we will feel that we have been restored and thus escape a final corruption which we fear to face. We need only to turn to the epic of Gilgamesh, which tells of the vanity of all human efforts to escape death, and the injustice of the gods in refusing man the gift of eternal life, to affirm what an old lament is expressed.

Childhood remembered as a period of innocence and happiness is a ready example of history being relived. Actually, no period in life compares with childhood in the number and intensity of regular disappointments and renunciations. Regardless of what play and pleasures characterize childhood, bringing the pleasure principle to heel is one of the cardinal achievements which the child's development must accomplish. Corresponding defenses evolve for each phase which through them is thus brought to maturation.

Each phase of psychological development holds strong demands for gratification. If development is to take place in some orderly fashion, they must all be modified. This process of accommodation, while supporting the aims of satisfaction, also brings the inevitable vicissitudes of the instincts; they are indicated, for instance, by the transformation of hate into love or repression into sublimation [8].

The primary object of libidinal attachment, the mother, must be forgone and substitutes must be accepted. The intense original relationships are doomed to be relinquished and modified for a time, later even repudiated altogether. The intense egocentric self-interest of childhood must give way to include an interest in others. Even though sources of gratification are many and frequent, they are outweighed by their repudiations and subsequent substitutions. As a period of disappointment and renunciation childhood has no parallel, nor is there a richer source of frustration, unrequited wishes, or expectations that fail.

Far from being a time of anguish, however, childhood is filled with hope; the drive toward fulfillment does not abate.

The losses strewn throughout childhood are recouped by restitution in the course of development. Thus the entire process of emotional development may be seen as filled with movement from one phase to another, each one driven by its characteristic repudiations, restrictions, and limitations, and forging on toward the next phase, with restitution taking place in each phase. What is renounced in one developmental period may be retrieved in another form in the next, in the course of which mastery over the instincts is won. As forbidden wishes give way to incomplete rewards, a repository of prohibited wishes remains in the unconscious. Restitution is always being made for these wishes, but frequently in no manifestly recognizable form, as through sublimation. For instance, the bookkeeper, the baker, the ballerina, the doctor, the public defender, the artist, are all engaged in occupations that are socially commendable. Psychoanalytically speaking, such occupations are not difficult to recognize in terms of their early childhood forms, which have undergone transformations from their humble origin or become socially desirable, elevated pursuits.

The bookkeeper's choice of occupation may stem from a childhood fixation with possessions; the baker may have an inordinately strong identification with a mother's role or with an ideal of a mother as a provider; the ballerina may once have been a child with an excessive interest in her body associated with strong childish exhibitionist tendencies. The doctor may have had a persistent curiosity about another's body or a wish to rescue others from danger as an expression of his own fears for himself; the public defender was perhaps once concerned with the common childhood complaint that conditions are not fair; the artist may be in revolt against a world he never made. These hypothetical examples are meant to show that all professions or occupations have some of their roots in some critical period of childhood. More important than a suggestion of their origins is the significance that from such ignominious beginnings desirable life work takes an impetus. This does not mean that circumstances do not play a great role, as do many other factors. It would be naïve to suppose that choices of occupations are made, even unconsciously, early in life and are then pursued without deviation to their goals.

The theme of loss and restitution and creativity is an enduring one not only for the individual; when it is woven into the fabric of a people and becomes a part of the culture, it achieves an imperishable quality. Myths are an example. In them the common experience is crystallized and some truth of both individuals and groups is revealed. Human experience, history, literature, religion, the arts, are replete with evidence of myths which perpetuate themselves and are constantly replenished in daily life everywhere. For this reason it seems desirable to call attention at this point to myth in one of its contemporary forms.

A fantasy of Western frontier life in America has so completely captivated an eager, credulous imagination that everywhere in this country it is reenacted by our children, revitalized and embellished for adults in our films, and retold in our literature. A myth with such power must satisfy a deep common need. It is evidently no longer merely a local or national folk tale because it has made its appearance regularly in East Asia, the Near East, and Europe. Once the continental boundaries have been crossed and the oceans spanned, we may be satisfied that our fantasy is probably not only a common one but an old one as well, simply arranged in our style. It is the story of the cowboy hero who triumphs over evil. The characters are rough, crude, and coarse. (In some instances their roughness is tempered by songs and they are dressed in comical costumes, with linen and batiste replacing leather and denim, and soap and water have been applied to what was rarely bathed. But these are insignificant alterations.) There are the prosaic vicissitudes and sacrifices and losses. The dimensions are greater than life in scale, and the outcome is regularly predictable. Justice is finally and regularly meted out to favor the good over the bad; what is lost, given up, or taken away is restored.

The play, however, is not merely a morality myth. It has deeper implications. The struggle is one in which lives are at stake. In the events that develop, some characters who are good die at the hands of bad men. The battle goes back and forth with more or less elaboration until finally the hero kills the villain, whose henchmen also either suffer the extreme fate of their leader or are punished. Here the story ends. What was lost, relinquished, or destroyed is restored. It matters not at all whether the scene is enacted on the plains between cowboys of the most common type, or between cowboys and Indians, or on the streets between constituted authorities and criminals, or in a further variation with more up-to-date properties, namely, modern warfare with atomic weapons. If we look closely, we see that the identification of the hero with the villain, the wish to be as strong and violent and as brutal and destructive as he is, becomes the emotional defense through which triumph is achieved, that is, the needed transformation to become frightening instead of fearful. As this transition takes place, the hero takes on the villain's behavior, which he now uses in the cause of good. The one who was abused becomes the aggressor, and with this acquired identification the myth can be brought to its proper conclusion.

The enacted myth finds its roots in early life. The young child three or four years old plays in this pageant no less than adults, who see it on film or read it in novels or record it in history.

The authenticity with which this myth depicts life owes

its vitality to the faithfulness with which it adheres to the
process of defense against aggression — to overcoming
anxiety — to resisting passivity — to undoing what was
done — to transcending previous limitations — and to a variety of other less obvious defenses the ego employs against
the demands of the instincts. The significance and the timelessness of the endlessly repeated and reproduced story lie
in its revelation of the universality of our experiences and
our emotional defenses that are associated with them.

A myth is true to life; not, of course, as a tale but as a
record of our defenses. A myth would lose its imperishable
quality and its common appeal were it not for the fact that
each myth relates experiences that evoke defenses from our
everyday existence. Each myth may have a particular
gamut of defenses which are associated with it. But a myth
that fails in this respect is not truly a myth and probably
becomes fixed to the period and place of origin instead of
being timeless and universal.

It would be a narrow consideration of the importance of
loss, restitution, and creativity to fail to observe the process historically; a path of vanished greatness is constantly
reconstructed by people everywhere. A deprived childhood
is often reconstituted on a grand scale, and even as an idyl,
in recollection. Many historical episodes have received this
treatment. One example is the efforts of the waning Assyrian kings to support their power — in particular the
efforts of Ashurbanipal (665–626 B.C.), who searched out
ancient tablets and had them copied and preserved in great
palace libraries in an attempt to add to his luster. Naboni-
dus (555–539 B.C.), the last king of Babylon before the
Persian conquest, organized excavations of old temple sites
with the intention of rediscovering ancient ground plans so
that he could reconstruct exact replicas of them and give
himself a better heritage than he would otherwise be
credited with [16, 17]. These efforts to restore a lost pres-
tige by the resurrection of a longed-for past are more than

an attempt to establish continuity. They are an attempt to elevate oneself to the past, beyond the burdensome impoverished present. The principal reason for restating a noble past or for creating one which is wished for is to add to a current doubtful stature. It is never to detract from it. In all cultures and in all times we pursue the past with the hope of adding to the present. If we are a wealthy, successful people it does not disparage our ancestors, but accords them a share in our affluence, when we make them more heroic, thus enhancing ourselves even more through them. If we are waning as a people, may we not, like the Assyrian kings, dig out some past which will add to our stature, refer to old heroes, identify ourselves with them, and believe ourselves the better for it? These practices are as old as history.

Is it simply the pleasure principle that perpetually turns losses into restitution, in the process of which creativity often results? Does man have such poor tolerance for limitations, whatever they may be, that he is compelled to attempt to exceed them? Does the pleasure principle set a liberating course which permits no lasting deviation from it? It appears not. Nor is it the pleasure principle and the reality principle acting in concert that brings about a resolution. According to Freud, it is the discrepancy between the two.

Freud stated that he had no faith in the benevolent illusion that human beings instinctually press toward perfection, high intellectual achievement, and ethical sublimation. He thought, moreover, the contemporary development of human beings required no different explanation from that of animals. He argued that, as a result of instinctual repression, the tireless impulsion appearing in a *minority* of people is the basis for all that is most precious in human civilization, and that no substitutive or reactive formations and no sublimations will suffice to remove the persistent tension from repressed instincts. Furthermore, he believed that the difference in amount between the pleasure of satisfaction *demanded* and that actually achieved provides the perpetual tension which will permit of no halting at any given position attained [10].

Freud explicitly stated that the "pressing forward unsubdued" of an elite could hardly be attributed to all human beings. In winnowing out that group of people who succeed to greatness, he has implied that a similar process is not characteristically present in others. In Freud's terms, the majority of mankind, although subject to similar dynamic and instinctual forces, because they do not produce the phenomena of human effort that are most treasured by civilization, contribute little if anything of intellectual or ethical value. Disregarding the cynicism of such an analysis of human effort, and not suggesting an egalitarian one in its place, Freud's judgment of what occurs when the instincts are subject to repression by social forces may be criticized. He leaves out of consideration the endless efforts universally expended by the many in relieving the human condition. He maintains that anything short of the greatest value is but a poor substitute and therefore of small consequence to humanity, because it does not represent what is rated highest — as if immortal works stood alone as divine revelations or as signs of a god's pleasure. In point of fact, they do not stand alone. Their value is supported by the vast majority of mankind. Otherwise they would constitute a priceless heritage appreciated and preserved only by a small minority. The Decalogue owes its continued significance to its appeal to the mass of humanity; Shakespeare is an immortal not only because he was a genius but because he has also been valued by masses and generations of people for four hundred years. The same is true of Mozart, of Buddha, Christ, Moses, of Leonardo da Vinci and others. The highest distinction given to that minority of humanity which produces what is most precious in human values rests on the fact that the majority, while falling short of greatness in its striving toward similar ends, often does not fail to support and recognize greatness when it occurs. This comment is not a polemic against Freud's view, but an effort to show that he has given only a partial explanation in his instinct theory to the question: What is the engine of change?

A more complete answer to that question evolves *not* only from the tension produced by the discrepancy between the pleasure and reality principles, but from the ordering principle of restitution which reconciles the two.

Unlike the other creatures whose instincts he shares, the human being is not free to pursue his instincts, by the very fact that he is a political animal, as Aristotle called him. He must live in a society which imposes certain restrictions. This fact creates a condition which distinguishes all men from other animals. As Freud described, there is a discrepancy between the gratification demanded and what is actually achieved. What is more, the lag not only exists at the outset but is also comprehended very early in life. It enters into the course of early psychological development. Furthermore, it seems not to be made up, either completely or for long, at any time. Thus the discrepancy serves as a constant source of striving that finds expression in wishes of fulfillment, dreams, and fantasies. These in turn are indicative of some of the effects of instinctual repression.

From this point of view, the most archaic experiences of deprivation may be observed in the infant's inevitable discomforts. The lack of gratification that ensues represents the earliest of instinctual vicissitudes. There is not a repression, but its prototype is being formed as the homeostatic balance is disturbed. As the child develops, the pleasure principle is modified by the principle of reality, and a rudimentary repression of instincts begins to take place. The difference between demand and satisfaction becomes a fact, and efforts to close this gap are put into effect. Thus, as has been stated above, the first principle of mental functioning modified by the second, is a step to the third principle, the altering of reality. The roots of wishes for fulfillment probably originate at this time from a lack of satisfaction, lack of pleasure, or frustration. Such experiences are always associated with the person who provides care and through whom fulfillment is achieved.

These early conflicts thus begin to take on their permanent social importance. The foundation is laid in the child for becoming a social or a "political" animal in the need for homeostatic balance which is characteristic of all living matter. But the human degree and duration of dependence on another person to reach or maintain this balance have no parallel in other animals. The attempt to attain a corrective equilibrium of gratifications is an essential part of human emotional development, but the modification of the basic principles of mental functioning and the effort to close the gap between what is demanded and what is satisfied are only possible through the help of another person. The introduction of the social process is thus axiomatic in achieving homeostasis. The process of homeostasis in the human is therefore not a self-regulatory mechanism to the extent that it is in other animals. Its regulatory function cannot be individually achieved during the early developmental years when the dependence upon another person for survival is a fact of life. Early conflicts in the young child and the derived ones of later life thus take on a social importance that they never lose; to achieve homeostasis is to include a social process.

The filling of the breach between the child's need and its gratification is accomplished, as we have seen, largely through the intervention of another person, and an enduring basis for a social relationship is established. The connection between this intervention and an emerging emotional development which is expressed in the child's attempt at mastery of a variety of functions, sensorimotor and intellectual, is highly important. If care is excessive, dependence is encouraged and the efforts at mastery are correspondingly inhibited. Inhibitions of mastery are also promoted when care is minimal. Countless examples of both extreme conditions show the process clearly. In the former condition the young child tends to remain emotionally immature; in the latter, retardation of normal developmental achievement (in speech, problem-solving, and social relations) is common, as can be observed in well-provided-for institutionalized infants whose care is not personal, but routine.

Under ordinary conditions of family care the young child's efforts at mastery will be in the service of meeting his expanding needs. The aims in striving for mastery are not antithetical to the essential relationship with an adult, but they help to free the child from being wholly dependent upon such a relationship. Mastery supplements the social condition for the child. It does not attempt to replace it as is commonly supposed. (See Chapter 6.) Mastery affords the child another course for closing the breach between wish and reality. One course develops through the child's social relationship, libidinal in quality; the other through mastery with its reinforcement of the ego, as represented by creativity. The two courses are not separate, but fused in the pursuit of restitution.

In later life the expanding needs of the child are replaced by the needs of the adult. Although needs are often acute in childhood, that is not the only period when inner wishes press for satisfaction and when variable conditions require adaptation. Childhood merely marks the beginning of these processes which extend throughout life. It is only in the realm of fiction and fantasy that the wisdom of years brings acceptance of a lack of satisfaction, frustration, limitations, or variable conditions of life. A closer examination of the period toward the end of life shows that there is at best only an apparent acceptance of limitations. The impetus to change should not be obscured by the wish of old age to resist change; the wish to restore what has been lost or forgone or to transcend one's limits is peculiar to no one period of life. Hence the process of restitution is a continuous one. Moreover, the prospect of its not being sustained in the face of inevitable losses brings out the pain of grief and the tension of despair. At these times depression may set in. Depression will remain, or mourning continue, until the processes of restitution are again operating and the lifelong cycle is once more established. In those instances in which restitution is not found, depression persists and tends to become pathological. No time in life is an exception other than early childhood. At that period the resources for restitution are most vigorous: substitutions, reaction formation, denial, magical thinking. In the absence of the oppressiveness of a well-developed superego in the child, despair is brief and therefore depression, in the ordinary clinical sense, is not demonstrable. Toward the end of life restitution is more difficult as losses prove to be less retrievable. Even then there is no actual resignation, or so-called acceptance.

For example, an eighty-three-year-old woman whose husband died after a lingering illness was exhausted from the care and demands from which his death finally freed her. At her advanced age she did not fail to realize that death was shortly in store for her, since she too was frail. She had been a scolding and critical wife for many years. In a brief time after her husband's death she mourned his loss genuinely and seemed to accept philosophically the inevitable. Publicly, she kept herself busy with her personal affairs, to the relief of her friends, who knew her to be wise and realistic. Privately, however, she was acutely attuned to remarks about her dead husband, which she weighed carefully. Any word which she felt to be a criticism of the man of whom she herself had been critical for years past excited her into

endless efforts to challenge it. Her life became solely committed to restoring her husband to perfection, to removing
from her recollection the scorn, derision, and disdain for
him that she had often either expressed to him or harbored
within herself when he was alive. She gave him an importance he did not seem to have had for years past, or indeed
ever, and marked his grave in a way that was not in accord
with what she had felt before he died. She extolled his virtues and thus reconstituted him into what she wished he had
been. Socially, she appeared to be a somewhat subdued and
resigned little old lady, making her rounds and doing her
errands.

We have noted that the loss of a personally important
relationship has its manifest and latent devastating effects
late in life, perhaps no less than it does in the earlier years.
There are significant differences in the elaborate defenses
which have been developed since early childhood but they
do not outweigh the similarities. It has often been suggested clinically and supported by popular views that the
losses experienced in later life are received with acceptance
or resignation and without efforts at restitution. Careful
study does not support these speculative ideas. Resignation
in the face of serious loss or a threat to life is more illusion
than it is fact. No new mental mechanisms develop in old
age; none really appear which were not previously present,
nor does an unwelcome reality late in life lessen the necessity to use over and over defenses which have been well
developed in the past, particularly those which relate to
loss.

True resignation and an acceptance of what the Fates
offer appear not to be human qualities. Such characteristics
are manifestly wishful if not fictional. The earlier chapters
of this book have attempted to show that there is no period
in life when naked reality is embraced. The commonly observed attitudes of resignation to adversity or apparent
acceptance of a serious loss are, to a degree, no doubt,

deliberately assumed. Actually they are largely dictated unconsciously. The behavior is the result of a powerful force that compels compliance with reality. It does not come from a sharp perception of reality as is commonly supposed. It is also not an application of the reality principle that supersedes, to an inordinate degree, other principles of mental functioning.

Resignation, acceptance, and submission to an unwelcome reality are a defense mechanism; a reaction, in other words, to a serious threat. An abhorrence of impending deprivation, disappointment, impoverishment, in short the threat of a serious loss, is changed at times into resignation or acceptance. Many examples are available in everyday life. Events which arouse or alarm the multitude leave some people unmoved. They show their curiosity or their interest in what is happening but they do not seem to become engaged as others do. They remain dry-eyed at the graveside; they watch a drama that grips and chokes the others in the audience and they mutter to themselves it is only a play.

A typical example is a man who passionately resists the dictates of an unreasoning authority. He is deeply concerned with adjudication and, in principle, matters of justice. He enjoys a profession that requires a high degree of personal discipline. There is no question about either his competence or his dedication to his work. The aloofness that is characteristic of him permits him to work without being distracted. The attitude is not a matter of his choosing. It earns him admiration and envy.

As we become familiar with his past, we learn that scenes of chaos in childhood showed him to be "mature" beyond his years. When his mother had tantrums that shook his father into limp ineffectiveness the boy, then nine or ten years old, regarded the scene with a dispassionate eye. He tried to calm his mother and to support his father. His private judgment was that his parents were behaving in "some ridiculous fashion." Similar episodes occurred be-

tween his parents when he was a small child. He was horrified by them. His principal defense then was to go to his
room, avoid hearing what went on, and concentrate on play.

What was unpleasant and threatening, and hence created
fears when this man was a small child, was countered with
strong denials to himself that he was frightened. The
details of other factors in his family life that supported his
reactions are not essential here, but they bolstered the boy
in his reaching for a level of "objectivity." There were
countless events that called for his participation. He rarely
lost his composure but he just as rarely gained in a shared
enterprise.

His adult life shows the same cool reserve that was
typical of him in his youth. The social and political events
which kept those about him in a state of ferment left him in
a dispassionate appraisal of his associates and the happenings. When his mother was discovered to have a fatal illness, the family and relatives received the bad news with
tears. He was dry-eyed. He went about comforting and supporting the others, much as he had done when he was a
young boy. His remarks were to the effect that we all finally
perish, that we must accept the realities as they are.

He is unaware that his calm and reasoned behavior is not
the result of a deliberate choice. We learned from extensive
study of him that an intricate web of denial of his real
feelings and an avoidance of the significance emotionally of
disturbing events left him with his stoical behavior. An attitude of indifference to events and their significance to him
does not mean that this man is unmoved. It indicates exactly the opposite. He cannot tolerate the frustration, the
distress of discontent with which events and his feelings
threaten to engulf him, so he stands aside.

There are common precedents for similar behavior in
children. This man's early history is illustrative. Frequently when adults are deeply disturbed in the face of
tragic events. and usually in the case of a loss, the children

who are witnesses often appear to be indifferent. They are regularly credited with a lack of understanding. Their indifference is alleged to be due to their inexperience or their youth. What is generally overlooked is that the young child appraises the events correctly, is keenly aware of their effect upon the adults, and cannot tolerate the disorder, the deprivation, and the danger that the circumstances and his reactions evoke. His reaction often is to play and romp about. The observation of his family is: "He acts as though nothing happened, as if he did not understand. He is too young." These remarks are correct insofar as the behavior of the child is concerned. But when the motives which underlie his actions are considered, his relatives are misled, they fail to understand him. An example of such an event was reported in the press a few years ago. Prince Charles was then a small boy of about six or seven years when his grandfather, King George VI, whose favorite he was, died. The entire nation mourned the king. The state ceremonies were many and long. Prince Charles was photographed during this period, as were others of the royal family. Charles always appeared playing, romping, sliding on banisters, and grinning. He was in no way unusual. These photographs are rare documents that show a child's typical response to tragic events that affect his family. Charles probably did not fail to comprehend the events in which he was involved. On the contrary, he showed a reaction found in children who clearly appreciate the reality but seek to avoid and deny its significance.

Like the man whose equanimity remains unruffled, the child who giggles in a crisis that calls for tears holds an underlying conflict in obscurity. Neither the child nor the man can tolerate a threat or the fact of loss. Massive ego defenses are mobilized to deny the fact or the fantasy of losses their importance. The losses are unconsciously acknowledged. Their emotional importance is repressed. What

appears in place of the direct response to loss or the threat
of it is negation (see Chapter 1, p. 4).

The reactions in the child as in the adult are not psychotic in the sense that reality has been abandoned. On the
contrary, as we have observed, the facts of reality are not
denied, but the feelings or emotions associated with them
have been repressed. The reaction is to loss *without* restitution. Far from being divorced from reality, actually it is a
sharp, often correct appraisal which because of its accuracy is repudiated.

Thus the clinical examination of someone who seems resigned and accepts the hopelessness of a condition of life,
for example, the experience of loss, does not reveal an
absence of the wish for recovery or restitution. Furthermore the effectiveness of the defensive mechanism of denial
is commonly underestimated as it leads the subject and
often the observer into mistaking manifest behavior, such
as acceptance, for the true emotional state. Instead, it but
shows the effectiveness of the defense in masking what is
truly underlying, the opposite of acceptance or resignation
which denial serves unconsciously to censor.

The timeless words of the poet Horace, "No one lives
content with his condition" — and, it may be added, children
least of all — speak of a general condition, even a principle,
rather than of a particular plight. The principle is not sea-
sonal, temporal, or conditional. It defines the human state:
it is the psychology of discontent. From the beginning the
child, and throughout his life the man, may seem to accept
his lot, but at best this is a superficial even though a useful
defense against the opposite, which his more genuine incli-
nations reveal. Thus, characteristically he continually adds
to what he has, aspires to what he wants, and permits no
giving up. At the two extremes of life, in childhood and in
the terminal years, a seeming resignation and acceptance of
the vicissitudes of living may be commonly observed. It has

led, as we have observed, to the frequent assumption that in early childhood there is a lack of full understanding of life, expressed in acceptance, and that toward the end of life there is much understanding, which affirms itself in resignation. In neither case is the assumption in accord with the facts. It is therefore misleading to assume that compliance is more than — at times — a suitable but unstable defense or form of adaptation. The opposite is closer to the truth. The child who mutely stands by as a witness to his blighted hopes is no more deceived than a grandfather who appears apathetically resigned to his own fate. Behind these effective defenses the wishes that are unfulfilled are perpetually being mobilized. The purpose of the defenses is to alter the press of circumstances, to undo the hobble of limitations from within oneself so that one can drive on to transcend frustrations. All is aimed at the relief of discontent. Acceptance and resignation carried to the extremes of indifference and apathy may defer the anger of disenchantment but they do not really suspend it. They only succeed in obscuring the workings of the principles of mental functioning: that reality is correctly appraised as abhorrent and that it must be modified in order to be compatible with the deepest wishes and needs that have not been full fed. Acquiescence and apathy represent an effort to postpone but not to relinquish the inner demands for gratification. There is a natural readiness to embrace these defenses for more than they are, as though they were proof of the suspension of the deeper disquiet of desires. It is therefore important to demonstrate that under the worst conditions and in the most abject apathy the rule of discontent is *not* compromised.

The pervasive apathy, resignation, and passivity commonly observed in Nazi concentration camps and among prisoners of war have been the focus of many studies and reports for twenty years [1, 4]. The miserable conditions of incarceration coupled with despair have been given as the chief reasons for such reactions. The apparent acceptance of their lot by the victims of the Nazis and the fact that they often gave only token resistance to their captors has been explained as the result of a grim reality that is accompanied by assertions, in the most general terms, about the social character of those who were incarcerated. The attention which has been paid to the intricacies of the Nazis' malignant social institutions has more often than not resulted in obscuring the effects that being victimized by other people had on the prisoners themselves. The conflict between the prisoner and his tormentors has been displaced from its proper focus onto its institutional framework. The prison camps and other means of Nazi oppression owed their nature to the people who conducted them. The prison camp was as it was to the degree and extent that other human beings made it so, not to the extent that it was instrumental to the policies of a regime. Under the degenerate living conditions produced in the prison camps it is not remarkable that the regressive reactions that occurred were widespread.

As deprivation by the jailors became more pressing, restitution continued to take place. The dreams, fantasies, and expressed wishes of the prisoners became correspondingly more primitive and, therefore, in some respects childlike. The wishes for release, recovery, and rescue were not relinquished, but on the contrary they acquired a more infantile and extravagant quality of expectation, in which the need for immediate gratification was intensified. The result was that the degree of disappointment was a measure of the extent of expectation. Thus regressive wishes were regularly entertained and regressive acts regularly committed. The often-observed vacuous apathy and acceptance of fate have not been regarded as a manifest expression of a rapacious latent process that finds its assertion in regressive behavior. Psychological studies of such victims since the end of the war, in many instances twenty years later, confirm the tenacity of the regressive reactions, and their persistence in somewhat modified but still very oppressive demanding behavior.

The conclusion of this study will be that commonplace apathy or resignation is intimately associated with regression. The regressive wishes and behavior (discussed above) are better accounted for if understood in relation to the psychodynamics of apathy that many individuals showed than when they are taken to be merely heightened eccentricities. These qualities, which are essentially sadomasochistic, are accentuated and evoked under the special circumstances. The defenses and particularly the sublimations previously effective give way to the full expression of the sadistic wishes and impulses, thus representing a return of what had been repressed. When regressive wishes and behavior are vented, apathy as a reaction is the crudest defense to sustain oneself. The satisfactions that take place in fact or fantasy are acted upon out of the necessity of overcoming a *sense* of severe deprivation and not simply the fact of it. They produce apathy as the response or the attempt to quell and hence to balance off the greatly heightened sadistic fantasies and acts that accompany regression.

In the Nazi prison camps, under terms of desperate deprivation which forced an indifference to others who were sharing a similar plight, life was relieved by bursts of abuse and destructive impulses toward one's fellow prisoners. The prisoners thus unwittingly acquired some identification with their hated jailors. Currying the jailors' favor may have been not only an unmistakable sign of defection but a sign of a return to childhood defenses as well. These defenses in the service of an individual's oldest desires are the familiar ones, such as wishing for special consideration, envy, jealousy, self-interest and a disregard for others or the consequences, the relinquishing of social aims for egocentric ones, and identifying oneself with the powerful tormentors. All such wishes and behavior, reprehensible on the one hand and rationalized on the other, enjoin a further conflict from early life. It is this old and previously resolved dilemma that is now intensified, one which is produced by the conflict between the demands of gratification and those of conscience.

To whatever degree rationalizations of regressive behavior may find reinforcement from reality in justifying such behavior to gain gratification, there is no escaping self-criticism in the final analysis. The more severe the conscience, the more extensively developed is the ensuing self-devaluing process that characteristically finds expression in despair, hopelessness, and resignation. The loss of self-esteem that comes about through regressive fantasies is rendered worse when they are acted upon. Moreover, the reality of being humiliated and reviled as worthless further compounds the injury. And the outcome of both the inner loss of self-esteem and the outer reality of being demeaned, acting in concert, is likely to be apathy.

It is significant that many neurotic symptoms, and even some severe forms of neurosis, went into remission during the experiences of inordinate hardship. Some disorders which were previously intractable were given up altogether, such as the severe phobias, hypochondriasis, and many recurrent types of psychosomatic disorders. After the victims were released from incarceration, many of the old disorders returned as though unchanged. These examples show that the force of circumstances may not play so exclusive a role in these disorders and that what has been overlooked is that regression should be accorded an important part. It appears that when regressive behavior is prominent, previously well-established neuroses abate, just as under conditions which maintain repression the opposite takes place, that is, the neuroses are magnified. The return of repressed wishes in a way of life which permits acting them out shows that the neuroses lose their impetus during conditions which lead to regressive behavior. Regression is thus seen to be nearer to wish-fulfillment. The way to gratification is considerably shorter through regression than it is through the tortuous course of neurotic conflict.

When a deep sense of loss is added to unmitigated experiences of deprivation and degradation, the need for gratification develops a unique intensity. Regression, under these circumstances, seems to be the principal means through which gratification may be achieved; it also becomes the mode of adaptation to those extraordinary circumstances in which the inner and the outer reality are joined. Regression, replacing restitution as the means through which what is lost may be restored, even if modified, gains its impetus as an effort to overcome the sense and realities of deprivation [18].

In short, the conventional view that a fateful outcome is met with acceptance or resignation appears to be an invention. It presupposes that these reactions are derived from an accurate appraisal of a grim reality. Although often the realistic judgment may be correct, it is rarely what brings about acceptance or passivity or resignation. In part it is a wish, followed by the belief, that such behavior when adhered to will serve to deny and perhaps even to postpone magically a present danger. Close examination reveals that apathy and resignation are but the manifest expressions of deeper underlying conflicts of emotional life, and that it is in these latent conflicts that the regressive wishes are to be found. They determine the outward aspects of apathy, acquiescence, and inhibition. The parallel to dreams about imminent danger, in which the dreamer is a helpless victim, inhibited in all his movements to defend himself and often voiceless to cry out his terror, is striking. It is a common experience in the analysis of such dreams to discover that their latent content reveals the dreamer's concealed aggressive, destructive, and regressive wishes.

That there is no actual acceptance of the finality of life is amply demonstrated by regressive wishes and actions, in that they represent the opposite of acceptance. They are the most archaic and desperate measures taken to sustain existence, for they characterize a period of life when gratification was sought as an immediate goal. Regression to an earlier mode of behavior is not the same thing as being in that state initially. To return where one once was is not the same as having been there and nowhere else. Hopelessness without doubt comes from the realization that the accustomed means for gratification through the ego are no longer possible and that only regressive behavior will sustain one. Many prisoners of the Nazis could not tolerate the confrontation with extremes of personal humiliation and loss; that is, they could neither accept nor be resigned to the primitive conditions of existence demanded in this type of internment, nor the premise that gratification could only be derived from regression. These perished not from a wish to die, though it often appeared so, but often from their inability to adapt themselves by resisting regressive wishes and by repudiating regressive behavior to satisfy such wishes.

It is not only the return of the regressive content of the unconscious but the fact that it is acted upon that promotes powerful archaic wishes and needs. The laboriously acquired functions of the ego — such as success in application of the reality principle to postpone an immediate need for a later gratification, the mastery of skills in service of the work principle, and the social relationships — all no longer available for the work of restitution, become fragmented. This means that these elaborate functions are reduced to archaic partial functions. For example, the urgency of gratification becomes once again associated with sado-masochistic impulses and sadistic acts to gain what is immediately desired; the relinquishing of physical and intellectual skills becomes converted into an abhorrence for work except when it promises to provide an immediacy of satisfaction; the scope of social relationships narrows to furnish only the security of dependence, accompanied by a heightened preoccupation with oneself to the exclusion of others. All these examples indicate that a reversion has taken place. Some of the mature aspects of ego adaptation are retained while others, replaced by immaturity and infantilism, are given over to the behavior of early phases of emotional development. Under these auspices there is no hope except of immediate gain: expectation yields to an appetite to be gorged, and the sense of loss is transformed into acute deprivation. No longer is there a press for restitution, but instead an indiscriminate rooting for replacement. With these profound alterations the social fabric of a person is destroyed. He remains gregarious but he is no longer a social being. The reverse of creativity takes place as regression succeeds. Creativity in periods of regression ceases to exist.

Creativity does not depend upon peace and quiet or affluence and optimism. Nor is it a restricted function exclusive to the gifted. It is basically part of the psychology of discontent and the striving to overcome it. It is a common and ordinary thing so long as regression does not replace it. Creativity is an expression of hope, of expectation, and of transcending one's limits. Man's persistent need for restitution from the unrequited wishes, frustrated desires, thwarted intentions, and grind of life is invariably revealed in his creativity — in his greatest inventions that enrich his life and in his little contrivances that comfort him. His curiosity and his daring, his explorations and his mastery over his environment, lay bare his hopes and his expectations straining toward fulfillment. Through creativity he repairs his past in myths; in his arts he remakes his present; and in his beliefs he fashions his future.

REFERENCES

1. Bettleheim, Bruno: *The Informed Heart: Autonomy in a Mass Age* (Glencoe, Ill.: Free Press, 1960).
2. Bibring, E.: The So-Called English School of Psychoanalysis. *Psychoanal. Quart.*, 16 (1947), 169–193.

3. Camus, Albert: *Carnets*, II (Paris: Gallimar, 1964).

4. Frankl, Victor: *Man's Search for Meaning* (New York: Washington Square Press, 1963).

5. Freud, S.: Formulations Regarding Two Principles in Mental Functioning. In *Collected Papers* (London: Hogarth Press, 1948), IV, 14–16.

6. ———. On Narcissism: An Introduction. In *ibid.* (1948), IV, 32.

7. ———. The Relation of the Poet and Day-Dreaming. In *ibid.* (1948), IV, 175.

8. ———. Instincts and Their Vicissitudes. In *ibid.* (1948), IV, 60–83.

9. ———. Leonardo da Vinci and a Memory of His Childhood. In *The Complete Psychological Works of Sigmund Freud*, Standard Edition (London: Hogarth Press, 1951), XI, 59, 131, 132.

10. ———. Beyond the Pleasure Principle. In *ibid.* (1955), XVIII, 20–21, 42.

11. Greenacre, Phyllis: The Childhood of the Artist. In *The Psychoanalytic Study of the Child* (New York: International Universities Press, 1957), XII, 47–72, 57–58, 178.

12. Hendrick, Ives: Instinct and the Ego During Infancy. *Psychoanal. Quart.*, II (1942), 33–58, 311–329.

13. ———. Letter to Editor. *Psychoanal. Quart.*, 12 (1943), 561–565.

14. Koestler, A.: *The Act of Creation* (London: Hutchinson, 1964), pp. 231, 263.

15. Kubie, L. S.: *Neurotic Distortion of the Creative Process* (Lawrence: University of Kansas Press, 1958), p. 141.

16. Moscati, S.: *Face of the Orient* (New York: Doubleday Co., 1962), pp. 95, 288.

17. Pritchard, J. B.: *Ancient Near East Texts* (Princeton: Princeton University Press, 1955), pp. 40–44.

18. Rochlin, Gregory: The Loss Complex: A Contribution to the Etiology of Depression. *J. Amer. Psychoanal. Ass.*, 7 (1959), 313–314.

19. Stein, M. I., and S. J. Heinze: *Creativity and the Individual: Summaries of Selected Literature in Psychology and Psychiatry* (Glencoe, Ill.: Free Press, 1960).

6

THE PSYCHOLOGY OF
FAILURE

Failure is one of the commonplace experiences in life.
Scrutiny of the most successful career will provide both
ample evidence of dissatisfaction and full catalogues of
limitations that show failures have appeared. Failure is
not confined to any single period of life, nor is there a
period without it. Failure is encountered in the beginning of
life, recurs throughout it, and characteristically marks its
waning. It is not always associated with those adventitious
circumstances which often prevail to make life miserable.
Nor does the realization of success preclude failure. It
seems that triumphs are naturally useful to conceal defeats.
Success and creativity have proved to be endlessly fascinat-
ing subjects for study. The psychology of failure, however,
has received relatively little attention.

The dynamic psychological processes involved in failure,
despite its ubiquity, have remained obscure. Failure has
been treated rather more as a literary subject than as a
subject of study in psychology. It has been dealt with by
historians in the procession of civilizations that have flow-
ered and then withered, and by biographers in those figures
whose lives have significantly influenced human events. It
has been the theme of legends, myths, folk tales, song and
art, in which confessions and acknowledgments of failure
have appeared throughout recorded time.

As a clinical phenomenon failure has been studied almost

exclusively in terms of the narrow perspectives of psycho-pathology. The psychology of failure, which comprises not only the event of failure itself but also the emotions that are associated with it, both influences and is subject to psychological development. It is therefore one of the deter-minants of behavior, perhaps no less than is success. Never-theless, the psychology of failure has been wrapped in nebulous ignorance. The unpleasantness and pain it causes may account in large measure for its neglect as a subject of investigation.

Development of the ego takes place when the child can begin to give up its complete focus on itself or, as Freud put it, depart from primary narcissism [14]. This process, which epitomizes emotional development, takes place in the transition from primary self-interest to interest in another person, from domination by the pleasure principle to a stage of compromise between it and the reality principle. These are the chief mental mechanisms by which the infant is transformed from a gregarious creature to a social being. The course of this development is initiated in very early life and much sooner than is generally supposed. Primary narcissism is very likely but a brief episode, which gives way readily and gradually, even though it persists partially in many ways for an indeterminate period and is never to be entirely relinquished. The child's readiness to follow the mother's needs, directions, and wishes, his responsiveness to and interest in the person who cares for him, support the hypothesis that, although the child's beginnings are utterly dominated by his hedonism, the value found in another per-son nevertheless appears quickly. This is not to say that its appearance is without conflict or that primary interests are not dominant, but rather that they can and do yield to in-terest in another person to a greater or lesser degree. Even the most emotionally disturbed children, those who are seemingly without any object relations, show that some form of this essential relationship is attempted and maintained even if in a remotely recognizable and pathological form [28]. Thus the infant's readiness to follow in the mother's tracks, thanks to the efforts and interest she expends upon him, shows his departure from his focus of attention exclusively on himself. The child's early search for the basis of a relationship marks the brevity of the primary state of narcissism and the onset of a transition that signifies ego development.

An infant is not to be contented by having only his physical needs met, however well they are ministered to. He requires a relationship which goes beyond such meager limits. In the case of autistic children, neglect in physical care is not found, whereas an emotionally empty relationship is a regular occurrence. It is characteristic of these children that they thrive physically but that they are serious and miserable failures emotionally and socially. If merely physical care is provided a child, the results are in the same coin; physical development takes place and in many instances is even precocious, but emotional development fails.

Recently a unique and excellent study has been made by Sally Provence and Rose Lipton [27] which compares the growth and development — physical and emotional — of infants raised in institutions with those raised in families.[1] Their study shows that normal infants and children "when deprived of varieties of experiences involved in good maternal care are not able to act except in an impaired and defective fashion." The study demonstrates that even an efficiently and competently operated modern institution will affect the development of normal infants and young children adversely. Children in institutions can only rarely be selected for regular special attention. Moreover,

[1] Direct studies of infants and their families are of recent origin. Psychoanalytic research of this kind has been in progress only since 1945. The scarcity of such studies is best accounted for by the great technical difficulties of conducting them and by the fact that few people are professionally qualified to do so. The careful work done by Provence and Lipton in 1962 is the exception.

they have few experiences in which an adult is directly responsive to the child's needs as they are expressed. Intimacy is lacking in an institution, where duties are of necessity divided among a group of people. By contrast, the variety of experience with a mother and household provides "an organizing and integrating force in the life of the infant that can not be overestimated" [27]. This is evident in the fact that the child without family care, living in an atmosphere that is quiet, bland, and tranquil, demonstrates unmistakable retardation in such essential functions as the development of speech, the maturation of sensorimotor activity, and perception. Even though the child is maturationally ready, without the influence of an intimate experience he shows failures. In both instances, family and institutional children have adapted well but the latter show (generally) consistent failures in development.

The significance of Provence and Lipton's study for the psychology of failure is that it provides a unique body of rich, directly observed, carefully gathered data on the early life of the child. It illustrates the relationship between deprivation of an intimate experience with a mother and failure in intellectual and emotional development. Development, manifest in the acquisition of skills by the sensorimotor apparatus, learning, curiosity, the desire to solve problems and even to encounter them, draws its impetus from the experience of family life. Care in an institution, however expertly administered, lacking the experience of family life, has a retarding effect upon the young child.

The study also shows that a stable, regular, and relatively unchanging environment, usually touted as desirable, is actually stultifying. The dullness of institutional existence, with its routines, its discipline, and its orderliness, borders on monotony. Even in good institutions, those that are well conducted and regulated, existence cannot be other than tedious and boring. Ironically, the good care which such an institution gives its child patients is reflected in the regularity of the appearance of intellectual and emotional failures among such children. By contrast, the child who is reared in a family is immediately and intimately exposed from the outset to a wide variety of experiences: the moods and temperaments of the household capture the child's attention and require his adaptation. The mother acts as a mediating influence as she chiefly conveys and interprets the members of the family and herself to the child. The resulting versatility of the family child is conspicuous when compared with the impoverishment of the institutional child. It would be false to suppose that all family life or all families promote success and that institutions only foster failures. This is obviously not the case. Families produce their fair share of failures, but in all likelihood not for the same reasons that institutions do. Perhaps no more significant conclusion can be drawn from the Provence and Lipton study than that ego development is critically dependent upon an association or intimate relationship with another person. When that fails, the child fails.

It is an important advance in development for the child to depart from his own primary egocentricity, to relinquish it significantly, and later even to wish to do so. The departure from infantile egocentricity, which is necessary for psychological maturation, is centered on the transition from dominance of the pleasure principle to increasing ascendancy of the reality principle, which defers satisfaction until a later time. As we have learned, compensations for the deferment are amply provided. The incentive to exploit or to neglect changes that may come with growth and maturation, however, does not depend solely upon the inherent qualities of the child; it also depends upon the quality of his relationship with another person.

A child left to his own devices has little impetus to put to use the changes that development brings. The critical factor in failure of the average young child is to be found in his relations with those who take care of him, with his family and particularly with his mother. It is her narcissistic needs expressed in her expectations for herself (which Provence and Lipton refer to as an integrating and organizing force) that give incentive to her child. When these maternal needs are excessive they are expressed in driving ambition which finds realization in her child as an extension of herself. The demands of her ambition are often detrimental to the child, for he is unable to fulfill them, feels helpless in the face of them, and frequently fails.

It is the mother's ego which serves the child before his own ego is sufficiently developed to assert itself. It is the mother's ego which supports his growth, helps to organize his environment, and thereby helps him in his adaptation. For example, a child may have matured to the point of being able to speak, but if this readiness is given insufficient direction, speech is delayed. Speech may remain retarded and thus becomes deprived of its value as a social function. Its cathexis is impaired, and when it develops later it is often a focus of conflict for the child. It is not uncommon to observe a mother who, from a variety of personal motives, speaks little, holds her own counsel, is shy and inhibited. She rationalizes her limited conversation with her young baby: "He is too young to speak"; "Why not wait until he is older? At present he would not understand what I'd say to him." Such a child's development of speech is often retarded, and when he does speak, infantile speech is characteristic.

Another example is a young mother who shops for a toy for her child. She wanders from counter to counter carrying her child, who, if she let him, would stroll with her. She decides against one toy after another. She remarks to herself that all the toys seem to be "too old for him." She finally settles for the purchase of what is virtually a rattle. Her complaint later is that the child seems to be immature. However, she herself is immature, regarding herself as a little girl and her child as a doll.

The children in these two examples have in fact complied very well with the mothers' unconscious dicates. The sensorimotor apparatus, like the development of speech, has remained infantile. The enormous libidinal investment of which the child is capable has not been made. Instead, the more infantile forms of gratification have been reinforced. The result is that they are relinquished with greater difficulty later; they are more readily a recourse during the frustrations which inevitably take place in later development. The readiness for regression to them is insured. These two illustrations of failure in development and achievement serve to demonstrate how little the child will promote himself independently out of his infantilism. He finds gratification there, and holds to it when the outer incentive to go beyond it is not provided him.

The child's progress during the early years of life is usually very rapid. Learning, achievement, and adaptation characteristically proceed relatively quickly, and gratification for these steps toward self-sufficiency is the reward for their being realized. But the child does not accomplish these great ends through sublimation, which comes later as a psychological process. These attributes are acquired and their mastery enjoyed during a period in life when the child is dependent, in many respects helpless, and when his egocentricity is best understood as narcissism. His narcissistic needs are very great. Such needs are also present in his parents, who act according to them where he is concerned. It is through parental narcissism that the child quickly comprehends that his accomplishments are highly valued and that his failures leave much to be desired. Thus the child's narcissism and his parents' act in concert to create a force to which the child cannot help responding.

The importance of the early mutual narcissistic relationship between the child and his parents is not generally understood as an immensely dynamic process, nor as one that plays a very significant role in the psychology of failure. The taproots of failure lie in narcissism. The child needs to gain mastery in more than a rudimentary way to serve both the pleasure principle and its modification by the reality principle. He needs to overcome his sense of helplessness, the sense of his limitations, and the oppressiveness of unfulfilled wishes. He is also driven by his parents' narcissism and his own to realize the values of growth and development, thus fulfilling their wishes and his own.

There is an ordered procession of failures and successes which typify the child's life. The attainment of each level of achievement in growth and development presages new efforts to fulfill the promises implicit in the preceding phase. It would be difficult to establish whether successes or failures exert a greater impetus to fulfillment. Is the mastery of a motor skill, such as walking, an incentive to become more agile and physically adept, or does the inducement to walk lie in the failure of the next effort beyond walking? Is the satisfaction of a previous achievement or the frustration of an unfulfilled effort the basis for making new trials? It is not avoiding the question to note that both aspects are present and inseparable in the impetus to fulfillment. Both are dynamic processes throughout the young child's life. We have seen in the previous chapter that whatever evokes the awareness of limitations creates a condition that is not acceptable and needs to be remedied. Thus the common experience of failure in realizing an enterprise, or even a wish, will produce a reaction to offset it, which may be a fantasy or an act or both. Thus in most important areas of his life the child succeeds in overcoming his inevitable failures. From these experiences the child may see that failure is not irrevocable. In this and other beliefs that the child evolves, nothing is irrevocable, neither failure nor the end of life itself.

There is little to blight the child's early life that is not associated with his relations to the people personally important to him. Nor can their importance be overstated.

For example, when the child becomes aware that the outcome of his oedipal wishes is doomed, he is confronted with a failure of a magnitude that he had not previously encountered. By any standard, previous failures are trivial and are dwarfed by the narcissistic injury that the oedipal failure creates. The oedipus complex is thus in the center of the psychology of failure. The loss complex is also relevant.

The fantastic expectations of oedipal fulfillment are brought to an end by the emergence of fears of castration. The result is to provide the child with a prototype for failure. The former experiences of failure are but little skirmishes in narcissistic humilation compared with this defeat. It should be borne in mind that the child has had not only his libidinal wishes dashed but concomitantly his intellectual curiosity about the intimate relations of his parents which had heretofore been energetically pursued. He sees that all his high expectations come to nothing and the enterprise has to be abandoned as insoluble [16]. Freud wrote that failure has a crippling effect on the child's whole future. Whether or not "crippling" is an accurate term, there is no doubt that the effect is profound. What is relevant is the recovery the child can and does make from the failure. The varieties and forms recovery may take will vary, not only individually, but also in accordance with the social customs and mores in which the child is brought up. It is not necessary here to discuss the varieties of recovery, since a voluminous clinical literature, beginning with Freud, has provided ample material. For the purposes of our subject, the psychology of failure, the deep narcissistic injury that ensues from failure is most pertinent.

The lasting effects of the failure of the oedipus complex are to be found readily in narcissistic humiliation, which occurs in the child as well as in the man who has not recovered from this blow to his self-esteem. In the expression of narcissistic humiliation, psychological conflicts from the psychoanalyses of children and adults are indistinguishable, particularly when each fears as a result of his fantasies that he lacks strength for some task that may in reality easily be accomplished, believes himself to be puny and inferior — and then worthless.

Some people fail to distinguish prowess from achievement. For example, one patient feared that in a new social encounter he would be put aside and that he would be left to watch, with envy, others who would be preferred. These fantasied fears result in fantasies of being neglected. He feels that he is not wanted and that everything will be taken away. These feelings are relieved by eating; all is not gone then. He becomes angry. He feels that what he wants is what he needs. What he receives seems not to be what he wants. The feeling that he does not get what he wants is to him proof that he is no good. (There is nothing in reality that he specifically wants or needs; he is not aware that it is esteem that he lacks and that he wants from others; he hopes to get it in some material sign rather than from the trivial things that he thinks he wishes.) Fantasies or cruelty and aggressive behavior toward others follow his fears and disappointment.

Another reports that he wishes to do nothing. He will only pretend he wishes to do what is required of him. He also wants to do what he should not do and quickly transposes it to the idea that he cannot do what is expected of him, when in reality he means that he would expect it of himself but dares not. Furthermore, because he is angry his wishes, he fears, would probably be bad ones. When he has sadistic impulses that may lead to destructive and aggressive acts, they confirm his fears and lead to his commonest defense, which is to claim that he does nothing. This is followed in turn by the claim that he wants to do nothing. Outwardly, he is idle much of the time and wanders about wondering what to do or waiting to be told what to do. He then resents what he is advised to do because it is not, he feels, what he would really like to be doing. Asked what it is he would like to do, he often answers that he wants to do nothing.

A third type shows the humiliation of narcissistic-oedipal failure, and the ambivalent wishes are expressed in complaints against a father who is a disappointing parent, that is, he is not wholly gratifying. "Maybe he will be sorry for me. He will see how I try but I am afraid I will fail. I could run away and then he would come and get me. If I don't try he will not want me. But if I work hard, I'll be safe. I don't want to be thrown out. I pretend I can take care of myself and that I'm not afraid. If you can't do things, you won't be liked." As a test and show of competence, "If I have to go somewhere, I have to know just where every turn in the road is or I'm afraid that I won't get where I'm supposed to be. I may forget; I have to be very careful to be safe because I don't want to do what is wrong. I make my father tell me what to do, then I can be sure he will take care of me. If I get angry with him he might want to get rid of me by leaving me some place. I feel weak and I get very angry when my father does not always come and help me. When he will not do it I feel I have failed."

A fourth example shows uncompromising oedipal wishes and conflicts that are associated with an abhorrence of the narcissistic humiliation that follows them. "It is repulsive to think that I can't have what my father has with my mother. In a way I only pretend that I am a son. I really want what he has. I see the position he has with my mother. I think, will I get it or not? I am not willing to consider anything else or any other solution. I won't look my father in the eye, he might see my intentions, so I stare at the floor when I am with him. If I gave it all up, with it would be [given up] the justification for being angry, and or even to feel violent. I can't get what I want as a son. If I gave up what I want then I would have to be quiet, defeated, with no complaints. But I am not willing to settle for that. It is worth the suffering and the tortures or the heavy penalties for wanting to be my father, or in his place and to have that ambition. I should suffer for it because to give up those wishes would be worse. Then I would be a weakling. Just to be a good boy is nothing, only nothing.''

The first example is from the analysis of a boy four and a half years old. The second patient is a lawyer, the father of three children. The third is a young mother of two children. The fourth is an early-middle-aged man who has had a very successful career as an executive of a large corporation. These excerpts from the actual mental content during psychoanalytic hours show that the material cannot be easily distinguished as belonging to a child or to an adult. The child's productions are not discernible from the adult ones, except perhaps in the choice of words and in facility of expression. The similarity of the conflicts is remarkable. Of particular importance is evidence that the fears, freely expressed and associated with failure, are based upon oedipal wishes that have foundered on the narcissistic injury that came with the realization that this heavily invested enterprise is a failure. Nevertheless, the insistent wishes have not been relinquished. With the exception of the child, each of these individuals has achieved real distinction and success while the experiences of a major failure have remained to exert an unmistakable influence on relationships. Like losses and other great events in life, failures are not carried forward from one period or phase to another simply as recollections of events; rather, they become expressions of conflicts which, set into motion, affect the formation of character, give rise to neurotic reactions and defenses, and govern behavior as long as they continue to have a persistent influence.

As in earlier and equally critical phases of development, one principle sets a course and another operates to achieve a balance. Some homeostatic level is sought even though, paradoxically, it is never really achieved in a dynamic system. As we have learned, limitations and failures in the early course of life may goad mastery. Under favorable conditions, successful relationships with those who take care of the child lead to the development of intense wishes that are doomed to fail. This failure inevitably brings about an unparalleled narcissistic injury. As a result, the balance must again be righted. The injured vanity compels that its injury be mitigated. A new developmental phase is ushered in to settle accounts. The latency period begins. The primary figures in the child's life commence to be relinquished and their place to be taken by substitutions; toward the same ends ego functions are further elaborated as the need for narcissistic healing is required.

It is among the tasks of ego functions in latency to begin their relief work in repairing the injury of the previous oedipal phase. The child shifts the focus of his interest from the primary objects of affection, his parents, to substitutes, i.e. to other adults such as teachers. The child takes a great step from being highly self-centered to having a genuine interest in others, especially contemporaries, in the form of friendships. These alterations represent not an increase in aggression but rather an intensive process of adaptation to reality and mastery of the environment made possible by the (further) development of the ego [7]. What Helen Deutsch wrote on the subject of girls in this period applies equally to boys: "The characteristically intensified activity of latency expresses the mobilization of the child's intellect, talents, aspirations and new identification" [7]. All of the child's ego functions press primarily toward some achievement to recover from the formidable unconscious aspects of failure in the previous oedipal phase and to restore self-esteem.

Development is always a crucial process, marking a turning point: that is, the resolution of one phase and the dilemmas of a new one. Latency owes its important place in developmental psychology largely to the fact that it represents the beginning of the child's emergence from the oedipal period. But failure in latency is also common. The high incidence of learning problems, regardless of what the child's emotional difficulties may be, is an important manifestation of failure. In recent decades failures in school have been the source of great concern everywhere, and considerable study and research has been devoted to them. Unfortunately, however, they have tended to be treated as a cause rather than as a symptom. The groupings and classification of learning problems and the study of them, even when they are regarded as having their foundation in oedipal and preoedipal conflicts, is reminiscent of the classification of fevers in the last century. The etiology of fevers was not understood as a reaction to an underlying disorder. Until learning problems are regarded as failures of ego function to restore a lowered self-esteem, they will remain confounding and obscure.

More attention must also be given to the fact that the school-age child has begun to make a transition from the family to the community, although his ties to the former are intense and his relations with the latter are tenuous. In this period, when his oedipal relations are still vigorous and the humiliation of their failure is still active, the ensuing narcissistic injury is correspondingly severe and continuing.

The ego functions on which the child should be able to rely in latency are often insufficient for the tasks that lie ahead. The usual burst of activity which is typical of latency, activity which organizes progressive adaptation to reality and mastery of the environment, is replaced by aggression. This is a common phenomenon. It is too often mistaken for the activity of adaptation, which, unhappily, it is not. It is actually a mobilization of the regressive phenomena of an earlier period. It often invokes passivity as a reaction; in any case ego development suffers. The child does not adapt himself but becomes instead intensely competitive, driven by narcissistic wishes which incorporate the aspirations, talents, and mastery characteristic of the previous period and now carried into latency. Even those children who succeed scholastically under such conditions are subject to constant self-harassment. The spector of failure haunts them no less than it does those children who actually fail. In both instances ego functions are disorganized: ability to adapt is limited, as is the ability to form new identifications, to accept substitutes for the parents with fewer conflicts than existed previously, and jealousy of peers shows no significant alteration from that which existed previously with siblings. The unresolved family conflicts are displaced to the community. From previous bitter experience the child acting on the basis of unconscious conflicts, chiefly involving narcissism, and finding himself in social difficulties, unconsciously responds to them in essentially the same way that he did before he left the family. As ego functions fail to develop, adaptation founders. The child has only his previous and now present devices to resort to; thus aggression is mobilized; the sense of limitations and narcissistic injury are played out in grandiose wishes. They are certain not to be fulfilled; intellectual achievement is inhibited and the old identifications are hardened. Sublimations, not easily acquired in any event, must fail.

We are concerned here with the failure that occurs in the time between the oedipal period and puberty. There is no need, therefore, to review any aspects of latency except those that apply to the failures common in and characteristic of this period. As the child attends school, going for the first time beyond the boundaries of home and outside the family, the failures that appear are the inability to form relationships on any other basis that the basis of his relationships with his siblings and his parents. Nor can the problems of aggression and sadism or passivity and masochism which existed previously within the family be easily turned to the activity of mastering a new environment. The

child's intellectual growth and development, his adaptation
to a new reality, his difficulty in repressing his deeper,
libidinal wishes that relate to his family, are modified very
little. His aspirations and his ideals, which are so closely
bound with his images of his parents, have evolved so
slowly that the distinction between them and others is
barely perceived, if at all. School, the outside environment,
and reality demand that accommodations take place, however. When they do not take place, the first manifestations
of social disorders appear. Prior to latency, the child's conflicts were played out within the home and with the members of the family. Now they are carried on outside. In view
of the impaired self-esteem that comes with the passing of
the oedipus complex and its attendant castration fears, it is
not remarkable that children should turn, in this phase, toward physical activities in the effort to convert fantasies of
prowess into some real success.

A seven-year-old boy, for example, has daydreams of
winning, conquering, proving that he is unbeatable. He has
fantasies of heroics, but they are not as before. When he
was only a few years younger, he wanted to have good win
over bad or to prove he was stronger; now he wants to be a
champion; he wants to win games; he takes great pleasure
in the development of his body and skills. He wants his
masculinity to show what he is. But these beliefs are not
unchallenged. He has many doubts and his self-esteem is
often in a precarious balance since his forming ego ideal is
often very difficult to satisfy.

These efforts represent the externalization of the previous narcissistic injury which, by the mobilization of the
need for ego healing through ego development, brings about
special emphasis on physical achievement, typical of this
period.

A heightening of narcissism as a reaction to narcissistic
injury and consequent lowered self-esteem is characteristic
in this phase as it was earlier and as it will be subsequently.

Heightened narcissism finds expression by making use of the new capacities of the ego. They have come about with the growth of intellectual development or functions and judgment, a further ability to postpone gratification, and the direct discharge of impulses through the adaptation to reality. The reduced intensity of direct sexual gratification is due in part to the repression that followed the lack of success of the oedipal enterprise. The active use of sublimation is thus initiated.

In short, failure during latency falls on the ego and its defenses. Earlier failures affect executant functions of the ego. Failure which takes place in latency manifest itself in defective sublimation. When failure takes place in the oedipal phase, mastery, elementary skills, and a relationship with primary figures (the parents) that served the ends of narcissism reveal the impairment. The aims of what then appeared as promising oedipal wishes, before they were recognized as coming to nothing, suffer inhibition.

Regression is the *sine qua non* of failure in the new phase. It is characterized in both fantasy and overt behavior as aggressiveness, and particularly sadism, or obversely as passivity and masochism (masking sadism). Pregenital behavior or an eruption of phallic behavior with clear autoerotic aims is commonly observed.

Which aspect of psychosexual development will come to the fore or predominate will be determined by a variety of factors. Among them, and of leading importance, will be the nature of the earlier fixations. Inhibitions in learning and social development may be manifested as acute phobias; they also may be expressed through unconscious denial, and become turned into bravado and fearlessness. The formation of clearly definable neuroses other than the occasional obsessional ones is not usually to be found, since the ego and its defenses have not, as yet, been sufficiently elaborated.

Much about the nature of latency is therefore to be

learned from the failures which occur in this period of life. From the signs that appear showing the properties of failure, it is evident that latency does not simply come about as an inevitable progression of development. It appears to be compelled by the stage which preceded it. The failure of the oedipal relation with its loss of self-esteem and injury to the child's narcissism is at the core of the forces which promote the child into latency.

The seduced child whose latency is delayed shows prolonged and far-reaching effects of his experience. The mother who binds her child, especially her son, more securely to herself, as she senses that the oedipal relationship requires termination, unconsciously loathes to relinquish him. The narcissistic ambitious mother will naturally be found in this category. She, especially, turns from her husband to her son. The child cannot avoid interpreting that the alliance she makes with him at this time is an action by his mother that shows her preference for him. This is a correct judgment on his part, though not for the reasons that he may suppose.

When a mother regularly supports her young son in wishes that defy his father, the boy's conclusion is that she wants a pact with him. How the mother conveys her intent to support her son against her husband may widely vary. The route may be through the growing boy's intellectual curiosity, or his early athletic or physical aspirations, or prowess of any sort. The choice is wide.

The mother may convey her purpose by way of food. For example, in a poor Jewish family, a father's orthodoxy was limited to observing his religious dietary laws. He insisted that they be obeyed in his house. The mother, whose scruples were not as strict as her husband's, surreptitiously often provided forbidden food, on poor pretexts, which she encouraged their son to join her in eating. The mother and the boy were in this way in a plot against the father. The son believed his father was too weak to break it. The result was predictable in two principal effects: first, an intensified and prolonged oedipal conflict was insured; second, the boy's latency development was correspondingly affected.

A persistent and distressing reaction that lasted for years was that the boy vomited almost daily after breakfast, on his way to school. He held a lasting conviction that he was unscrupulous and false. He was actually meticulously honest. He could not seem to rid himself of the unfounded feeling that he had deceived others, when in fact he had not. Toward older men whom he knew well and whom he liked, he felt that "he was not a true son." There were many self-destructive fantasies that were associated with depressed moods. There is no doubt that the compact with his mother led to these reactions.

A partial indentification with his mother, that is, based on fantasies of her passivity, was inevitably strengthened. Passivity, a deep source of conflict, became one of his characteristics. The two qualities found expression in marked obesity and in a tendency to provoke his father into attacking him. Incestuous fantasies continued unabated. They were displaced to his next youngest sister. On the one hand the boy wished to be rid of his mother's excessive attention, yet on the other he enjoyed her favors. His castration fears were naturally intensified and persistent.

This mother took satisfaction in the belief that she was primarily serving her son. She is correct and truthful. She lacks, however, a real understanding of her motives. Her conscious wishes were to indulge her son and to deny him as little as possible. The mother rationalized that he was not to be deprived. It is a common atttude for such women to take. They readily justify it by pointing to the reality of their limited means. For this mother to have realized that the basis of her feeling impoverished might have been within herself, rather than in a lack of material goods, would have required introspection which would be alien to her and which she would resist. She cannot recognize that her unconscious

resentment at being a woman leads her to an insatiable narcissism that she acts out with her son to gain her own satisfaction. She attacks the boy's father. It is as though her
husband were receiving well-deserved punishment for his
failure to gratify her deep-seated narcissistic wishes. It is
the reason for her behavior toward him, but it is not based
on her insight.

She belongs to the group of envious women who are only
vaguely aware of their envy of men. Their narcissism is
intense. They find little gratification in themselves — neither
in their bodies nor in their accomplishments. Their grievances pour out as scorn and scoldings on their passive men.
Typically, this woman demands from her husband satisfaction that he cannot furnish her, and abuses him for the
deprivation that she experiences. Holding him responsible
for her condition, she personifies him as demeaned, inadequate, and hence lacking in masculinity. This view of her
husband is, however, indistinguishable from the one she
holds of herself. She would vehemently deny that she sees
herself as devalued, and would insist that she is discontent
because of her marital circumstances. It is true that she is
an ignorant woman; nevertheless her denial rather than her
lack of insight explains her attitude.

As occasionally happens, the husband became financially
successful. The wife has indulged herself in their affluence,
but she remains disgruntled. Without the earlier basis for
her rationalizations, she searches in vain for explanations
of her continued misery. The ones that she finds are not as
good as those she had when she was poor. She is no less
narcissistic, demanding, or abusive of her husband. Her
guilt over her aggressive impulses, in the absence of the
rationalizations she previously relied upon, results often in
depressive symptoms. They are frequently of a hypochondriacal nature. Her unconscious wishes have not altered.
She feels there is salvation; it exists in relation to her son.
He is the key to her narcissism.

The problem is not characteristic of a certain segment of Jewish lower-class life. The same aims may be carried out by an upper-class Protestant mother with her son. For example, a mother was alarmed at her discovery that her son enjoyed sadistic acts. The boy indulged in cruelties to animals. He tortured them and finally, after he had satisfied himself, he killed them.

The mother had provided her son with endless ingenious and often original entertainment. It was, she believed, her obligation to make up for her husband's neglect of their son. She tried to interest the father in the boy by exaggerating to him his son's virtues. It was her vain hope that in this way the father would give up being aloof and cold and that he would treat the boy with less formality. She did not succeed. The mother felt fully justified in her conviction that she must rescue the boy from the father. It gave her the reason she needed to bring the boy closer to herself. The mother too suffered from the father's coldness. She regarded his temperament as indifference to her rather than as a limitation in her husband. The aggressive demands that she made for her husband's attention increased his inhibitions and passivity, which he expressed in aloofness.

The mother believed that she must let nothing interfere with constantly offering her son new pleasures as a means of offsetting the deprivation she was certain the boy suffered. She was not aware how much the feelings of deprivation applied to herself. She did not relate finding pleasure for her son to her own deprived feelings and the vicarious gratification she had from her relationship with him. She took great pride in the boy's precocity. For years, she read and studied his books along with him, ostensibly to be more understanding. But it was a living out of his life; she identified herself with him and the boy with herself. In her view, the boundaries between them were blurred. Her son seemed at times uncertain whether he was more boy or girl. He also felt that regardless of what he did, he could be certain his mother would protect him against "any terrible thing I might want to do." He might want to do something to his father, he thought, but his mother "was there to save me from doing anything against my father. My mother's first thought is always for me. She looks after me first. If my father ever came into the room when I called for help, I would know she was dead and he had come to hurt me. . . .

"Mother's first thought is for my safety. I remember a conversation about me being sick. I overheard her say she should come in and see if I was sick. My father thought I was big enough to say when I was sick. My mother would not give in to this, she would make life miserable for him until he agreed. She would like resistance from him because then she could throw a fit and make him give in. If he said 'the boy is my son, too,' she would give him a real battle. She would lay down her life for me. . . .

"It bothered me to feel she was so attached. I like it. But it puts my father in second place. I feel I wish I knew he was always first. I'd like to know that he was first and I was not. If he is first, who will look after me? We both need her. She might have to choose. I want her to pick me. If I truly want to be first then she will have to stand between us and he will resent me. He will want to do away with me.

"If I am dying, she would come to me no matter what my father thinks. How could I keep him from carrying out what he might want to do to me? He would be right to want to do it. If I could get on my knees and beg my mother not to put me first, it might be better. It is bad to have my safety in her hands. I guess a better solution would be if I gave up my ambition to be first. Then I could throw myself on my father's side. I would turn away from my mother. But my father would not care."

There were many signs that showed the boy how weak his father was and the powers his mother had. He resembled his mother and he knew how weak he felt, how frightened and often in panic he was. His similarities to her in many

ways troubled him. It made them seem more intimate. He
felt he needed to be free of her. The identification with her
as a woman was frightening. To be cruel to her, he hoped,
might put down his fears. It gave him satisfaction like that
of torturing the animals. This behavior did not succeed.
The boy may have been dimly aware that his mother was an
unusual masochist. The degree and extent of abuse and
torture that she could take from her son seemed without
limit. Its effect on him was to increase his guilt and to reinforce his sadism. His mother, therefore, was an unwitting
but willing partner to his sadistic behavior. Both parents
were passive objects of sadistic abuse. The boy was often,
however, a passive subject of torture in his fantasies. The
main feature of the "family romance" was a sadomasochistic drama.

Another example offered a different setting and action
yet the significant psychological problem is the same as in
the preceding illustrations. The son of a distinguished,
famous father and devoted mother was in despair over the
difficulties he was having with his schoolwork. Moreover, he
evaded responsibility and wished to avoid engaging himself
in any enterprise. He felt guilty, anxious, and was fearful
of what would happen to him in the future.

His mother regarded her son's activities with an eye to
finding in them characteristics that were similar to her husband's interests. She extolled the boy openly, much to his
embarrassment. He privately enjoyed his mother's praises;
she savored remarks from teachers, friends, and virtually
anyone who commented to her on her son's average achievements, which she used to support her wishes that the boy
was showing signs he was extraordinary. The boy was
divided between fears that he would distinguish himself and
that he would do nothing. His fears often became acute in
the midst of some work. He usually anticipated the outcome
of his efforts. He feared that the results would be poor.
Impelled by these fantasies, he would abandon an enter-

prise and then be left with self-devaluing feelings. His mother's reaction, though she did not know her son's mind, was to try to find a substitute satisfaction for him or to deny the importance of what he had given up.

The father was an indulgent man who was inclined to convey to his son that he expected little of him. He encouraged no initiative; the boy's reaction was not to take any. He thought of his son as young, and therefore there was no urgency to accomplish things. They had better be left to the father. Superficially, the parents gave the impression of being exceedingly permissive. Actually, the boy saw his lot as one in which he was always in a period of development that seemed never to mature.

The father treated the mother in much the same fashion that he dealt with his son. He expected little from women; the weakness and inadequacy which he assumed were common to them all made them fit for household chores and little else. The mother, before her marriage, had a very successful professional career. She had long since given it up. She thought of herself as having once been a clever woman who had somehow become stupid.

The son had a frequent fantasy which was of "getting something I want, but not having to do anything to get it." The way that forbidden wishes would be realized was by doing nothing to bring them about. He spared himself all accusations in his imagined achievements by the reassuring argument that he had done nothing. He was so afraid of what he might want to do that he countered it by making certain that he did nothing. Moreover, he issued a private proclamation to himself which disavowed all motives. It was, he said, "I have not taken over my father's place! I couldn't! I haven't! I am not interested! I never would do it! Besides, I can't! I haven't anything! I don't know how!" He behaved in a way that he said made him feel "like a girl, or foolish" and that they were "the same thing" to his father. He said of his father, "He looks at women like he does my mother, they can't do things on their own, they are no threat to anybody. I guess I am not either.''

The son's proclamation declares an intention to find a passive solution to the intensified oedipal conflicts. He was to gain his aims through a more complete identification with his mother. The result was a crippling inability to work, that is, inhibition to do his work. It brought him to being utterly dependent upon his father, who for obvious reasons approved his son's position of weakness. The father, in effect, approved and supported his son's passive feminine wishes. In a word, the boy was castrated.

The mother's narcissism, like that of the other two women cited, was founded upon a deep unresolved infantile envy of men. The result in each case was that the women felt themselves to be deprived and angry. In the last example, the woman was intelligent and capable, but she had come to think of herself as stupid and acted as if she were. From the time of her marriage, she probably began to feel old conflicts of deprivation and impoverishment, which were evident from her periodic depressions. Her narcissism, however, found no measure of gratification until she turned to her son. Though her alliance with him was to give her a degree of satisfaction she otherwise did not have, she succeeded in reinforcing his passivity.

In contrast to those women who find a solution to their narcissistic ambitions or strivings through their sons by supporting the boys in the formation of their ego ideals, the mothers here cited remain in an active erotic relationship to their sons. The instinctual wishes in the relationship are not renounced in favor of supporting an ego ideal. The women in the examples have in common, among other features, not only the penis envy all women experience, but also an intense variety of narcissism that prevents them from enjoying their femininity. Instead, it heightens their envy and hence their aggressiveness. Their hopes are to have their infantile wishes assuaged through their sons. Their efforts, instead of promoting the boy's ego ideal, which he requires to mature, press him into a seductive relationship with his mother which cannot benefit him and against which he must defend himself. The inevitable result is that the oedipal conflicts are furthered by the boy's unconscious incestuous wishes. There is actually not a delay in the boy's latency so much as a carrying of the oedipal conflicts into the early latency period. This is normally a time of strict superego formation. But when, as in these instances, erotic conflicts are heightened and the ego ideal is compromised by seduction by the mother, in which the son was an active partner, the decrees of the superego are most stringent; stricter repression is required. Increased aggression is common behavior at these times. Often denial as a defense is further developed; it is expressed as elation coupled to aggression and takes the form of increased activity.

The boy's reaction to women, drawn from his passivity in relation to his mother, is often expressed in being excessively aggressive toward them. The mother is not forgiven for her active sexual role. Her son is in a rage that he succumbed to his mother's sexual wishes or to her seductiveness. He denies his own incestuous intentions but at the same time acknowledges by wishing he had renounced them. He rightly blames his mother. She *is* really to blame; it is her function to help the boy realize his ego ideal instead of seducing him.

In accepted psychoanalytic theory, the latency period is considered to be ushered in with the resolution of the oedipus complex and the establishment of the superego. Most authors, in discussing the onset of latency, confine themselves either to the phenomena of the passing oedipus complex (with emphasis on castration fears as marking its final phases) or to the developmental onset of a conscience which dictates with increasing severity the most rudimentary standards of conduct. A central issue, the fate of the child's narcissism, already deeply affected by the oedipal failure, although occasionally referred to by inference and implication, has not received a fraction of the attention it deserves under these altering conditions. The child's severely wounded self-esteem, resulting from doomed oedipal wishes, has been referred to by Freud as an outcome which is inevitable. Nevertheless, the critical role of impaired narcissism, which demands the recovery of self-esteem, in ushering in latency and starting a new level of development has inexplicably remained obscure. The vicissitudes of narcissism and self-esteem appear to be a unifying thread which is woven throughout the entire fabric of human development. As a consequence the fate of narcissism in all stages of development has a determinative influence and bearing on the outcome and dynamics of any one of them.

The immense literature on adolescence is a good index of the attention that this period of life has always received. Plato's complaints and observations about the fecklessness and misbehavior of the young are famous for their durability. No better description of the adolescent exists than in Aristotle's *Rhetoric* [2]. Nearly two millennia later, when Italian schools in and about Bologna, Padua, Florence, and Venice provided an equivalent of our boarding schools for young people, concern was often expressed because they presented serious problems and because these young people were frequently failures [33]. One critic among many was Dittorino, a famous teacher, who found it difficult and discouraging to govern his school at Padua. His students were earning no favor; they were too lost in dreaming and intemperate in their habits. The gymnasium was ill-ordered; its students took too much liberty and they failed in their studies. In desperation he moved to Venice in 1423 to become a private tutor and escape the lack of reward he found in Padua [33]. He found it, however, in Mantua where, in the school he established there, he reached his great fame. For over a quarter of a century, he educated many who became the great humanists of the Renaissance. The problems presented by adolescence have not changed with the times. The despairing outcries of the older generation seem to remain the same ones that have been recorded for tens of centuries.

That the relation of the adolescent to his society has never lacked special attention may be due in part to the fact that adolescence is the period in life when the individual is formally introduced into society. He is no longer a mere child of the family but has a place in the adult community. It is significant that the rites of passage in all cultures are so important that when they fall into disuse, as in our own culture, the youth fashion rites for themselves which they observe. This is exemplified in the group associations they form, the symbols of status they wear, and the modes of behavior they adopt, which are all intended to testify that they have begun a passage from family to community life. Until recently, the adolescent's inner turmoil and his corresponding external disorder were well understood as phenomena which normally took place as the individual attempted to relinquish his family bonds and sought new ties beyond it in society. Because the study of "culture" has received deeper scrutiny since 1945, it is inevitable that behavior during the adolescent years would be explained as the product of cultural influences.

Prior to World War II, the literature on the psychology of the adolescent tended to emphasize the role of the child's biological maturation in conjunction with his behavior. The problems were defined chiefly between these two factors. The influence of culture was a new factor. Although perhaps implicit in most of the presentations or discussions in the recent work on adolescents, the two earlier factors seem

to have been almost excluded. Our discussion is concerned
with the unconscious conflicts of the adolescent, subject to
the influence of society, behavior, and biology. All are fully
represented in the child's inner life. They are, however,
often obscure, even obtuse, and always variable factors.
Adolescence is, by definition, marked by the beginning of
adult physical maturation. This period is characterized by
behavior that is remarkably similar in adolescents widely
separated in culture, space, and time [22]. Aristotle's description of adolescence, St. Augustine's confessions of
delinquency, the distemper and failure of students at the
Renaissance school in Padua, and countless descriptions in
today's periodicals show that the problems of this period of
life have not fundamentally changed with the times any
more than adolescent behavior has basically altered with
cultural differences. Furthermore, the complaints of the
older generation remain the same.

The successes which youth enjoys are many; but, regrettably, so are the failures. It is important in discussing this
matter to confine our attention to those factors which are
essential to the psychology of failure in adolescence. Most
simply stated, the task for the youth of both sexes is to
develop physically and socially from childhood to adulthood. The gap to be bridged appears wider and more difficult than previous ones. The failures that occur at this
period are not as easily offset as earlier ones. They are also
often compounded by previous failures. We have learned
that the young child leaving for school goes forth with his
ties strongly fixed to home and tenuously attached to the
world outside of it. With the onset of puberty and the coming of youth, a further extension involving similar processes of the school child's previous conflict between family
and community takes place. Granting that in the meantime
ego development, meaning both its functions and its defenses, has been elaborated, the tasks in adolescence are
nevertheless correspondingly greater. The old bonds to

home are further strained and loosened, without the loose
ends becoming fixed. Less metaphorically, the wish and the
need of the child and of the adolescent is to give up the old
oedipal objects and to replace them with new ones that are
less in the image of the parents. The wish to do so mobilizes
and renews the conflicts of childhood, which are clearly revived in adolescence. The fact that the new substitutes have
not yet been firmly established raises anxiety about being
without the old, close relationships. The reaction to loss of
the parental objects is a sense of loneliness and abandonment. The loss complex, to which loneliness and abandonment are central, increases narcissism. Feelings of
loneliness and abandonment are common complaints of
adolescents, and narcissism is the dynamic process underlying them which, as we shall see, has a direct bearing upon
failure.

A previous transition, from the oedipal period to latency,
was characterized by activity. Direct observation of young
children indicates that throughout the early phases of
psychological development a "thrust of activity" always
typifies the process of transition from one phase of development to the next, just as it often does on a smaller scale
when lesser achievements of ego function or mastery and
the development of skills are in the making. Helene
Deutsch, in 1925, was the first to describe the thrust of activity as the principal characteristic of prepuberty and to
say that it "represents not an increase in aggression but
rather an intensive *process of adaptation to reality* and
mastery of the environment made possible by the development of the ego; "The intensified activity characteristic of
prepuberty serves to mobilize the child's intellectual and
artistic [creative] talents and his aspirations, affective
hopes, new identification tendencies, etc."; "Its source lies
in the inherent drive of the ego toward growth and independence. From earliest infancy there exists in all normal
individuals the urge to grow up and to achieve something.

This drive is particularly strong in prepuberty'' [7]. For reasons that are not apparent, the observations of Helene Deutsch which she first reported forty years ago [6] and further elaborated upon twenty years ago [7] have not been generally accorded their great importance in psychoanalytic studies of ego development, despite the wide recognition that her now classic work on the psychology of women has received.

In each of the significant transitions which occur in the course of psychosexual development the thrust of activity may be observed. Nevertheless, there is present in each transition a regular hazard: instead of a thrust of activity, aggression may occur. The distinction to be made between them is that a thrust of activity represents a development in the ego which utilizes the aggressive drives toward mastery and adaptation to reality, whereas the thrust of aggression indicates some fault in ego functions which do not turn aggression to such constructive purposes.

With aggression instead of activity direct instinctual gratification is sought; consequently, regressive aims are reinforced in place of being sublimated. When regressive aims are promoted an increase in narcissism is to be found at the center of adolescent conflicts. In the failures that occur during adolescence, we observe two constant elements: an intensification of aggression instead of activity, and increased narcissism. The fusion of these two regressive phenomena lies at the root of the psychology of failure in adolescence. Furthermore, both aggression and narcissism are naturally heightened with adolescent biological development. Ego functions laboring under extreme conditions are more subject to aggression, narcissism, and regression. They tend to falter and often fail.

Emotional development will not proceed in an orderly progression at any given phase. There are endless interruptions such as illness, injuries, separations, deaths of members of the family, expectations which end in disappoint-

ment. In other words, a constant procession of experiences
evokes normal neurotic reactions at the very least. There is
no point in adding a catalogue of all the events that could
occur and reactions that could take place to upset the adolescent. What is important is that any experiences that
heighten narcissism and aggression, whether derived from
reality or from inner life, will tax ego development, often to
such a degree that achievement is relinquished for regressive gratification. While this relationship between narcissism and aggression holds throughout life, and is therefore
relevant to any period of development, it is especially significant in the adolescent years.

Clinical experience bears out the belief that earlier aspects or disorders reappear in adult life. Adolescents differ
significantly from adults in that the defenses of the ego,
reaction formation, and a way of life have not yet been
established, whereas in adults these processes may function
supportively. In the course of development such assets are
not sufficiently secure to be relied on. Therefore, the failures which develop during adolescence are those in which
specific aspects of the youthful ego have been unable to find
adequate adaptations. The fate of the active sexual needs in
these years is also greatly influenced by these essentials of
character. The joint course of narcissism and aggression
has a direct bearing upon the active sexual life that is
typical of youthful development, and determines the quality
of object relations and the degree and nature of sublimation
in adult life.

Considerations of adolescence must include the process
of identification. Like other phenomena of character development, it is a long time in preparation. It goes through a
variety of earlier phases. And in each of them it serves the
ends of a solution. The identifications of the preoedipal
period, which are virtually imitations of parental figures,
are essential to achieving the mastery of functions. Later,
during the oedipal period and latency, identifications as an

essential solution are too obvious to require detailing here. In adolescence the previous functions of identification are carried further. They are pressed into the service of the new aims which are particular to this phase. As the old bonds with parental figures are lessened, the identification with them is also somewhat freed to permit relationships with others. The search to reestablish old identifications with new figures leads away from the realm of fantastic and mythical characters toward figures in reality. The figures in reality, however, are often invested with qualities carried over from the paper ones and heroes of latency. The models' existence in turn found their inspiration in the oedipal period.

From the type of identification that is made by the adolescent the nature of his narcissistic and aggressive conflicts may be discerned with certainty. No case histories are better or more illustrative than those which Helene Deutsch presents in her *Psychology of Women* [7]. One typical example is the case of "Dorothy," whose emotional life became empty. Her struggles to win some measure of independence from her parents, and particularly her mother, led her to asserting herself by defiant and marginal delinquent behavior. Her narcissism was inordinately heightened. "She tried to fill her life with something that would secure her superiority at home, to win the respect of her gang . . . she was absorbed in aggressive (acts and fantasies) tendencies in relation to her mother to which she gave free rein . . . asserting her toughness" [7]. The development of real object relations, the unification of affection and instinctual drives, is precluded when narcissism and aggression become aims in themselves. Deutsch provides many examples which illustrate this failure in the ego development of adolescent girls.

In many respects the problems to which adolescent boys succumb are not essentially very different from those of girls. Narcissism and aggression pose a problem for the

youth of both sexes. Passivity tends to be less of a dilemma
for a girl than for a boy, provided that it does not threaten
her with masochistic surrender and thus bring her under the
influence of infantile sadistic fantasies. Boys, on the other
hand, frequently founder on the fears of passivity which
have not lost their oedipal significance. In adolescence all
qualities and attributes need, in some measure at least, to be
tested in reality. Fantasy alone is an insufficient measure of
one's powers and affirmation of masculinity. Absorption in
self-examination is common.

An inventory taken under his own auspices often reveals
to the boy a discrepancy between his vaulting aspirations
and his achievements. As in latency, prowess rather than
success becomes an aim. The maturing adolescent biological
assets are put to use in asserting masculine goals. The disquieting wishes for passivity become alarming through fear
they may arrest masculine achievement. Sadism often becomes the common defense against passivity. Sadism may
also express itself as intense masochistic cruelty which
takes the self as an object of the heightened aggressive
wishes and impulses. A defense frequently resorted to by
such boys is to turn the sadism on others. The boy desperately needs to overcome his strong identification with a devalued woman, a mother who appears to have surrendered
passively to the father. This need is plainly seen in boys
asserting their brutal masculinity, in which aggression is
inevitably fused with narcissistic gratification. When narcissism takes this course, failure in object relations is assured. The fusion of narcissism and aggression can also
affect intellectual functions, with the result that learning
and work are drawn into the ensuing morass of longing and
expectation. Work and learning then become part of the
test of superiority and a measure of prowess. When narcissistic expectations are amalgamated with aggressive conflicts, intellectual activity and work must take a secondary
position.

The following is an example which parallels Deutsch's "Dorothy." An eighteen-year-old boy, Tom, came to Harvard from a small Midwestern town. He had been very successful scholastically at high school. He had few creative interests, that is, none that he pursued. Doing well at school, preparing for college, seemed the sole focus of his attention. Socially he was shy. He was merely an acquaintance to other boys. Although he wished that he had some intimacy with girls, he had none. He could not bring himself to be forward. After a party where he would at times encounter a girl more bold than he, there would be some limited sexual play. Afterward he would elaborate fantasies, while masturbating, of what someone else might have succeeded in carrying out with the girl. He envied such a boy and identified himself with him in his fantasies. In reality he shrank from acting on his extravagant wishes.

Tom came to college confident of his intellectual abilities but he was only hopeful that he would overcome his shyness. Being away from home for the first time gave him both a sense of relief and a sense of anxiety. The boys with whom he roomed seemed to him to enjoy a license that he did not possess. Tom became more absorbed in his studies. He tried to dismiss the behavior of the others with the rationalization that they were dangerously neglecting their work. It was true that they were. A new anxiety arose. He had previously not been aware of it. What if he did not do well in his studies? The humiliations which such fantasies produced were not only burdensome but they became a constant source of concern and preoccupation. He had not been noticeably compulsive before, but now his aims became rigidly fixed upon perfection. A growing anxiety developed over what would become of him if he were not to excel. Although he studied hard, it was now by rote, and for longer periods than he had previously needed to master a subject. Also, he found that his standing in the class was mediocre. The disappointment was great. He became depressed. The symptoms of depression were mild. He complained of being tired, listless, lonely, and said that no one cared about him and that he had a low opinion of himself. He felt that his intellectual abilities, upon which he previously prided himself, were inadequate. His inability to work became a serious matter; he was not turning in his assignments on time, whereas previously he had been meticulously prompt. He was threatened with failure. These were the immediate troubles that brought him to treatment.

From the time he was fourteen and had begun to show signs of physical maturation, his concern with shyness had increased. He confided it to his mother. She conveyed the substance of his complaints to the father. Tom could not bring himself to acknowledge his shortcomings to his father himself. On the basis of the messages the father received, he encouraged Tom to become more athletic. He offered himself repeatedly to Tom as a model of self-assertiveness, confidence, impeccable rectitude, and shrewdness, whom no one, except at his peril, would attempt to best. In addition, although he was then about fifty years old, his physical powers, he claimed, had in no way diminished from the time he was twenty. He was still an active gymnast and boxer. He enjoyed going to the YMCA and bragged about wins over men half his age. The boy, although big for his age and powerful, viewed himself as weak. He was often invited to contest his father, in relation to whom he was physically much bigger and probably stronger. He avoided all such encounters and devoted more time to his studies, arguing that he needed to insure that he would be accepted at college. There were other children in the family. Tom was the eldest by four years; next to him was a sister. He was often the baby-sitter when his parents were away. During those evenings he usually studied. The erotic fantasies that he had about his next oldest sister were quickly repressed with severe guilty feelings.

The incestuous wishes were unconscious. They mani-

fested themselves in a reaction of passivity, especially in
relation to his father. Tom's father thought of his son as a
very good boy, who was obedient and who took seriously
the teachings of the Bible. The father, a fundamentalist,
was pleased with Tom; it was the father's rationalization
probably for the satisfaction he took in his son's passive
submission.

Tom was eager to be off to college. He wanted, among
other wishes, to leave the alarming sexual fantasies involving his sister behind him. Perhaps most of all, he wanted to
escape what he believed to be his father's rigid prohibitions. The father's sanctimonious self-righteousness and
his persistent preaching of the Decalogue were oppressive.

Toward the end of his first semester, in which Tom
learned that he had not realized his freedom from his old
conflicts, he attempted to occupy himself even more with his
studies. He also hoped that in this way he could avoid the
regular confrontation with his roommates' behavior with
girls, which he regarded as promiscuity. Their license was
intruding and exciting his fantasies so much that he could
no longer study except in an increasingly compulsive and
ritualized fashion. His books and papers had to be arranged in a certain way and he needed to count over and
over again the pages that he had to study. Tom felt himself
to be deprived of pleasure. Now more than before he identified himself with his friends, the roommates, with whom he
was not really intimate but whose activities with girls he
envied. He began to appear to give up his shyness and persuaded the boys to procure girls for him. Seeming to disregard his father's strict injinctions of caution about girls and
drink, he could not bring himself to study and instead gave
himself over to fantasies all day and plans for what ad-
ventures he would have in the evening with girls and drinking. At night he spent long hours in adolescent ambivalent
acting out of sexual experiences that represented feats
rather than pleasure and in drinking that afterward usually

made him sick. Tom's guilt was oppressive and his studying became an increasingly mechanical operation.

There were deeper effects from the apparent changes that had occurred. Tom's physical needs seemed to call for a vigorous expression which he found first in judo lessons and then in karate. Intellectual pursuits were no longer satisfying. They had, in fact, become dull, boring, and compulsive exercises. They were replaced by attempts to prove himself through winning adulation for his prowess. He began to believe that he must protect himself against some assailant — no one that was identifiable and none who actually existed, an anonymous attacker. His rationalization was that the streets were dangerous. The newspapers were constantly reporting the evidence of lawlessness. The victims he was referring to were really women who had been strangled. At the time, Tom was not aware of the deeper significance of these events to himself. He more regularly attended his judo lessons than he did classes at college. In a short period he became very proficient. But he was still unsatisfied that he could protect himself. He shifted from being expert at judo, which he regarded as a defensive art, to karate. With this new course of action he became a potentially murderous adversary of whoever attacked him. The identification with the fantasied aggressor satisfied him in a way that judo did not. Incidentally, these exercises and newly acquired skills made Tom a very powerful youth in fact, although he tended to minimize this. The gratification his prowess afforded him superseded all other pleasures except for his increasing sadistic fantasies of attacking and mutilating girls.

The father disregarded the mother's complaints that their son was in difficulty and suffering. Neither one had any knowledge of Tom's shift in interests. They were only aware that the boy, a former excellent student, was now failing. The father insisted that the boy was lazy, probably self-indulgent, too much influenced by other boys, and above

all extravagant. The boy's allowance was actually a nig-
gardly one, owing to the father's penny-pinching and not to
real financial need. It was the father's principle that one
should not indulge oneself except in hard work and privation.

Further changes took place in Tom. He became secretely
resentful and openly stubborn, whereas before he had
been compliant. His fantasies, increasingly more conscious,
were of being superior to all. He began to play at being
grandiose. He so longed to excel that he could not write
course papers, and finally even some examinations, from
fear that he would reveal how little he knew. He could only
think of the immediate future and his need to find some
scintillating occupation that would assure him instant
success.

He considered "Being a diplomat on intimate terms with
all the great ones and settling the trouble spots of the
world. Perhaps I'll go to where new countries are emerging
where I'll be recognized as great. It would prove my power
and independence. I read the life of a president of a big
corporation. If only I could be in his place, but the work to
get it is too much. I want to be appointed. I don't want to
concentrate on anything except to be a world historical figure. I know this is peculiar to want to be like Hitler. I know
if I am lucky I'll just be mediocre. But the other side of me
says there is greatness and vast power for you and having
will and foresight you will be like Bismarck. The trouble
with all the people I choose to want to be is that they are all
unsavory types. When I was younger I used to wish I was
Superman and had bullet proof vests and have an island
empire. I put people in upper and lower grades. My ships
were unsinkable. I liberated countries and I was against
crime. Being little was frightening. My image of myself is
in constant danger even now. I can play great the first time
I go out with a girl. That is why I take them out only once
and then get another one. The figure I want to think of

myself is that I am great. The second time I might not be able to bring it off. Just like I don't like dark streets. I might get my invincibility smashed. The thought of losing is a peril. I won't play games for that reason. The idea of not being the 'most' is very frightening.'' The sadistic fantasies about girls were of subjecting them to extremely humiliating and cruel acts in which they were bound, whipped, and raped while they in turn were enthralled with his powers.

Tom's analytic treatment proceeded along a stormy, difficult course. The elements which contributed to his failure materially were not significantly determined by the appearance of new, traumatic, or even dramatic events. They were simply that Tom's increasing physical maturity called for corresponding adaptation to reality. The immediate difficulty which led him to founder was based upon what his situation required of him. What was called for was activity that would be carried forward to sublimation and a relationship with girls in which more than an exercise was expected. Tom brought a heightened narcissism and aggression to meet it. The fears of passivity had existed long before but were now met with extravagant sadistic self-assertion. Herculean powers in fantasy hid his fears of exposure as weak and worthless. Few sublimations had been achieved in latency. Superman was retained as a hero, as virtually a paper ideal. Little allowance was made for enrichment by achievements other than schoolwork. Later, judo and karate were limited solutions to problems requiring the fusion of affection and instinctual needs. Compulsive studying became a poor remedy for gratifying intellectual aspirations.

A stern father and a yielding mother like Tom's are more common than unusual. The parents' narcissism for a long time was realized in their son's scholastic achievements.

His oedipal conflicts were especially difficult to resolve as both parents, each with separate fears, unwittingly needed to bind the boy to themselves. They had little conception of what is meant by giving a child freedom. They confused it with license that both of them dreaded. Tom regarded his father primarily as a sadistic man. The father's demands that the boy comply with his wishes were not to be debated. He would allow no one in the family to challenge his will, that is, to be free of his control. He was a petty tyrant. Tom and the other members of the family submissively accepted their designated places. In Tom's view there was no alternative. Rebellion would be met with the strictest censure. Tom was too intimidated to risk the consequences he feared that openly defying his father would bring. Tom's split identification with the father, whom he saw as a brutal and punitive man, on the one hand, and with the mother, whom he saw as a weak, unassertive woman who had succumbed to her husband's will, on the other, reinforced Tom's passivity as he increasingly identified himself with her. She provided him with a model of passivity as a solution to his oedipal wishes. But it was an indentification he was obliged to reject consciously by way of his grandoise and sadistic fantasies. They were present during latency.

When Tom came into adolescence, he was called upon to act. His increased narcissism and aggression did not lead him into finding sublimations. There had been very few in preparation in earlier periods. Instead, the previous defenses of earlier phases were enlarged and extended, such as sadomasochistic fantasies, daydreams of invulnerability, and an increase in narcissism. His ambivalence about his wishes increased. The acts he carried out did not show a better adaptation to reality. His narcissistic expectations multiplied, and with them his fears of failure mounted. He began to fail scholastically as well as socially. The gratification Tom received from intellectual pursuits became minor in comparison with the demands of his instinctual and social needs. His response to the demands was in poorly adapted instinctual behavior.

Tom continued to fail until after a long period of treatment. When his agressive aims and narcissism gradually modified, his object relations improved. For the first time he fell in love with a girl whose importance became real. In relation to boys he remained aloof and somewhat wary. He began a professional career after graduation from college and after a time was reluctantly content to go on without spectacular success.

Acknowledging that adolescence displays all the diversities of behavior peculiar to both the child and the man, and that such behavior is characteristic of adolescence, we must inquire further and more deeply into the powerful forces that bring about the conglomeration of childhood and adult life into one period. Two factors in particular are significant. The first is the long phase of helplessness that is characteristic of human biological and psychological development. A necessary dependence upon another person has not only a profound but a continuing influence upon all phases of development throughout life. (See Chapters 4 and 5.) With growth and development and by a variety of activities that involve the acquisition of skills and mastery, helplessness is slowly forced to give way to independence. Concomitantly with these changes an alteration takes place in relation to the parental figures. The initial deep attachments to the family are loosened normally by the child's development to yield to the natural acceptance of substitutes. While much remains to bind the child to the family, his own needs for survival requires ego development. His maturing ego does a great deal to promote relinquishment of his dependence upon the members of his family so that his growing need of freedom from them may be realized. Both forces are working simultaneously. Which of them will be fostered depends upon the circumstances and upon the character of the parents. If independence or loosening of close ties are vigorously resisted by the family or if circumstances support clannishness, then the child's own experience will compromise the independence he might otherwise cultivate. The liberty to develop relationships with others is an acquired quality. If the growing tendency toward freedom is not supported, obvious limitations become imposed on the child's ego development. These may be observed in the nature and quality of object relations, which are apt to be egocentric and shallow.

Neither the child's helplessness nor his acquisition of skills, regardless of his level of development, fails to be meaningful to a parent and thus to also have a lasting effect on the child. For example, the mother of a three-year-old child encouraged physical prowess in him because of her wish to overcome her own anxiety about heights. She was eager that her child not suffer as she had. She also tended to doubt her own good intellectual capacities, and she was therefore equally ready to encourage the beginning intellectual interests in her child. The capable young child quickly showed mastery, and skills followed in a relatively easy sequence. Virtually every day was ended with a review for an admiring father of the accomplishments of the past twenty-four hours. Both parents wished to give the child a free rein to discover and perfect his talents. An unexpected result that puzzled them was that the child, by the age of four, tryannized both over them and over his playmates with his precocity and competitiveness. The child's virtues had become the basis for the parents' complaints.

Whatever achievement is fostered in the child during the early years of life will at the same time support the actively present narcissism and aggression that is typical of this period. Because these qualities become associated with the gratification that mastery provides, they cannot readily be dissociated from such gratification in later development. In the child described above, achievement and precocity were encouraged while social expectations were minimized, perhaps even rationalized away in favor of accomplishment. The child's intellectual talents were cultivated assiduously but his social relations were neglected. His abilities, although they were real and admired, became instruments of the child's tyranny which finally led to his difficulties at nursery school and at home. What occurred with this child is commonly observed in precocious children with ambitious or zealous parents. Such children, who show early a quick intelligence, a talent, or a skill, are exploited by parents who, in their narcissistic zeal, seize on what the child presents. They enjoy his demonstrable capacity, promote its development, and thus gratify both themselves and the child as well. The young child's achievement may appear to presage sublimation, and it could in reality be sublimation serving libidinal aims in a socially adaptive fashion if aggression were not intimately associated with it. Sublimation neglected, however, is what the tyranny expresses. Social reality and hence object relations are forgone. Instead of really serving the aims of a developing ego, social reality and object relations become secondary to the instinctual gratifications that are overriding, and thus narcissism and aggression are supported at the expense of object relations.

Those precocious children within whom gratification is strongly bound to narcissism and aggression become increasingly exhibitionistic during the latency period, often highly competitive, and frequently successful insofar as they tend to lead others. But in adolescence their failures become conspicuous. These children hold high hopes for themselves in the belief that a personal relationship may be acquired as their skills had been, or that being admired for their accomplishments is a substantial enough vehicle to carry a relationship. But since adolescence calls for a heightening of all relationships, these youths have only their skills to offer instead of themselves, which, in their narcissism, they cannot part with. They often wish desperately to discard their gifts in the vain effort to overcome their loneliness. It may be commonly observed in such youths that they deliberately try to conform in their dress when they were indifferent before, try for mediocre achievement in school whereas before they were avid students, try to become social in the hope that the pretense will not be discovered. Their honest statements are that they just want to be an average student at college or to be employed somewhere in an ordinary job. They have correctly recognized that their talents have not led them to making relationships with another person, but just the opposite. Thus the helplessness that characterizes the first period of life may be overcome in the second in a manner that brings on loneliness in the third.

The second factor that plays an important role in bringing about failure in adolescence is the long period of maturation, which, like the long period of dependence, has a unique effect upon psychological development. The child's active sexual life, we have long since learned, begins very early. It is both an extended and a protracted process. Actual genital maturation requires at least a decade and often extends into the second one before it is realized. Adolescence is the period of sexual life when the gap between childhood and adult sexuality begins to close. In a real sense adult biological maturation has finally joined with the child's sexual wishes, fantasies, dreams, and conflicts. It is in this adolescent period that the diversities of the child and the man meet. After the long night of sexual immaturity, the most significant sexual problems, the oedipus complex and the castration complex, have arisen. And to an important extent, their resolution has had to be found. Thus in both the conscious and the unconscious life of the child, biologically immature for most of the time, the entire spectrum of sexuality has been rehearsed and reviewed over and over again in wishes, dreams, fantasies, and play, beginning in the years before latency and extending into it.[2] Thus the

---

[2] It should be remembered that latency, far from being an inactive period as is generally supposed, is actually a recovery period. It is a time in which recovery from the oedipal and the castration complexes may be accomplished.

long maturational process of latency may be observed to be useful for two important purposes: to recover from the conflicts of the oedipal phase and to prepare for adolescence. In this respect only may this intervening phase of development be called latency. The extended maturational process of latency permits ample time to prepare for adolescence. The child in adolescence is called upon to carry out in fact what heretofore could be conducted only in fantasy and in play. In a real sense a confrontation takes place. Whatever a child may have wished sexually may now become a reality. Sexual wishes and conflicts are present with a biological reality to implement them that did not previously exist. It is at this point that the failures of adolescence often begin, as we shall see.

The adolescent confrontation of fantasy with fulfillment also marks the period when the child becomes a member of the community. We have pointed out above that regardless of culture, time, or place, family taboos are replaced by social laws.

Many writers would have us believe that because we belong to a new era in which social, economic, and technical revolutions are taking place, and our adolescents are correspondingly confronted with new problems, requiring new solutions, their present behavior reflects these current social transformations. Some, like Eisenstadt and Riesman, argue that youth is so deeply affected as to have become shallow-minded and even empty. They have developed what Riesman calls a "cult of immediacy" [11]. Emphasis is placed on the fact that our youth in universities long for some isolation from adults and demand autonomy for self-realization [25]. Bettleheim expresses his concern that the middle-class society has become "tamer" and that youth is afraid to come into its own [25]. But a splendid anthology edited by Norman Kiell [22] reveals that such observations and comments about adolescents, their conflicts, dilemmas, and behavior, and adult reactions to them have been made countless times (the description in Aristotle's *Rhetoric* is a famous early example) and that many adolescents have themselves written eloquently about their condition. Adolescents appear to have changed none of their typical characteristics.

Little is to be gained from a compendium of the interests that youth shows at one time or another. Whatever a society or culture may offer, youth will use it to serve its own ends. If the culture is a meager one, youth has less to use, perhaps, but the aims will not alter. In every society or culture, adolescence is that time of life when youth must prove itself: must test its assertions and its maturity and free itself from the commitments of childhood. Simply stated, a boy must prove himself a man and a girl prove herself a woman. The ordeals and tests of youth are to be the proof of maturity and thus of what youth expects of itself. Maturity for the adolescent is a realization of his narcissism. Whether he achieves it through idealism, through sexual prowess, intellectual accomplishment, feats of heroism, endurance in athletics, or through extravagant fantasies (romantic, ideological, or adventurous), so long as the affirmation of self-esteem is forthcoming, the aims of this phase of life are met. If in the course of this pursuit youth shows strong attachments which are quickly broken, shallow ones that rapidly deepen, causes upon which prodigious energies are expended and then abandoned, or long periods of sleep and idleness with fantasies that are completely absorbing, these are all only indications that the ego of the adolescent is highly adaptable. The rapid succession of whims, changes and extremes of tastes and interests, commitments — or the sudden lack of them — testifies that the ego as an instrument of accommodation is capable in adolescence of widely diversified interests for its investment.

In no other period in life does the ego show such rapid adaptability. The quick adjustments made by the plastic adolescent ego cannot be, and as a rule are not, sustained. The adolescent ego is therefore characteristically unstable. The conflicts between instinctual needs and wishes and the forming of mature object relations, the conflicts between holding to the old family ties and giving them up for a more autonomous way of life, the conflicts between the security of what is familiar and the uncertainty of what is not, require of the ego a series of modifications of the heightened instinctual needs which takes the adolescent from one horn of a dilemma to the other, often with failure resulting. What determines failure is whatever restricts essential functions of the ego which, in turn, are determined by the demands of adolescent narcissism to be satisfied.

No other psychological factor has so much effect upon the outcome of emotional maturation as the course which narcissism takes throughout life. An illustrative example is a sporadically hard-working, ambitious clerk in an office. His efforts justified some measure of success, which he had received. But when he saw that another clerk received some deserved recognition, he immediately despaired and went into a barely concealed rage. He wanted to have special status in the eyes of the office manager. He believed he was entitled to it — "It is due me, I deserve it." Closer observation revealed that the hard work he had done was governed by the wish to justify his envy and greed, and the presupposition that he was deserving of and therefore entitled to special consideration. "What is the use of it all if they do this to you?" he complains in his loss of self-esteem. "I was there first, it was promised me that I was special." There was no such promise. It was what he wished for and felt he needed. "I want to be special, I feel it was assured me. That gave me a right to it." His need to be special had an unconscious precedent in the past. A younger sister's arrival had never been accepted. "What right had she to be given preference that is mine? It's a betrayal for them [parents] to do this to me. I am the victim, I can't believe that I want to wipe them out for it, or still want to eliminate her after all this time. How could I be so calculating, but I am. It is so.''

Another example of adolescent narcissism was demonstrated by a capable young junior executive. Although he was twenty-five years old, he was still a neurotic adolescent. ''I prefer to have someone in charge of me,'' he said. ''I'll take a position below my ambition. I have to hide my wishes. I get very angry when I can't have what I want. I have to hide that too. I am ambitious and I want to be a leader. But then there are limits, you get this and you can't have that. This is too galling to admit. It is better to pick things to do that are sure to succeed. Failing is such a humiliation, like having limits, it depresses me. I get angry and feel degraded, isolated, lonely. I masturbate and think of beautiful women that I never otherwise get. I refuse to answer the telephone, and overeat and oversleep. I think cruel thoughts about the world and do little meannesses. It depends upon how bad the disappointments are, how cruel I get. But if I am weak and helpless it is better. Then I can think of having things conferred on me. Being on my own is to make the future too risky, earning my own way would ruin my system. It would mean I'd have power; then I would have to be invincible, to ward off the risks. But if I am sure of getting favors, it's like having something inherited, it would prove my importance without my having to do anything. The place for me in the world is to be given it. I would give up too much to be my own keeper.''

While the ostensible task of the adolescent is directed toward establishing his independence and to confirming his growing maturity, there is a deeper process which the adolescent's quest for identification rarely fails to reveal. The process is of meeting the needs of heightened narcissism, in an individual who doubts his own value, which has not yet been proven in reality, regardless of how forcibly it may be asserted. The common feelings such as those just cited support this observation. Literary works, especially memoirs, diaries, autobiographies, history, and often fiction, also provide an abundance of rich material illustrative of the narcissism of the adolescent.

A casual familiarity with Milton's seventh *Elegy* reveals the adolescent's high aspirations, vanity, and his frank despair over the conviction he held of his worthlessness [10]. Boswell, who had set his heart on fulfilling his ego ideal, was very depressed when the discrepancy between his wishes for self-aggrandizement and the real Boswell became only too plain. It brought him to weep over his lack of worthiness [4]. Marie Bashkirtseff's *Journal of a Young Artist* has often been cited as a superb example of an adolescent's passionate and desolating love affair. What has usually captured readers' attention is that Marie fell deeply in love with the Duke of H, whom she never really knew and whom she had seen only from a distance. More arresting is the fact that she identified herself with the kind of devastating woman who could cause the multitude to prostrate themselves and who would dazzle the Duke of H by her mere presence. These fantasies gave her a lasting excitement. Her wishes were, of course, not fulfilled. She tells us that she had not a moment's peace, nursed "wounded self-love," and complained of her torment. Underlying the identification that carried her along is her failure to recognize that the petard she was hoisted by is her vanity. It was deeply injured when her grandiose wishes came to nothing. She is almost purely narcissistic, writes Helene Deutsch [7]. While narcissism is not the only factor in Bashkirtseff's experience, hers is a typical adolescent one [3].

Kiell in his recent anthology on adolescence [22] describes the archetypal hero taken from the novel by Thomas Wolfe, *Look Homeward, Angel*: Eugene Gant who was unable to identify with anyone. He extravagantly acted out his need for identification by knocking on strangers' doors, in strange towns, and identifying himself as a carpenter or as Thomas Chatterton looking for a gentleman by the name of Coleridge — Mr. Samuel Coleridge; or he would sign hotel registers as Ben Jonson, Robert Browning, and other famous poets. Kiell gives as an example of a passionate identification illustrative of adolescent ambiguity that occurred in fact, William Ellery Leonard, teacher, poet, and biographer. Throughout most of his life Leonard made a successful career out of his intense identification with Byron. He was Byron in mood, manner, and theme. Before he was able to create and value his own more individual identity in late middle age, Byron's served him. Eight hundred years earlier, a daughter of a provincial Japanese governor made an entry in her now famous Serashina Diary. In her romantic fantasies, she identified herself with an exalted beauty. She then waited and languished for the arrival and love of the Shining Prince.

The use of identification to elevate self-esteem is not merely a literary construction. These examples, fictional, autobiographical, and historical, reveal themselves as expressions of a longed-for identity. They gain more meaning when we observe in countless such cases, clinical or literary, that at the center of adolescent life narcissism plays a more basic role than identification. The search for identity and the so-called "crises" of identity simply overlook that they are but the vicissitudes of adolescent narcissism.

In the postwar studies on adolescents much emphasis is placed upon the social circumstances, social patterns of behavior, changing social orders and, in the United States, on the special problems introduced by the increased longevity of the older generation, which adds to the difficulty that youth has in becoming socially, economically, and emotionally independent. Since 1945 the large literature on adolescence has been considerably increased by writing from the field of social relations and anthropology.

Erik Erikson recently has revived a subject which, while not lost sight of, has had little new emphasis for a decade:

namely, the role that the adolescent's search for identity plays in his development. Erikson pleads for reexamination of both old and new psychoanalytic writings on the subject. Freud's famous "Dora" case, together with his own experience, Erikson argues, supports the premise that "adolescent development comprises a new set of identification processes both with significant persons and with ideological forces which give importance to individual life by relating it to a living community, to organizing history and by counterpointing the newly won individual identity with some community solidarity" [12]. Although he acknowledges that "Dora was an hysteric and that her symptoms were psychosexual," Erikson presses his view that "perfidies, familial and communal, cause adolescents to regress in a variety of ways and to a variety of earlier stages." With metaphorical eloquence Erikson emphasizes the destructiveness of the deceptions that parents of families practice on youth. He stresses that, while on the one hand "Dora" is made privy to the sexual peccadilloes of the adults around her (particularly her father), on the other hand the adults do not acknowledge their behavior that disturbs her so deeply. With that "Dora" falls ill [12]. Erikson suggests that the deception which isolates the child from her family also works effectively to interfere with the identity formation, which is thus denied the child. Identification accordingly becomes distorted. To whatever extent Erikson's theory may merit credence from his reexamination of the "Dora" case and from his own experience, he not only has placed his chief emphasis upon the process of identification, but he believes it to be the critical factor in adolescent development, and hence in the disorders of adolescence as well. It is therefore also relevant to failure in this period of life.

If the dynamics of the "Dora" case hinged, as Erikson claims at some length, upon "the psychosexual centering of the girl's story in matters of fidelity," then Freud missed the point in the case. He concentrated upon and discovered "the symbolic meaning of her symptoms and their history" [12], which empirically demonstrate the essential role of unconscious wishes in producing conflicts and symptoms and have a bearing upon behavior.

Erikson cites the "Dora" case, one of the most familiar in psychoanalysis, to show that a better understanding of the girl would have been gained through a further examination of the social facts of her life. He states: ". . . the meaning of her symptoms was psychosexual; but the sexual nature of her disturbance and of the precipitating events should not blind us to the fact that other perfidies, familial and communal, cause adolescents to regress in a variety of ways to a variety of earlier stages. . . . There is a pathognomonic picture which all sick youth have in common and which is clearly discernible in Freud's description of Dora's total state. This picture is characterized first of all by a denial of the historical flux of time, and an attempt to challenge retrospectively, while retesting in the present, all parental premises before new trust is invested in the (emancipated) future" [12]. These remarks relate to what Erikson calls the social symptoms of adolescent psychopathology.

Writing in the same vein two years later, Erikson urges that we should undertake a study of "biocultural history," as he termed it. "A total configurational approach — somatic, historical, individual — can help us to see the differences of functioning and experiencing in context rather than in isolated and senseless comparison." This is a post-Freudian position that will, Erikson suggests, "transcend trauma and defense" [13]. He states that the psychoanalytic view of womanhood has been strongly influenced by the fact that "first and basic observations were made by clinicians whose task it was to understand suffering and to offer a remedy; and that they by necessity had to understand the female psyche with male means of empathy'' [13]. It is his view that "many of the original [3] conclusions of psychoanalysis concerning womanhood hinge on the so-called genital-trauma" [13] and the defense against that injury.

Erikson has frequently referred to the discoveries in psychoanalysis as "biased by the task of understanding suffering and offering a remedy," and has asserted that psychoanalysts to encourage themselves (and as an argument against others) have stated that human nature is best studied in a state of partial breakdown [13]. His explicit purpose is to call attention to the fact that what we have learned about human conflict has come chiefly from the psychopathology of neurotic people. It would have been better, he clearly implies, to have studied as well those who have no neurosis; but he has not suggested where such people exist.

Erikson makes plain his regret that the course psychoanalytic psychology has taken has led to some formidable deficiencies. In summary they are that Freud sacrificed understanding social reality by his interest in symbolism; for example, that the treatment of suffering introduces a bias, as illustrated by Freud's attention to Dora's needs on account of her anguish; that the views psychoanalysts have taken of women have led the clinicians into making senseless comparisons between men and women; and that drawing conclusions as to normal function on the basis of clinical findings was narrow and isolated from the main stream of normal life.

The "Dora" case owes its notoriety to the fact that Freud achieved a specific aim in publishing it. His chief objective in presenting the patient was to illustrate the novel value the interpretation of dreams has; not only for psychoanalytic treatment, but for understanding the im-

---

[3] By original, Erikson probably means Freud's original contribution; but no analyst has contributed more to our present views in the psychoanalytic psychology of women than Helene Deutsch. She could hardly be said to have a "male means of empathy."

portance to the individual of his reality. The time of publication was 1900. The immense significance of Freud's use of the dream was that by analysis it was to enrich the understanding of individual psychology, that is, to deepen our knowledge and to discover the role that circumstance plays at the deeper levels of the unconscious that govern behavior. Freud showed explicitly that the facts of Dora's social life and her emotional experience could neither be separated from each other nor be understood independently [21].

The dynamics of the "Dora" case actually center upon the *significance* to Dora, and not merely the social facts, of her relationship to her father and the other adults in the household. While it may be that the behavior of the adults caused her anguish, she was not really betrayed. There were no social facts that she was a victim of faithlessness as she believed herself to be. Briefly, Dora, a girl in late adolescence, became intensly obsessed with her father's illicit relations with his friend's wife. Freud made it very clear that "she felt and acted like a jealous wife." Putting herself in her mother's place, she gave her father an ultimatum to put an end to the affair. She threatened suicide. "She identified herself both with the woman the father once loved [her mother] and the woman he loved now. She was almost incessantly prey to the most embittered jealousy" [15].

Dora believed herself rejected; her vanity was deeply wounded. She not only had had unconscious incestuous wishes which were beyond being realized, but she was obliged to refuse to acknowledge them. Yet, despite the denials of her incestuous wishes, her belief that she was deceived by perfidious adults did not correspond to the social reality. None had given Dora promises. Her conviction that she was being betrayed was patently derived from her unconscious wishes. The peccadilloes of the adults about her served the rationalizations she required to distort reality and that she was being abused. She sought revenge in the hope of healing and compensating herself for the narcissis-

tic injury she felt she had suffered from her father's neglect. Dora reacted to these events in her adolescence, i.e. to
their meaning to her so extremely that her vanity, her expectations, and her denial of reality reached near psychotic
proportions.

Twenty-four years after Freud had seen Dora, she
suffered from some disturbing somatic complaints. Her
physician could not account for her symptoms on the basis
of actual pathological changes. He decided a psychiatric
study of his patient was indicated. "She was now a married
woman, 42 years old. She had for some time become bed-
ridden because of her illness." Felix Deutsch was consulted.
After she reported to him "a detailed description of the
unbearable noises in her right ear and of dizziness when
moving her head . . . the patient then started a tirade about
her husband's indifference toward her sufferings and how
unfortunate her marital life had been. Now her only son had
also begun to neglect her. . . . Resentfully she expressed
her conviction that her husband had been unfaithful to her,
but she could not decide what to do. Tearfully, she de-
nounced men in general as selfish, demanding and ungiv-
ing." She went on to furnish details of her experience in the
past with feckless men, especially her father. "This story,"
wrote Deutsch, "sounded familiar to me. My surmise about
the identity of the patient was soon confirmed. She began to
chat in a flirtatious way inquiring whether I was an analyst
and whether I knew Professor Freud. I asked her in turn
whether she knew him and had he ever treated her. As if
waiting for this cue, she quickly replied she was the 'Dora'
case, adding that she had not seen a psychiatrist since her
treatment with Freud."

Approximately thirty years after this episode her death
was reported. Her son had long before brought her to the
United States from France. She clung to him with the same
reproachful demands that Freud reported half a century
before [5]. In the fifty years, with three generations, her

father, her husband, and her son, her relationship to men remained unaltered.

Erikson does not treat explicitly or thoroughly the fundamental fact that narcissism is basic to adolescence and to its disorders. Narcissism is basic to the problems of identification as well. The severe narcissistic injury that Dora underwent because her unconscious incestuous wishes were not satisfied provides the simple key to her disorder, as Freud made plain. She was never to recover from the failure of her unconscious wishes to be gratified. Her subsequent sad history confirms it.

In the attempt to understand adolescence, Erikson correctly deplores the tendency to encompass the complexities ''by the 'clinical' reduction of adolescent phenomena to their infantile antecedents and to an underlying dichotomy of drive and conscience. . . . Adolescent development,'' he says, ''comprises a new set of identification processes both with significant persons and with ideological forces which give importance to individual life by relating it to a living community and to ongoing history, and by counterpointing the newly won individual identity with some communal solidarity'' [12]. He does not suggest that infantile antecedents, drive, and conscience are not operative, but how they function as powerful determinants in the child's adolescence in relation to the new set of identification processes is not clear.

The process of identification has much broader implications, as Erikson views its development, than have been accorded it from individual psychology. He has been able to fashion from the psychoanalytically familiar mental defenses and processes a philosophical homily. He makes a benevolent prophecy; no longer a comment on a child's development but a formulation of a universal ethic. ''Moralities sooner or later outlive themselves, ethics never: this is what the need for identity and for fidelity, reborn with each generation, seems to point to. . . . In the near future peoples of different tribal and national pasts join what must become the identity of one mankind. . . . They must put a vain super-identity of neonationalism in the place of their much exploited historical identity weakness. . . . The overriding issue is the creation not of a new ideology but of universal ethics growing out of a universal technological civilization'' [12].

Perhaps no more remedies are offered the individual than are offered society. Erikson suggests that what he has learned from individual psychology he would apply to society as a corrective for its needs. For the future he would press for the creation of a universal ethic. Popper has aptly called such engineering of society, in which a blueprint is drawn to be followed, ''utopian engineering.'' It is an ancient and noble pursuit. Plato is its most profound and influential advocate. But Popper regards it as ''the kind of methodological approach to attract all those who are either unaffected by historicist prejudices or reacting against them. This makes it only the more dangerous, and its criticism the more imperative'' [26].

The child's attempts to acquire and to preserve an individual identity often cause him to belittle authorities and parents. What is regularly overlooked in the focus on identity is that these efforts on the part of youth are aimed to establish a sense of worth, not only in the eyes of the community, however important that might seem to be, but in their own eyes. No behavior is more typical of youth than to seek self-aggrandizement, to establish self-esteem, and to attempt to remove the doubts about it. The youths who make ''a plea for being recognized as individuals who can be more than they seem to be, and whose potentials are needed by an order that is or will be'' [12] show how little real value the untried, unproved youth feels he has, and that the narcissistic needs of youth or adolescence are indeed great.

There are important distinctions to be made between what a youth aspires to and his attempts to realize his aspirations. As we have learned, the child is particularly and constantly confronted with the gap to be bridged between his wishes and his achievements. Each phase of development mobilizes aggression that ushers in the thrust of activity to serve the aims of the period. When the thrust of activity fails — that is, when aggression is not put at the service of the ego but is bound to instinctual needs — maturation does not follow. Instead, regressive behavior follows. Immediate pleasure or gratification is sought and maturation is postponed. The reality principle is compromised for the sake of pleasure. The need to establish self-esteem (one way is through identification) becomes more pressing as the demands for immediate gratification become urgent. Development is thus put in jeopardy often by the very aims themselves; that is, while narcissism may promote growth, it may also support regression.[4] In such cases, adolescents give up things which bring deferred pleasure; they forgo the tedious application of skills for future mastery in favor of immediate indulgence, relinquish the demands for a more mature social adaptation in favor of protesting against it, often through antisocial acts. The search for immediate gratification may be masked by social protest and may thus superficially give the appearance of a social movement with altruistic aims of freedom or liberty, or it may be expressed as rationalized delinquent acts. Identification is often made with figures who represent violence, revolution or, more likely, anarchy.

As an example, one adolescent caught up in such aims reported, "I am either omnipotent or impotent! Success is to have great power. I want to be able to do what I want without fear of retaliation. My mind is filled with power. It might make everyone mad, but if I have to give up violence,

---

[4] Identification is only a part of the process; it follows the course set by the developing ego rather than the ego being directed by identification.

I won't do it! I want to be a single unit. No ties to anyone. I don't want to need another person. The only thing that is important is *me!* What a pleasure to think they all want your place, if they hold no envy for me that would be no fun. I want to be able to flaunt the envy in their faces. I don't want to kill anyone. I just want to punish them and torture them, if they were dead they would be beyond my reach, I want the pleasure of my punishing them. I want them to think, What have I done to this boy? I have done something awful to him and I should be punished. The worst thing they could do to me is to treat me as if I was like the pattern of wallpaper, just to go unrecognized. I would mind that worse than if they wanted to get rid of me."

This young man attempted to achieve a sorely needed self-esteem through prowess and sadistic fantasies and daydreams which he then acted out in a variety of ways. He cruelly seduced girls whom he met socially. At work he would do what was assigned him very carefully up to a point and then contrive to leave things undone at the very last moment; or he would procrastinate until the last possible moment, when the completion of a piece of work would require his utmost effort, and then do it with the fantasy that but for him the whole venture would fall apart. He was actually very capable, but barely escaped being dismissed because of his erratic behavior. He came for treatment because of acute severe phobias about heights and not because of what is reported here about him. His initial complaints were about self-destructive impulses. He had urgent wishes to throw himself from high or dangerous places.

We have seen in earlier chapters that the fear of losses and the dread of abandonment are expressions of helplessness and dependence that are characteristic of the anxieties of the early years of life. The drive to acquire skills and to achieve mastery is often accompanied by grandiose wishes that are coupled with magical beliefs in the power of such wishes. These are some of the principal means employed to transcend a life that is intimately dependent upon others.

Daily experience, the realities of which enforce the truth that limitations exist, perpetuates a conflict throughout life that only under the extraordinary conditions of psychosis appears to be resolved by relinquishing reality. These mental mechanisms, devices, and efforts, indicating magical thinking, childish in their origins, are but slowly given up. They are never abandoned altogether. They begin as individual efforts; as the child becomes an active member of his community, they are expressed in communal organizations or institutions — of which religion is the most powerful — that express the aims of transcending the conditions of life. Myths, legends, rites are among many other joint communal efforts to resist natural forces, some of which are effective, such as communal provisions against hunger, privation, pestilence, and disease, or for the care of the aged. All serve the same ends to relieve the constant press of limitations.

A further and no less important means to security is expressed in the process of identification. Granted that it is a universally observed human quality, it is an acquired one. It first manifests itself in the young child in relation to those who are of immediate significance to him. It is a discrete and discriminating defense. It binds the child to those upon whom he depends and thus provides part of the defense against the early conflicts which center about loss and abandonment. Identification is thus an indispensable part of the child's early defenses and of his effort to overcome his limitations. It is every young child's unshakable belief that adults are unfettered. At least they appear so to him. This conviction, together with others about adult powers, and the effort to be like adults carry the process of identification from its earliest form, imitation, into the more sophisticated internalized identification which goes beyond being *like* the principals to *becoming* them. With the formation of the superego, identification is launched into its maturing form — a lifelong process. Identification is the means through which the entire environment, the whole of one's culture, is absorbed into and becomes a part of the individual.

The latency period that follows the oedipal years shows the thrust of activity. The doomed oedipal wishes bring home, as no doomed wish did before them, that the child is utterly defeated in his highest hopes. Karl Abraham considered this debacle the theoretical basis for primal depression. That is, he considered that this severe injury to infantile narcissism was the prototype for subsequent depression in its repetition throughout later life [1]. He reconstructed these dynamics from his analysis of adults. Recently direct clinical psychoanalytic studies of young children have borne him out. The activity which is characteristic, as latency follows the passing of the oedipus, appears to arise, in part at least, as a reaction to the severe narcissistic injury inflicted by the lack of fulfillment of wishes and the sense of limitations that are evoked from the failure of the oedipal aims. In latency, the child again employs his previous defense, his magical thinking, and all the old devices in the effort both to carry himself beyond his present limits and to begin to loosen his old ties to the parental figures. With development in latency, and hence a clearer sense of reality, the discrepancy between the child's excessive wishes and reality becomes plainer. He begins to employ more than fantasies of achievement, and thus the beginning of sublimation is initiated; ego functions and libidinal aims are more socially than narcissistically directed. But, as we have seen, activity instead of working for sublimation may turn to aggression, and with that, wishes for achievement may become intensely narcissistic. And the means to secure a measure of independence from parental figures and a gain over the limitations of reality is not won. Still, no period in human development brings all these elements together in a more pronounced way than is to be observed during adolescence.

The activity that follows on the heels of narcissistic injury, the experience of the deprivation of wishes, and the humiliation of limitations are the signs of depression. The depression may be brief, prolonged, or persistent. On close study, the typical moodiness of the adolescent reveals that the dynamics center on the vicissitudes of narcissism, as the examples cited show. The early years, and also latency, show aggression as a common form of expression of narcissistic conflicts; it occurs in conjunction with social estrangement and isolation. In the adolescent, however, the more typical adult aspects of reactions to narcissistic injury begin to become manifest. The earlier elements are all retained. They are, however, on a larger scale in adolescence than in previous periods; aggression, despair, and social isolation often may go on to their more psychotic forms. The psychoses of adolescence are frequently temporary, although they are often alarming in their clinical manifestations. When the principal earlier defenses are organized increasingly about a denial of conflicts, then excitement, ecstasy and even mania begin to appear, as they do not in young children. When narcissism has been the principal system of defense, the severity of an injured vanity is often expressed in the psychotic disorders that are characterized as narcissistic, for example, in the schizoid personality, and in schizophrenia. At this time of life schizophrenic symptoms tend to be acute, limited in duration, and deceptively severe. Recovery from them is usually rapid and followed by activity. Nevertheless, the fact that psychotic dissociation from reality occurs and that the needs of narcissism are so demanding as to require relinquishing reality, rather than compromising narcissism, indicates the depth and gravity of the problem regardless of its transitory manifestations and the uneventful recovery.

A relationship exists between work and the psychology of failure. Since we recognize that failure begins early in life, the question arises, When in development does work begin? Young children do not work; they play. There comes a point in development when most waking hours are no longer given over to play but are devoted instead to work. One might argue that the child at school or the student at the university works and that labor should include the formal educational experience. But in both the conventional and the pragmatic definition of work, attendance at school or university, even when arduous and demanding, seems not to be synonymous with labor. The least frivolous students often admit that only when school is completed will working begin. Other aspects of the life of the student tend to support the view that the libidinal pleasure derived from studying is so prominent that it is in contrast to the satisfaction to be derived from an effective performance for its own sake. The perpetual scholars, unlike the students, have converted a large measure of the libidinal aspects associated with their pursuits into an ego ideal. Repudiating the instincts for the sake of unconsciously serving the ego ideal, they are free to engage their aims, scholarship for its own sake. (It would be a naïve oversimplification to think that conflicts do not remain despite the repudiation of the instincts, or that though they are given up in respect to certain pursuits, they fail to make demands in other areas of behavior. The extent to which the ego ideal is fulfilled is an index of the extent to which the instincts have been deflected. The instinctual gratification that the scholar often finds may, when dissociated from his scholarly activity, be very regressive in nature.)

Before the passage of laws prohibiting their exploitation, children were barbarically used in industry. In some narrow definition of the word they worked and earned a wage. But many children who work earn no wage, and many who do earn are not really working. In most rural communities or among agrarian people children are found working. For the purposes of our discussion it seems more useful to regard such children as doing chores. Work is not easily defined. Because it is so difficult to explain, in its unabridged definition it is one of the most extensively qualified words in our language.

Work is so much a part of daily life that any consideration of adult emotional life must assay the role of work. Despite this fact, work as a psychological motive has seldom been a subject for intensive study. Psychoanalysts from the outset have used the ability to work effectively as a criterion for health just as they have similarly used the capacity of a person for good object relations and love. Nevertheless, the latter has received meticulous attention, while work, by comparison, has been given only cursory notice.

The frankly neurotic acting out of emotional conflicts in work is well known. For example, there are inhibitions which make occupational performance poor when it might be excellent; under some conditions conflicts arise in the individual over his simultaneous needs for dependence and independence; other work difficulties are directly related to conflicts which involve the superego and are reflected in compulsive types of reactions to work. Some such conflicts center about the need to work, in which a day free of work is met with an anxiety that can only be relieved by working. There are countless ways in which work becomes a highly gratifying form of sublimation for genital conflicts, as in the case of the engineer whose structures are to him phalluses, or of the woman scientist who has overcome her castration fears by "performing as well as any man." In these instances work is regarded as such an integral part of the neurosis that, if there is a further significance to its importance, it has been overshadowed by the manifest aspects of the emotional disorder.

Work of a manifestly creative nature has received special attention in the literature. In such circumstances, it is not the work but the creativity which attracts the attention. A great deal of interest has been shown in creativity and far less in the work related to it; perhaps even less notice has been taken of the relation of failure to work. But the motivation for certain types of work has often received attention.

The motives for creativity rather than work have been tracked back to their libidinal elements, and often by a clinical reduction to their infantile antecedents, in numerous publications. The motivation for working received no dynamic study until Ives Hendrick investigated the subject approximately a quarter century ago in 1943. Hendrick's paper is recognized as original and a valuable contribution to the problems of motivation in work, but it has not stimulated other investigators to follow Hendrick's lead and make further contributions to the subject [17a].

Hendrick's paper reveals aspects of work that are important and useful to the psychology of failure. His paper is a discussion of certain relations between work and the pleasure principle. He states that the pleasure and reality principles do not account adequately for the total psychosocial activities of the organism. Hendrick introduces the concept of the *work principle,* which explains the dynamic significance of gratification from the performance of well-integrated ego functions that enable the individual to control or to alter his environment. It has been taken more or less for granted that ability to work, in the absence of physical or mental obstacles, is a result of normal ego organization. Focusing on the study of defense mechanisms, anxiety, and the superego, psychoanalysis has almost completely neglected those integrated functions by which perception, appraisal, and manipulation of the environment are carried out through mastery. Hendrick calls these functions the *executant functions* of the ego and says that their infantile precursors are partial ego functions. (For example, the infantile use of organs of perception, including the tactile ones.) He raises the question of what it

is that is drawn upon or provides the energy that leads to
the developing of integrated functions of the ego. He believes it to be a drive that impels integration, skillful performance, and hence the exercise of ego functions. In his
opinion, it stems from a need to master and differs from
"the other sexual or sexualized instincts; its aim is to control or alter a piece of the environment. . . . This is the
drive impelling to integration and skillful performance, and
therefore the incentive to the development and exercise of
the ego functions which are mentally and emotionally experienced as the need to perform work efficiently. Work pleasure is, therefore, assumed to be an expression of the instinct
[need] to master and is attained by the skillful use of the
central nervous system, whereas the affect that characterizes sexual pleasure is primarily a discharge of tensions in
the autonomic system." Hendrick writes, "I would therefore suggest that work pleasure yields pleasure by the
effective use of psychological and motor instruments providing mastery of the environment." He anticipates that a
cursory examination of the work principle may suggest
that it is no more than a rewording of the reality principle.
He insists that there are more than superficial resemblances between the two. He is mindful that "psychoanalysis has always recognized work capacity as a cardinal sign
of mental health but it has by no means generally recognized work pleasure as a primary psychological motivation."

Hendrick's study of work has produced his theory that a
need exists to perform efficiently. What follows in the
service of this impelling need is the integrated use of skills,
first as partial, then as complete ego functions which are
indispensable to affect, alter, or manipulate the environment. The expression of this need is what we call work. It
was not Hendrick's treatment of the problem of work or his
original contribution of the conception of partial ego functions which drew criticism so much as it was his calling for

an "instinct" to explain what initially leads to and provides the impetus for integrated functions of the ego. He would happily abandon the word "instinct" for "need," which he on reconsideration now prefers [20].

A series of discussions of Hendrick's theory among prominent psychoanalysts (which he reported later in 1943) centered on the "instinct to master." The important points made in these discussions were that it was simpler for the current views of ego function to keep ego function separate from instinctual needs, and that the classification of instincts then in use was sufficient to include the functions Hendrick referred to. Hendrick's answer to his critics was that he was not offering data, but a theory; hence, it was not a question of rightness or wrongness, but of usefulness as a concept. He stated, moreover, that concepts of the ego as dynamic must be based on concepts of its dynamic properties, and that the conventional classification of instincts did not take account of the ego as a dynamic organization in the area of problems he raises. Hendrick warned that the necessity to describe every phase of life in sexual terms was too limiting. Interestingly, at these discussions the main emphasis was on the matter of only *where* in general psychoanalytic theory Hendrick's contribution could be made to fit.

It has generally been acknowledged that most if not all manifestations of a drive to master our functions and our environment cannot be differentially separated from the instincts with which it merges. This general idea may well be valid because the drive to master, if taken as an instinct by itself, would be far too short-lived in the sense that it rapidly combines with the libidinal instincts in early infancy. For example, there is no doubt that the nursing infant's activities show that neurological patterns exist then and that their use is inherent in the physiological pattern. But the process of an orderly and efficient exploitation of these reflexes and patterns indicates a primary need that adapts the infant to the conditions of nursing. The behavior is performed with dispatch and not left to the simplicity of a set of patterns or reflexes alone. Although reflexes, in all likelihood, are what set the behavior in motion, the continued impetus for an efficient performance probably draws on what is best understood as a *need*. When Hendrick proposed his theory he had meager examples to draw upon. This is a common experience in science when a new theory is offered; the data are frequently scanty and in some instances even incorrect. Copernicus formulated his new theory without the benefit of good observation. As Sarton remarked, if the early astronomers had been given excellent telescopes, they would have been so bewildered that they would have been unable to understand anything [32].

In the last decade, many direct studies of infants have been conducted. The most notable is that by Provence and Lipton, referred to earlier in this chapter. What may be learned from their work has an application here which they, for one reason, and Hendrick, for an entirely different one, did not make use of. Hendrick referred in his papers to the work by Gesell, but it required a more sophisticated piece of research than Gesell's to be of substantial use in the context of the problems he was concerned with. Gesell and others described the child's emerging development of function as "appearing without special training or responses to the maturation of the neurophysiological apparatus necessary to perform them." Gesell "has shown that neuromuscular ability appears at very definite times in the infant's life. But their effective use of neuromuscular ability is not immediately established: each is practised over a period of time" [17].

Provence and others have confirmed these findings, but she has shown that, while it is true that certain neuromuscular abilities appear in a calendar-like fashion, they do not persist to maturity; in fact they are relinquished when the libidinal investments accompanying them are absent. As

Provence and Lipton have shown, a family child more
nearly follows Gesell's calendar. But a similar child in an
institution without the benefit of stimulation, without a personal object specifically and intimately related to him,
shows retardation. It follows, therefore, that for maturation to take place a neuromuscular pattern, a use, and a
personal object are indispensable. In the absence of an
object in relation to whom the child's libidinal instincts are
exercised, the need to master is given up. It seems, then,
that the need to master is intimately related to libidinal
satisfaction and does not exist, at least empirically, alone.

The next consideration, easily demonstrable, is that in
the presence of libidinal satisfaction from an object, the
work principle is heightened. The two operate in conjunction with each other and it seems doubtful that either one,
under ordinary conditions, exists for long without the
other. What we observe is that the pleasure principle is
fused with Hendrick's work principle and this fusion
brings about the normally expected healthy maturation.
The importance or significance of not relying upon the
pleasure principle alone for maturation is that, of itself, it
does not induce achievement, efficiency, or for that matter
adaptation. On the contrary, the pleasure principle as a
primary source of motivation tends to support the status
quo, to pull toward regression and to *oppose* adaptation.
To whatever extent partial ego functions are performed by
the child and indicate that the need for mastery is operating,
it is in later development that the need for mastery is plain.
It will be recalled (see Chapter 4, Loss and Restitution)
that the child's need to overcome the awareness and facts of
his limitations promotes and encourages the use of efficient
behavior to adapt to his environment and to alter it in his
favor, in fantasy if not in fact. While the theory of mastery
may be appropriately applied to emerging motor achievements, its application should include the earliest manifestations of the child's effort to overcome the limitations he

experiences. It thus appears that the need to master is subject to development and that mastery of new skills is
required in the various phases or periods of psychological
development. The process of acquiring mastery is established early in life and continues thereafter, propelled
constantly by limitations and frustrations, by a discrepancy between wishes and realities. What begins as a need
for the efficient application of skills and partial functions,
finally ripens into full functions of the ego. It seems to be
continually in demand throughout development. Each phase
of development will draw on the need for proficiency in
order to overcome the limitations perceived as peculiar to
it. Whatever the stage of development, the relationship
with the object which carries with it the libidinal gratification that is demanded is a critical factor in the emergence
of mastery.

May not the reality principle, which is constantly pressing to be met, thus be realized by the carrying out of ego
functions in the need to master? If so, the corollary is that
when the executant functions of the ego fail through object
relations, that is, when personal relationships as a source
of libidinal gratification are seriously diminished, and when
the requirements of reality become inordinately burdensome, the development of mastery fails; or if it has been
achieved, it may be relinquished and hence lost. A course of
regression is then initiated in the search for gratification.
Resorting to the pleasure principle follows when the reality
principle is rejected and the work principle with it. Thus
the failure in ego functions, the forgoing of gratification
from a well-integrated performance, is also a failure in
work. The reaction to failure of ego functions is experienced in the same way as is the loss of any valued function:
the individual feels humiliated and demeaned. Self-devaluation begins and ushers in the typical symptoms of self-
denigration and depression. Relief may then be sought in
the satisfaction derived from regressive behavior.

Careful scrutiny of the young child mastering his varied functions, and doing so in relation to those who take care of him, makes it evident that he finds gratification in achievement. But his satisfaction is a mixed one. As we have previously noted, achievement either ceases or is retarded in the absence of someone libidinally important to the child. It may therefore not be possible to draw distinctions or perceive differences between what pleasure is derived from achievement or the exercise of mastery and what comes from libidinal sources in the child's accomplishments. The fact that the child plays, and does not work, although pursuing accomplishment, upholds the conclusion that the pleasure principle rules play. But work in its final performance is satisfying for its own sake and fulfills both the pleasure principle and the reality principle.

There are few instances of young children working under six years of age. For one thing, the young child's limited physical abilities preclude it. It is no longer a common practice to employ the somewhat older child in latency and preadolescence. When such usage of children did occur it was in civilized societies, such practices being unknown in primitive society. But the exceptions are useful in attempting to judge the effect upon a child of compelling work before pleasure.

Children can be coerced to work, and the exploitation of child labor in times past has been notorious. Exploitation of children in large numbers occurred during the rising industrial period of Europe and the United States, but it has virtually disappeared since the early twentieth century. The first child labor laws were adopted in England in 1802 in an attempt to control the notorious exploitation of child labor in the English cotton mills. It was nearly twenty years later that an enactment prescribed that child employees be at least nine years old. The international labor movement received some of its chief impetus from the imminent dangers in work to both the physical health and the morals of children. The labor movement's main concern about the child has been to protect the preadolescent child from being used as a source of cheap unskilled labor.

It is difficult to determine historically what the psychological effects were upon a child who was obliged to work during the period of latency and preadolescent development. It is no wild speculation, however, to surmise that a serious disturbance of the child's play life would produce a lasting psychological distortion of ego development. A harsh reality requiring work demands the child's adaptation to circumstances for which he is probably ill equipped emotionally and physically. These assumptions are based upon the child's limited ego development, the uses to which he may still find play essential (even as an early adolescent) in evolving resolutions to his conflicts, and the probable nature of his relations with the adults who would employ him. The child's experience would in all likelihood be characterized by a masochistic relationship toward those who used him. There is much in the psychology of the young child that is ready to be masochistically abused. The child's alternative to this reaction is to identify himself with his employer; this would support the sadistic modes of behavior as a defense. Not all who would employ a child would be sadists, but a child would be inclined to regard those in authority in such a light and would then perhaps tend to identify himself with those people. Psychodynamically, a sadomasochistic relationship under such circumstances would promote this aspect of the child's character to his possible permanent detriment.

Training young children for the ballet is one example of a severe discipline introduced at an early age. Play in the conventional sense is sacrificed under these conditions, and in its place a high degree of narcissism, which is especially focused on the body, makes compensation to which the young child is naturally well prepared to respond. Since the vigorous course of physical training is under the close tutelage of a master, the libidinal aspects of the training, that is, its emphasis on physical narcissism, may be expected to find full expression in which childhood narcissism may become fixed.

In the child's view, work is done not for himself, nor for social reasons, but for the sake of someone on whom the child depends. In fact, there is little likelihood that work has meaning for its own sake until much later in life. The child's training is thus distinctly different from adult work pleasure in which the libidinal elements have given way naturally and sufficiently to the satisfaction of doing work in the service of the ego rather than chiefly the libido.

An outstanding example of a young child being put to a task is furnished by the eminent nineteenth-century philosopher, economist, and champion of liberalism, John Stuart Mill. It is fortunate for us that he wrote so candidly about his unique experience. His father determined that he was to be the boy's sole tutor and undertook his son's entire early education to the exclusion of all else. Mill's formal education by his father was said to have begun before the boy was three years old, although it is not clear just what that education might have been. However, within a short time he was fully occupied with his father's fanatical intentions and objectives about education. At the age of three years Mill was being taught the Greek alphabet and given endless lists of Greek words with their English equivalents to study. Long before he was eight years old he had read the whole of Herodotus and the dialogues of Plato, had studied history extensively and was carrying a curriculum that was common in the universities. But John was not endowed with genius.

His astonishing education has received wide attention and criticism, but it interests us less than the experiment of putting so young a child to work. What is of first importance to our discussion is that the elder Mill was a tyrant. He was contemptuous of emotions, except his own, and ruled his son John with a discipline that placed the task at hand, his education, before all else. It requires no psycho-analytic knowledge to understand that the father, to achieve his ends, cultivated an intense sadomasochistic relationship with his son which was thoroughly masked by an educational scheme of his own creation. The boy was obliged to exhaust himself solving countless educational problems set forth by his father before he was eligible to receive help with them. He was deliberately not openly praised and was given no comfort or relief from his efforts. He was thus raised on a gruel of work and accomplishment with no concession to pleasure.

This relationship of father and son is an example of the work principle being exploited that derives from the child's pleasure principle. It succeeded in developing an extraordi-nary precocity of the ego and a remarkable education. In commenting on his educational experience in his *Autobiog-raphy*, Mill said of his "analytic habits" that they may "strengthen the associations between causes and effects, means and ends, but tend altogether to weaken those which are, to speak familiarly, a *mere* matter of feeling." These habits kept a "perpetual worm" at the root of his passions, virtues, desires, and pleasures: "My education, I thought, had failed to create these feelings in sufficient strength to resist the dissolving influence of analysis, while the whole course of my intellectual cultivation had made precocious and premature analysis the inveterate habit of my mind." John's sense of being valued by his father was to be estab-lished only through the means set by the elder Mill. Al-though work, learning, and the sacrifice of pleasure were held up as prizes, it appears that it was neither work nor education but his father's approval that was necessary to the boy. It was that for which he constantly slaved through work, and it was by means of his education that he tried to gain it.

The masochistic surrender of the boy to his father as

part of the curriculum is obvious. Many references in his *Autobiography* show how Mill might have hurt his father and just as regularly put down his hostility and decided against it. His case demonstrates that the pleasure principle even when tortured pathologically in a child turns the work principle, mastery and achievement, to serve its own libidinal ends. Mill was an unhappy man, given to recurrent depressions, which he describes in some detail. He quotes two lines by Coleridge that were often in his thoughts:

> Work without hope draws nectar in a sieve
> And hope without an object cannot live.

Mill's greatest work was *On Liberty*. Throughout most of his adult life he was most outspoken against social tyranny. Despotism destroying development was his frequent theme and warning. He did not extol work but was a champion of freedom — an experience he evidently never had [23].

Labor, unlike play, consumes years of human life. It is performed for the sake of its products to enable the individual to sustain himself, support his family, and contribute to the community. Most of adult life is give over to it. Unlike any other aspect of human existence, it has no real precedent in childhood. The child's life, by contrast to the adult's, is given over to play, and the younger the child the more is this the case.

Probably no greater transition takes place in human development, both psychologically and physically, than the turn from play to work. Play distinguishes itself from work in that it serves only the individual. Its products if important are significant essentially to him. It is the opposite of toil. The great importance of play is that it is the child's medium through which he expresses both the immediacy of external events that press him and the ever-present personal conflicts that remain until they are resolved. In play the invariable emotional conflicts attendant on growth, development, and maturation, together with the vicissitudes of living in a world of events meaningful to himself, give the child endless and recurrent themes, plots, problems, and dilemmas (from which the child is rarely far removed or divorced) to make the fabric of his play that he regularly weaves in a great variety of patterns.

We know that in the child's world of causality, all things are given meaning, and that events, personal as well as external, are explained. The interpretation which the child gives to events may not be in accord with reality, but this does not mean that the child is lacking in interpretations; in fact he makes them readily.

It is not the events or circumstances of life that differentiate the child from the adult so much as it is the way in which the child deals with them. Births, deaths, illnesses, celebrations, the activities of the people around us, the events recorded in the daily news, are part of the child's world as well as the adult's, whether he is a participant or merely a witness. What they mean to the child however may be expressed in his play. Determined by many considerations, what actually goes into the child's play depends chiefly upon what are personal items to him; the child does not find objectivity the virtue that the adult claims it to be. One outstanding characteristic of child's play which differentiates it from adult activities is that events are given a personal significance which is reflected and translated into play, rehearsed repetitiously, and may become a basis for behavior. This is to a degree true of adults, naturally, but not to the impressive degree that it is in children. There are many remnants of this aspect of child's play which are carried over through adolescence into adult life, often in forms so modified that they are difficult to recognize and would require careful scrutiny to find.

The great significance that play has for the child explains to a large extent the tenacity with which it is held to and the reluctance with which it is given up. The fact that play operates under the aegis of the pleasure principle makes it all the more evident that to relinquish play for work implies modifying the pleasure principle sufficiently to allow for a way of life which previously had only a rudimentary existence. To find pleasure in work is a contradiction for childhood.

We have seen that the mastery of a skill or the acquisition of an accomplishment leads to behavior that represents an efficient solution to a problem that arises early in life. By the age of three years, mastery has become a form of behavior which is indispensable to fulfillment of the child's needs, to his growth, and to his development. While it is the root from which the pleasure of work stems, it does not fulfill the definition of work and should not be mistaken for the fruit of work. The aims of a child are essentially egocentric. In other words, to whatever degree a child laboriously toils to learn, to master and perfect his skills, he does so for his own ends. Self-serving aims may be no less strong in many adults, but ordinarily they are not the sole ends of effort as they are in children. There is little doubt that much adult play is childish, however meaningful it is to the adult; but despite the similarity, there are important distinctions between the adult and the child at play.

With rare exceptions, work becomes the adult's way of life. It consumes his energies and his years. He finally gives it up only when he can no longer pursue it. Universally, the adult suspends the rules of work for the deliberate purpose of play. Conversely, when the child labors, the rules of play are partially remitted. Play as a phenomenon of the child's life thus undergoes transition with growth and development. The resolution of some personal conflicts and a deeper and broader adaptation to reality find less ground in play as maturation takes place. Increasing demands of reality reduce the time and effort given over to play and change the auspices under which it has been carried out. The content of play is indeed retained in fantasy, but the latitude of behavior in relation to it becomes restricted. As more is to be learned and more experience is to be gained in order to resolve the conflicts of life, the inroads on play increase. The need to alter, influence, and modify the environment is omnipresent, and the maturing child realizes that while play served these ends once, it can no longer fulfill in fact the aims that were set out for it previously. The old discrepancy between wishes and receipts and the limitations inflicted by reality are plain. Play is given up as a way of life probably for the simple reason that it is no longer functional.

The preparedness to relinquish play is further strengthened when the rules of work are imposed. Work will not necessarily bring about the desired results. But there is a better chance that it will. It should be evident that the severity of the conflict between the wish to play and the need to work is felt in adolescence. The earlier periods of development were not occasions to distinguish sharply between the two. The threatening contention between these two modes of living becomes a common basis for failure in adolescence.

The tenacity with which play is held on to should not be taken as evidence that it is solely a source of pleasure. This would be a narrow and conventional view of play. There is no doubt that play provides pleasure, but as we see, it also does far more. It is a way of life. Children play regardless of how emotionally distressed they are, and in truth they probably play more rather than less with greater disturbance. As a rule even the most psychotic child plays. His play may be bizarre, restricted in its scope, endlessly repetitious, and give the appearance of being empty and meaningless. But it is not readily relinquished and it is often impervious to entreaties, distractions, or any attempt to externally modify it. A four-year-old psychotic child whom I treated for some years without much success may illustrate this point. His play was stereotyped, monotonous, and very simple in its plan although it was not always clear. There was a long period of many months, during his frequent visits, when he was mute. His sole interest was focused on a toy comprised of varying lengths of smooth, narrow, dowel-shaped sticks to be used for building. He would bite them and chew and swallow their ends repetitiously. Fifteen years later he telephoned after an interval of no communication for a few years. He wanted to report that he was well and pleased with himself, working as a farm hand. He directed the conversation to his visits for treatment many years ago. He remembered that he had chewed up virtually boxes of the sticks. Asked what he had intended by that behavior, his answer was prompt. He replied, "I was very angry and now I must go visit my mother! Good-bye."

The persistence of infantile play at whatever age speaks for itself and hence requires no elaboration here. But the goal of play and its encroachment on the rules of work (which is often expressed in the constant search for diversion and distraction from the work at hand), while characteristic of the lazy and procrastinating early adolescent who feels acutely deprived when confronted with the prospect of giving up or postponing his pleasure, takes on significance that suggests failure when it persists into adult life. It is not the little childish act that has importance as an indication of failure but the principle involved, to which the individual cannot accommodate. It is typical of the adolescent at work to be as fickle toward it as he is toward every other aspect of his life. He keeps no permanent attachments to his play, his interests, his contemporaries, or his work. While his commitment may strengthen suddenly, it can just as quickly dissolve. In relation to work as to other aspects of life, he can make a good, rapid, effective adaptation but one which cannot be depended upon to be stable. This degree of lability is permitted in most societies, if they are not Spartan, and society can take these transitional characteristics into account. But when they persist into later periods of youth and then into adult life, they have become anachronistic and form the basis for failure.

Perhaps no other aspect of man has been written about so much as sexuality. The literature on the ego ideal, while it may not be as extensive as the literature on sexuality, is probably in many instances no less passionate. We have called attention to the enormous influence that a relationship with another person has on an individual's development [31]. The effective development of the ego ideal depends more upon the quality of a relationship with another person than upon any other factor.

Ego-ideal formation, like that of object relations, develops. The level of maturity that it reaches is probably determined by the nature of the object relations that are formed. The aims of the ego ideal are not simply to keep oneself an object of value or to retain an archaic self-love (as has often been suggested). If that were the case, then libidinal needs alone would be self-sustaining. We know that they are not.

The fact is that the ego ideal exerts a repressive force which directly affects unconscious wishes. Nothing suggests that the ego ideal is a mere psychological fact or an abstraction. It is a process. The formation and development of the ego ideal reveal its essential functions. It increases the demands of the ego and is the most powerful force favoring repression [14]; and it mediates the conflict between the gratification of instinctual needs and the requirements of the ego. The result is that some of the vicissitudes of the instincts in human beings, affected by this unique process, undergo repression.

The ego ideal is the repository of cultural ideas. It fixes the standard for the individual. Through it he may acknowledge that an inner measuring of himself and all else in relation to himself goes on. He is not aware, however, that it is in constant operation. It is chiefly unconscious. His freedom from its tyranny is only for the time when he suppresses it. The ego ideal thus makes claims on him. Whatever impulses oppose such ideas and claims will be subject to repression, which "proceeds from the ego; we might say with greater precision from the self-respect of the ego" [14].

The mental functions that the ego ideal enforces are chiefly aimed at making important object relations more secure and insuring social adaptation. In effect, it keeps us social rather than gregarious creatures and binds us more securely to objects whom we need. It defends us from the pull toward a more hedonistic existence and it attempts to contain egocentricity within bounds. The ego ideal is a civilizing influence.

From its impairment, we have learned that regressive behavior returns, repression being then lifted; object relations suffer when regressive aims serve narcissism. That narcissism is not a self-supporting process becomes evident when the ego-ideal fails. The examples cited from Murray [24] and Hendrick [18] later in this chapter show what an inadequate substitute narcissism is for the ego ideal.

A too strict adherence to the ego ideal, that is, to its dictates, which become a source of pleasure, may combine with enjoyment of the decrees of the superego. However, the expression of moral rectitude supporting social and cultural aims actually takes its impetus from what these two mental functions have repressed. Our readiness often to mete out justice, to defend aggressively a moral position, and to support our cultural and ethical principles may be a reaction to wishes that threaten the self-respect of the ego.

We are all subject to the erosion of our self-respect by the return of our early instinctual wishes. At most times they are successfully repressed. But through dreams, through free associations, and through fantasies they often escape censorship. They are then constant reminders, frequently disturbing, that the demands of the ego, the ego ideal, and the superego are in conflict with instinctual wishes that make their claims heard despite our personal exhortations to the contrary. We thus undermine our own self-respect, which we then seek to recover. The ego ideal which we on the one hand support, we on the other hand subvert.

To whatever extent an object relationship is indispensable, the relationship to oneself is no less important. It is plain that a mere hedonistic narcissism is not adequate for us. In fact, to our hedonistic childhood narcissism we add the qualities of those who are important to us. We enhance our own attributes with the characteristics we admire in others. However, taking others into oneself in this instance does not mean narcissism in its earlier form; otherwise the ego ideal would merely be a later edition of narcissism. Nor is the ego ideal merely narcissism transformed, as some have suggested. Rather, the ego ideal provides a new level of narcissistic satisfaction. It is also more than an effort to restore to ourselves the lost narcissism of an earlier period.

Infantile narcissism was given up for the sake of an imperative commitment to those important objects of infancy without which one could not survive. It is retrieved, however (because, as we have seen nothing is really given up without at least a substitute to take its place), as the ego ideal. Thus the ego ideal replaces the archaic self-love. The ego ideal is dealt with as though it were an object. It is idealized and its value overestimated in quite the same way that our love of another person aggrandizes and exalts that object of our attentions [14].

The formation of the ego ideal is not entirely a self-contained internal process:

If we look at the attitude of affectionate parents towards their children, we have to recognize that it is a revival and reproduction of their own narcissism, which they have long since abandoned. The trustworthy pointer constituted by overevaluation, which we have already recognized as a narcissistic stigma in the case of object-choice, dominates, as we all know, their emotional attitude. Thus they are under a compulsion to ascribe every perfection to the child — which sober observation would find no occasion to do — and to conceal and forget all his shortcomings. (Incidentally, the denial of sexuality in children is connected with this.) Moreover, they are inclined to suspend in the child's favour the operation of all the cultural acquisitions which their own narcissism has been forced to respect, and to renew on his behalf the claims to privileges which were long ago given up by themselves. The child shall have a better time than his parents; he shall not be subject to the necessities which they have recognized as paramount in life. Illness, death, renunciation of enjoyment, restrictions on his own will, shall not touch him; the laws of nature and of society shall be abrogated in his favour; he shall once more really be the centre and core of creation — 'His Majesty the Baby', as we once fancied ourselves. The child shall fulfill those wishful dreams of the parents which they never carried out — the boy shall become a great man and a hero in his father's place, and the girl shall marry a prince as a tardy compensation for her mother. At the most touchy point in the narcissistic system, the immortality of the ego, which is so hard pressed by reality, security is achieved by taking refuge in the child. Parental love, which is so moving and at bottom so childish, is nothing but the parents' narcissism born again, which, transformed into object-love, unmistakably reveals its former nature [14].

In the parents' joint participation in their child's development, in which each parent has a direct influence on the formation of the ego ideal, the mother's contribution is the more significant. Ordinarily the superego is more nearly the father's province. The parental roles may be reversed but they more naturally tend not to be. It is the part that the mother plays in influencing her son's ego ideal which is of special interest. The complex libidinal relationship to a daughter, although at times creating anxiety because of the mutual unconscious homosexual components, constitutes a threat that is significant only when these components are intense and excessive. It is not a serious source of danger except under the mother's need to maintain an active intimate relationship. Even then, the intensification of the daughter's identification with her mother may find its solution in femininity. It is particularly the absence of an incestuous relationship which sets the mother and her daughter off on a different course from the one with her son.

The relationship potentially least trammeled by ambivalence is the gratification that a mother may receive from her son. But the satisfaction that she gets from him often carries her to an awareness of her erotic interest in him. The threatened danger of incestuous wishes that are not present in relation to a daughter is a persistent and disquieting source of anxiety where a son is concerned. This may be especially enhanced in the best kind of good, healthy relationship where the mother enjoys her son's masculinity. This pleasure for a woman is the real index of her femininity. She relishes her husband's masculinity and her son's too. But even under these favorable conditions her erotism leads her into fears of incest. Her reaction will be to repudiate her sexual impulses toward her son, which results in their repression. She then is found to be idealizing him, as a reaction formation, thus depressing her incestuous wishes. The child need not be very old for these phenomena to begin to take place; mothers often come to this point when the boy is only an infant, and the entire experience just described takes place in fantasy before the boy has shown many male qualities. The same process goes on in those women to whom Helene Deutsch has referred, whose pathological emotional life blights their love for their sons because of their aggressive hatred of men, which emasculates their sons and drives them into passive feminine characters.[5] Such mothers are frequently seductive, especially when they characteristically develop heightened defensive reactions, that is, additional defenses against their hostility

[5] An example is the Ismeric March which is very famous in Turkey. It says, "My mother brought me up to protect and love my country. She said to me, 'I'll regret the milk I gave you if you do not attack the enemy bravely.'"

toward men. These women thus find themselves then confronted with their incestuous wishes, which they too consider abhorrent. As a defense against the fears of their incestuous desires they attempt to drive their sons — and often succeed — into an intense idealization of the ego ideal which may also be then coupled to a severe, meaning punative, superego.

There is a marked contrast between incest of fathers and daughters, which is not uncommon, and incest of mothers and sons, which seems unheard of. To my knowledge, there is no authentic clinical or biographical documented example of incest involving a mother and son, that is, an actual seduction by a mother of her son is not known. The desire for incest and a defense elaborated against it has been plentifully demonstrated in every medium of communication. It indicates that the greatest anxiety is expressed in the strictest incest taboo, which operates between these two members of the family.

The unique relationship of mother and son contributes materially to formation of the ego ideal. Helene Deutsch has written that under certain conditions, in a religious atmosphere and among simple-minded people — for example, among uncritical believers in Catholic dogma — the Holy Virgin and the Christ Child play an immense role. The son will fulfill his mother's fantasy of immaculate conception and sanctify her to holy virginity by becoming the future bearer of religious perfection and saintliness — the ascetic priest. The example is not confined to such people exclusively [9].

It is a more common occurrence perhaps among the lower classes, where the opportunity to realize the mother's wishes are fewer. In a somewhat modified form similar aims are carried out among Jews, often in the form of the student given over to a Talmudic life; even though later married and with his own children, his life is that of an ascetic. His wife regards him as one. The ghettos of Europe

furnished many examples of such asceticism. In this country, other professions serve the same ends. There is a more
modern version of this practice, one not so strict in the formal sense: the scientist who repudiates the flesh for his research seems to be carrying out the same mission. Among
the so-called primitive peoples, the ego ideal may not be so
rigidly observed by the renunciation of the instincts, but the
encouragement to fulfill the tribal ideal comes more often
from the women of the tribe — that is, the mothers — than
from the men. To the men of the tribe or to the man of the
family falls the responsibility for invoking proscriptions
and proclaiming sanctions rather than promoting the ego
ideal as directly as the women do.

One need only be reminded that *ad maiorem dei gloriam*
in the present context speaks for the ego ideal. Moreover, it
applies also to those theologies that are not the revealed
ones. What religion fails to be for a god's sake and in turn
for one's own sake? In Chapter 3, on the origins of religious belief, we observed that the longing for paradise and
the need to transcend one's limitations, while driven by the
need to close the gap between what was wished for and what
there was, stood for the striving toward an ideal condition.
It is clearly not enough to wish for a paradise. One requires
credentials to enter it. The qualifications are to be attained
by acquiring the character reference of an ego ideal. The
tremendous force that is constantly being exerted to realize
the ego ideal cannot be measured but only marveled at.

The most renowned example of the ego ideal is Jesus
Christ. He represents its complete attainment and to Him
have gone the rewards. He, the only one who has perfectly
observed the Ten Commandments, is the epitome of perfection; in His repudiation of the flesh, He transcends the limitations of life, and the laws of nature have been abrogated
in His favor. He embodies all the qualities of the ego ideal
that the fondest parents could have wished for. It is however, together with His mother that the unit of the ego ideal

is brought to perfection. She gave Him life by immaculate conception and virgin birth and is Herself free of the flesh and hence of sin. Mother and child both achieve the ideal. The Holy Virgin and the Christ Child thus represent the most perfect unity, in which the instincts are disavowed and the ideal fulfilled. The Son holds the future as the bearer of the ego ideal [9]. And to insure its aims the prohibitions are embodied not in the ego ideal as has been generally supposed, but in the superego that supports the ideal and becomes its guardian. The libidinal impulses that would subvert the ego ideal are therefore renounced or at least strictly governed. The task of the superego is clearly set forth.

The unity of the Holy Virgin and the Christ Child, unique as a model of the attained ego ideal, is in part reproduced in the birth of a son. It is reasonable to assume that the prototype of the ego ideal would not have its power or its durability if it did not have some foundation in everyday life to keep it alive. The motives for myth-making suggest that they correspond to a wish, to a fantasy, to a specific defense, to a desired or an actual experience. A myth also meets some necessity in life in that it serves as a defense in the solution of a prevalent conflict. Through it the incestuous wishes of the mother find a way to be repudiated and yet a way to be gratified. The striving for realization of the ego ideal is evidently an important effort in that direction. The birth of a son offers a unique opportunity for such an aspiration, particularly as the child is quite naturally the focus of self-realization. Idealizing of the son by the parents, and expecially the mother, launches the entire process. It thus forms a solution to the oedipal relations and also goes deeper. Idealizing the son reaches into the incestuous conflict of the mother.

From this point of view the emphasis on the son's future exhorts him not so much to achievement as to a renunciation of his instincts. The child for some time to come is not prepared to make this sacrifice. In the meanwhile, the developing superego begins to prepare him for the time when he may wish to do so. Countless examples could be cited. Clinical practice invariably provides some of them. One outstanding historic instance is that of St. Augustine and his mother, Monica. Even at this distance in time it seems that she must have idealized her son, who turns to her directly from the scene in the garden, the place of his triumph of the spirit over the flesh. However profound his preoccupation may have been with the problems of the day, philosophy, and sectarianism, there is throughout these preoccupations the conflict over libidinal issues in which the ego ideal struggles and is finally successful in putting them down. Monica was no intellectual companion to her son and probably had little to contribute to the resolution of this aspect of her son's conflicts, but his union with his mother is complete when he forgoes the flesh for the faith and thus fulfills the ego ideal that she promoted.

The ego ideal, that "who-one-wants-to-be" part of the self, shaped by many vicissitudes in childhood, youth, and adult life is tempered between the heat of wishes, fantasies, imitations, projection, introjection, identification with the parents and their surrogates, the libidinal needs, superego demands, and the cold of reality. No other aspect of psychological development is more a result of the transformation of other processes, or more subject to them, than the development of the ego ideal.

In adolescence and early adult life the ego ideal is put to its severest test. During this period the oldest inner conflicts are coupled with the novelty of biological maturation. Not only are the libidinal demands more intense and the superego correspondingly more pressing, but the requirements of reality are more exacting. This was not the case in earlier periods of life. The issues that are contending can no longer, as they did in the past, depend upon being dominated by fantasy, play, and the pleasure principle. A young woman at this time begins to be a wife and a mother, and a youth must function in reality as a man, a husband, and a father. There remain ample opportunities for the ego ideal to assert itself, which it characteristically does, in romantic idyls, social and political movements, creative activities, joining the company of men in the so-called primitive societies, and in the pursuit of commonplace aspirations that will elevate self-esteem. In other words, the turn to reality and a further adaptation to it ordinarily are compelling and support the effort to attain the ego ideal.

The failure of the ego ideal, while having its roots in early periods of development may not become manifest until late. To have one's ego ideal outside oneself, contained in the person of someone else, is a manifestation of early failure of ego ideal. Consider the cases cited by Murray [24]. One was a very competent air force gunner who was unable to continue in the service after his ego ideal had been killed; another was a forty-five-year-old clergyman who experienced a serious emotional disorder when his bishop's behavior toward him severely attacked his self-esteem and the values of his ego ideal — the bishop — were lost. Hendrick explains a similar case in which a woman in her mid-thirties developed a schizophrenic-like disorder, about whom he states, ''This woman patient's destiny was [also] ruled by the imperative need to be like her dead hero brother, her ego ideal since childhood. . . . The ego ideal . . . represented externally by an actual person . . . was necessary for healthy, libidinal gratifications during better phases of adjustment, so long as a real relationship with that person was possible'' [18]. In each instance, we observe clinically a reduction or loss of self-esteem. The subjective experience of the failure is not perceived as an impairment of one's ego ideal any more than the superego is experienced as the governing institution which it is. The superego is perceived as bad conscience or compelling obedience to a model or to an aspiration, that is, to an ''ideal'' [19]. The ego ideal when failing is perceived as a lowering and a loss of self-esteem. It may reach a point of clinical depression when it is severe or intense. As we have learned, there are many experiences which try the ego ideal and lower self-esteem. There exist inner conflicts, centered about unconscious wishes associated with aggression which affect the ego ideal; circumstances in external reality may arouse similar conflicts. In both cases narcissism functions to repair the damage that occurs to the ego and the ego ideal.

Narcissism is no mere fact of life or a simple characteristic of it. Narcissism is a part of the process of self-preservation; and whenever that is threatened, narcissism protects it. Regardless of what transitions take place in respect to narcissism in the course of development of object relations, narcissism is indispensable to offset the dangers to self-esteem. Nor is self-esteem a mere aspect of the human condition. It too is a complex process held in precarious balance that relies in great measure on narcissism to right it. The excesses to which narcissism may be developed are always related to the fragility of self-esteem. Moreover, careful study of narcissism has shown that the restoration of a lowered or lost self-esteem requires, in addition to vanity, an object relationship for libidinal gratification even if it must be gained in a pathological fashion [30]. Narcissism is the libidinal component of the instinct of self-preservation [14], and self-esteem is its ego manifestation. The executant functions of the ego, by skill, mastery, achievement, by controlling and manipulating and thus affecting the environment so as to provide a better adaptation to reality, sustain self-esteem. Conversely, when the executant functions do not develop sufficiently to make such aims possible, self-esteem suffers and a sense of one's precarious position or failure prevails.

The development of the executant functions of the ego, essential to the process of adaptation to external reality and to the reality of inner conflicts as well, makes the ego ideal more secure by supporting and raising self-esteem. When self-esteem is reduced and the self is demeaned, the mechanisms of denial and projection are often resorted to. They are incompletely effective, however, and self-accusations, self-inflicted injury of one's narcissism, and wounding of the ego ideal develop with self-destructive impulses and their acts, to be followed by depressive reactions. The depression may be literally a matter of moments, caught in a fleeting fantasy, as brief and transient thoughts, or it may become a mild or severe chronic preoccupation. The mental content varies more in degree than in kind. In fact the relief from such oppressive reactions often depends more upon the mechanism of denial and projection than it does upon a *test of reality*. Further expressions of lowered self-esteem are voiced as self-accusations. They come from sado-masochistic impulses and from admonitions by the superego. Although appropriate, perhaps these inner demands on oneself are all private confessions of failure. The disavowal of failure and its implications deploys the unconscious use of denial and projection, which is frequently shown by varying degrees of elation and euphoria and, in extremes, mania [29]. The fluctuations in mood may be accounted for in large measure by the dynamics of these mechanisms, through which attempts at a balance of self-esteem are made.

The view that failure in an enterprise or exploit may be attributed solely to circumstance needs for a basis the conviction that there is little or no personal involvement in an undertaking. It is associated with an absence of effort or initiative. It is also founded upon a belief that events occur without an aroused curiosity and without a searching need for explanation in a world of only random, fortuitous, and adventitious happenings. If such a view exists, it must be exceedingly rare and is applied to few experiences. Moreover, it has little or no precedent in either individual or human history. There is no time in early life during which such opinions are adhered to, nor is there any later period when such opinions would be satisfying.

The child's conception of causality fashions a world in which whatever occurs is designed, deliberate, and intentional. What is more, animism — that is, perceiving the world as having the qualities and characteristics of oneself and as being governed by the talion principle, and looking upon it as a place where deeds can be undone and punished and in which magical thinking and magical happenings occur — is part of every child's existence. These prevalent beliefs bring the child into an immediate and deep involvement with his functions, acts, and experiences. His awareness of the world about him is not comprised of his awareness of the real physical elements in nature, but of his growing awareness of his own feelings, which he believes are connected with the physical elements of the world he lives in. There is much to show that such concepts of causality persist throughout later life. Despite increasing adaptation to reality and a sharper perception of it that contradicts childhood causality, childish beliefs are not altogether replaced; instead, the adult beliefs are added to them. The two coexist.

It is common to retain in adulthood a conviction that circumstances are governed, and that there is a master plan, or that the order of things is part of a vast design in which we are a friable part. This does not mean that such concepts can be reduced to their childhood antecedents; on the contrary, it indicates that early concepts of causality are elaborated in adult life and are endowed with immense importance. An illustration of the way in which circumstances and forces are personified is furnished by the young woman (see Chapter 4) who fell from her horse and temporarily injured her back. It seemed quite natural to her to discount the fact that the horse balked unexpectedly at a jump. Although the episode could have been avoided had she not been riding that day, such reasoning is irrelevant to the fact that she did not believe she was caught in a set of circumstances over which she had neither influence nor control. She believed that she did affect the circumstances and hence their consequences. She secretly blamed herself. She did not do so through a clear perception of the reality that persuaded her to so reason, but from the conviction that causality was directly linked to her motives. They were drawn from those occasions when she was reckless and when she entertained self-destructive wishes and fantasies, some conscious but many others unconscious. There are countless instances in which a similar sequence of events takes place. The occurrence of a common cold in a small child provides an appropriate example. For example, his mother warned him to wear boots, he neglected to heed her. His cold, he believes, is more a punishment than an infection. A sense of responsibility for what happens is prevalent in the child and it is present in the adult as well. This is not to suggest some inborn sense of guilt, but to illustrate that we are aware of our impulses and desires and that there is no escaping their consequences. The tendency to hold ourselves accountable for the unfavorable outcome of our efforts should not be attributed so much to the inevitable occurrence of human error as to a conviction of our culpability. To try to find out how to influence, control and affect the environment in our favor is not entirely a rational endeavor. Each of us knows that our limitations create a gap between our wishes and their fulfillment which we strive to bridge, and that our failure "is not in our stars . . . but in ourselves . . ."

REFERENCES

1. Abraham, K.: *Selected Papers: Development of the Libido* (London: Hogarth Press, 1942), pp. 458–469.

2. Aristotle: *The Nicomachean Ethics,* translated by H. Rackam. (Cambridge, Mass.: Harvard University Press 1956), pp. 70–188.

3. Bashkirtseff, Marie: *Journal of a Young Artist* (New York: Cassel, 1889).

4. Boswell, James: *London Journal, 1762–1763,* edited by Frederick A. Pottle (New York: McGraw-Hill Book Co., 1962).

5. Deutsch, Felix: A Footnote to Freud's Fragment of a Case of Hysteria. *Psychoanal. Quart.,* 26, (1957), 159–67.

6. Deutsch, Helene: *Zur Psychoanalyse der weiblichen Sexualfunktionen* (Vienna: Internationaler psychoanalytischer Verlag, 1925).

7. ———. *Psychology of Women* (New York: Grune & Stratton, 1944), I, 5, 5–6, 91–148, 108–109.

8. Freud, S.: On Narcissism: An Introduction. In *Collected Papers* (London: Hogarth Press, 1948), IV, 48–49.

9. Deutsch, Helene: Clinical Consideration of the Ego Ideal. *J. Amer. Psychoanal. Ass.,* 12 (July, 1964), 514.

10. Diekhoff, J. S.: *Milton on Himself* (London: Oxford University Press, 1939).

11. Eisenstadt, S. N.: Archetypal Patterns of Youth. *Daedalus,* Winter, 1962, 45.

12. Erikson, E.: Youth: Fidelity and Diversity. *Daedalus,* Winter, 1962, 23, 18, 19, 26.

13. ———. Inner and Outer Space, Reflections on Womanhood. *Daedalus,* Spring, 1964, 582–606, 600–601.

14. Freud, S.: On Narcissism: An Introduction. In *The Complete Psychological Works of Sigmund Freud,* Standard Edition, edited by James Strachey (London: Hogarth Press, 1957), XIV, 73–102.

15. ———. Analysis of a Case of Hysteria. In *Collected Papers* (London: Hogarth Press, 1948), III, 68–71.

16. ———. Leonardo da Vinci and a Memory of His Childhood. In *The Complete Psychological Works of Sigmund Freud,* Standard Edition (London: Hogarth Press, 1957) XI, 78–79; and The Sexual Theories of Children, in *ibid.,* (1954), IX, 217.

17. Hendrick, Ives: Instinct and the Ego During Infancy. *Psychoanal. Quart.,* II (1942), 42.

17a.———. Work and The Pleasure Principle, *Psychoanal. Quart* 12. (1943) 311–329.

18. ———. Narcissism and the Prepuberty Ego Ideal. *J. Amer. Psychoanal. Ass.*, 12 (1964), 525.

19. ———. *Facts and Theories of Psychoanalysis* (New York: Dell Publishing Co., 1963).

20. ———. Personal communication, September, 1964.

21. Jones, E.: *Sigmund Freud; Life and Work* (London: Hogarth Press, 1955), II, 289.

22. Kiell, N.: *The Universal Experience of Adolescence* (New York: International Universities Press, 1964), pp. 14–16.

23. Mill, John Stuart: *Autobiography* (New York: Liberal Arts Press, 1957), pp. 86–93.

24. Murray, John M.: Narcissism and the Ego Ideal. *J. Amer. Psychoanal. Ass.*, 12 (1963), 477–481.

25. Naegle, K. D.: Youth and Society. *Daedalus,* Winter, 1962, 66, 71–74.

26. Popper, Karl R.: *The Open Society and Its Enemies* (London: Routledge and Kegan Paul, Ltd., 1949), pp. 138–139.

27. Provence, Sally, and Rose C. Lipton: *Infants in Institutions* (New York: International Universities Press, 1962), pp. 17, 19–29.

28. Rochlin, G.: Loss and Restitution. In *The Psychoanalytic Study of the Child* (New York: International Universities Press, 1953), VIII, 295–296.

29. ———. The Disorder of Elation and Depression — A Clinical Study of Change of One State to Another. *J. Amer. Psychoanal. Ass.*, I (1953), 456–457.

30. ———. The Loss Complex: A Contribution to the Etiology of Depression. *J. Amer. Psychoanal. Ass.*, 7 (1959), 301.

31. ———. The Dread of Abandonment: A Contribution to the Etiology of the Loss Complex and to Depression. In *The Psychoanalytic Study of the Child* (New York: International Universities Press, 1961), XVI, 461.

32. Sarton, George: *Sarton on the History of Science,* edited by Dorothy E. Stimson (Cambridge, Mass.: Harvard University Press, 1962), p. 108.

33. Symonds, John A.: *Revival of Learning,* Capricorn ed. (New York: G. P. Putnam's Sons, 1960), pp. 84, 211.

7

THE LOSS OF FUNCTION

Disabilities, impairments, or the loss of a function are such distressing experiences that no matter when in life they occur, they rarely fail to produce lasting emotionally disturbing results and influence behavior more than has been generally recognized. The loss of function inevitably draws attention to the disability itself and tends to divert scrutiny from some deeper conflicts, which, although characteristic of all disabilities, are inclined to be overlooked. Attempts to judge the psychodynamic effects of a loss of function have been conventionally expressed in terms of pregenital conflicts and those which refer to castration anxiety. These reductions have brought out only a portion of the effects that impairment may evoke. Because the emphasis has been placed upon the libidinal aspects of reaction to loss, its effects upon the specific parts of the ego have been neglected.

The loss or the impairment of a function occurs as the result of a disorder, an accident, or longevity itself. It represents a serious loss to the ego, which then sees itself as subordinate to circumstance and the inevitable. The imposition of this awareness upon the ego inevitably engenders conflict within it. In the conventional interpretation of loss of function, the fact is often overlooked that its meaning dates from early childhood, the period in which the profound significance of losses begins to be firmly established. Most of the immediate emotional effects of the loss of function, such as the anxiety of deprivation and the need for restitution, owe their principal importance to the fact that these conflicts are prevalent in early childhood and continue throughout life to influence and govern some aspects of behavior. Furthermore, the young child often equates the loss of a function or of certain functions with death. Hence a disability or impairment of function or a loss of a part of the body has a causal relation to conflicts which center about loss and restitution and the relation of the loss of function to dying or death.

By the age of three or four years the child gives some functions a place of special or vital importance. Activity, involving the use of the body, for example, as expressed in gross motor pleasure, comes to represent properties of life to the young child. An arrest or loss of motor functions to such a child may become a definition of dying. This was the case when a simple fracture of the leg immobilized a daring and venturesome child of five years whose characteristic and preferred mode of play was in gross motor skills, climbing, swimming, and bicycling. Another child, for whom vision had become a highly cathected experience, defined death simply as being unable to see. She enjoyed satisfying her curiosity through what she could see rather than do, and was a keen and contemplative observer who from an early age had acquired a detailed knowledge of her neighborhood and learned to judge people by what she closely noticed in their behavior. A visual disability developing in this child would have a far more serious implication than it would to the child for whom gross motor activity represents life.

Thus the loss or impairment of a particular function has found much of its potential significance, ineradicably, long before the actual event may occur. It is given a place in the unconscious in the course of emotional development. When a loss of function occurs, its childhood history has preceded it and will have a direct bearing upon a contemporary disability. This influence upon the loss of a function is not

simply conveyed from the past to the present as an historical recollection, nor is it fashioned extemporaneously to
meet a current crisis. Previously well established in the
course of early development, the importance of a function
finds expression in the governing effects it exerts on
thought and behavior in the event of illness, disability, or
the loss of the function itself.

The heavy emotional or libidinal investment that is made
in a function demonstrates that libidinal investments are
not relinquished without a sense of loss, nor is there a failure to search for ways to replace them when they are forgone.

The abhorrence of losing a function is also related to
abhorrence at losing the part with which it is associated.
The libido is invested not only in functions but in the parts
of the body as well. Some parts of the body, such as the
organs of locomotion, perception, and sexuality, draw their
significance more from their performance than from their
existence; some — for example, the form, breasts, muscles,
hair — draw it more from what they represent. The distinction is not a hard or fast one. All parts have powerful
narcissistic importance. The loss of parts of the body can at
best be adapted to only slowly and painfully. The adaptation is an achievement that is a gain over narcissism, and is
normally limited to regenerating parts: excrement, hair,
and fingernails. We know from ample clinical experience
that neither parts nor functions can be given up without
arousing deep conflicts. Nor is there much doubt that some
parts as well as functions carry a higher value in the
narcissistic scale than do others. The values, however, are
set in childhood rather than in adult life. They are subject
to little change. For example, the removal of a breast or the
loss of a leg is a highly traumatic event, whereas the removal of a section of the intestinal tract, which may be
affected by a far more serious disorder, may create less
distress and perhaps even distress of a different kind.
There is no natural inclination to give up any one part of

the self any more than there is, as we have learned, to give up anything else that is valued. Giving up a part of the self requires a cultivated and disciplined act that is remarkably similar to the process that may be observed in mourning. But because a lowered self-esteem is unconsciously and regularly associated with a loss of function or a part of the self, the implications are more serious.

Emphasis upon the restoration of a function in recent writings has tended to obscure the elaborate and complex phenomena that are associated with its loss. Whether the privation belongs to the motor, vegetative, or sensory systems, or involves an organ or a part of the body or intellectual capacities or emotional responses, and regardless of whether the basis of the privation is real or not, the experience or the sense of loss is always present and evokes a reponse which is attributed chiefly to the reality of the loss. This attitude is misleading because neither the manifest despair accompanying losses, impairments, and illnesses, nor the losses, impairments, and illnesses themselves account for the regularly observed responses of denial, increased egocentricity, hypochondriasis, and regularly altered relationships that are commonly associated with them. Regardless of whether the losses of function are temporary or prolonged, minor or severe, defenses are called for. These defenses bring on wishes for regression and elaborate fantasies that are attuned to a process of restitution as a reaction to the underlying conflicts which are specifically associated with what has been lost.

A ready example may be found in the sufferer of a common cold who inadvertently reveals many emotional effects that are associated with that trivial and pernicious infection. He demonstrates that some conflicts which arise in a minor or transient disability are remarkably similar to those found in major physical catastrophes. The victim of the infection, to take him at his word, attributes his plight to self-neglect. He expresses self-reproaches freely and readily voices his guilt; he displays regressive wishes in his demands for care and perhaps exceptional treatment. The discomfort that develops and the vague aches and pains that arise, instead of being dismissed realistically as inconsequential, are often associated with fleeting fantasies of morbidity. Some hyprochondriacal preoccupation and increased self-interest are typical reactions to a cold. While all these phenomena, which are related to a simple temporary disability, may be short-lived or ephemeral and may thus escape clinical attention, they are not without clinical importance. It seems, therefore, that even a slight disability reveals unconscious conflicts which show that narcissism and sadomasochistic and regressive wishes have increased. Restitution associated with these conflicts is unconsciously sought. The far-reaching implications of these conflicts and defenses may account for the frequent untoward reactions that follow inconsequential disorders. The following clinical example illustrates the impact of a serious loss of function and some of the unconscious conflicts associated with it.

A young editor of Danish ancestry whose family lived in a small town in western Canada had, in a few months, become partially blinded because of an eye infection. His visual impairment was so severe that he could no longer read. He became very depressed during this period and gave up all activities and his many interests. He was chiefly preoccupied with cursing his fate and making excessive demands upon those who took care of him. After a few months he seemed to begin to recover from his despair and set out to learn braille quickly. He was evidently resigned to the loss of his vision. His physicians had informed him that full recovery from his loss was doubtful. He prepared to begin working by employing readers to serve him; with them and the use of braille, he felt that he would be able to resume his occupation.

The editor came from a small, middle-class family. They

were all Spartan in their habits, frugal, earnest, diligent, humorless, and ambitious people. The family was closely knit and its members were not given to open conflicts with each other. Moreover, this did not mean they were under constant strain to prevent outbreaks; they lived together compatibly. Each tended to keep his own counsel. All were physically well; no one had ever suffered more than a temporary infection. The family seemed so alike in their energies, their ideals, the exactions of their superegos, that their similarities appeared to outweigh their differences. If a family could be said to share a common neurosis, theirs was a compulsive obsessional one. Some members of the family, including the editor, had a few hysterical features in their character, but these were not striking. Kindliness, charity, and Christian principles were the virtues they all practiced. They were highly respected in their community, perhaps envied for their stability and capacity for hard work, and appreciated for their concern with the needs of others. The ideals upheld were masculine. Femininity was a condition to be alleviated. Both mother and sisters encouraged the attitude that there be no distinction between the members of the family because of sex. The father and brothers complied with these strivings on the part of the women. There was so much sharing in virtually all activities that there was not much distinction between masculine and feminine family members. In their strained efforts to be fair to each other they succeeded to the point of having only ambiguous feelings toward one another.

The physical impairment of vision precluded the editor's working. He felt, over the six months of active infection, that the rapid loss of the use of his eyes for his work was a catastrophe that deprived and impoverished him. His helplessness not only increased his dependence upon his family, to whom he returned to convalesce, but it also led to his making excessive demands upon them. It had been tacitly forbidden in his family that any member should receive more than another, even when it came to distinctions and honors. All were to share alike. He had always harbored private wishes to be favored, to be greater than the others, to outshine them all, and especially to dazzle his mother with his achievements and his personal qualities, which would not depend upon what he did so much as on what he was. The only way that he allowed himself to realize these wishes was to make inordinate demands in the name of his infirmity. He had behaved the same way when he had a minor infection as a child. Now he solicited the pity of his family and their support, which they freely gave him. It added to his guilt that he felt undeserving of these attentions; perhaps, he thought, he was even taking their help under false pretenses. Although he did in fact require considerable help, this reality could not relieve him of his self-accusations. It was not only that the world was a poor place for him to be, deprived and helpless as he now was, but, more important, it was his own low estimation of himself which caused him the most anguish.

He became further preoccupied with himself as a blind victim. His vanity was deeply hurt. He felt that he had been cruelly treated by fate in suffering the loss of his sight. At times he felt that it was perhaps what he deserved. It will be recalled that no one in his family had had any significant illness and he was exploiting his own symptoms to gratify wishes that were and always had been implicitly forbidden. The others in his family prided themselves on their good health as though it were a virtue. He, as the exception, blamed himself. There was more to his guilt than the current situation. As he reviewed his past life, he recalled it as secretly filled with anger and jealousy toward his siblings. He resented the fairness with which his parents had dealt with their children. He had privately wanted to be accorded special favors. He was particularly angry with his mother, who failed to satisfy him by only giving him ideals to strive for, and toward his father, who, he believed, considered him unworthy of special attention or recognition.

His estimation of himself diminished as his disability continued. The anger that was directed toward others turned away from them to himself. He became alarmed at the frequency of his self-destructive wishes. Not only did he believe that he was currently of little consequence, but as he reviewed the past, which he was prone to do often, it seemed to be as true for the past as it was for the present. His good relationship with his siblings and his parents seemed to him to be really superficial because it masked his hatred. Here he referred to his competitiveness, the secret pleasure he took in a success over the others or in his constantly seeking favors and whatever advantage he could surreptitiously find. He concluded that he did not really have a good relationship with the members of his family. In his ruminations he became convinced that they must have hated him in the past as they probably did now. He hated them in turn for their hypocrisy. He developed fantasies that no one really wanted him and that all were against him. Although he knew that there were no real plots to harm him, he was still suspicious of the seeming good intentions that his family showed him. His father, he was certain, was contemptuous of him. The loss of the use of his eyes, he believed, rendered him useless and earned him the resentment of whomever he depended upon. His self-criticism was severe, far more than was deserved or appropriate, but it was fed by what he thought was in the minds of others.

He privately believed he was the cleverest in the family. In the past he had taken delight in showing off his intellectual abilities to the supposed detriment of the others. It had always been typical of him to attempt to prove himself superior. From the time that he had learned to read as a small child, he pursued reading assiduously, using his precocity aggressively to assert his self-esteem. He read in order to gather up information and become a human almanac. He retained what he read and used it to flog the others with facts. He thus assured himself that they were stupid and ignorant while he was brilliant and informed. That he later turned these aims into rewarding scholarship in no way detracted from their serving him as a constant source of narcissistic aggrandizement, guilt, and anxiety. His success served his extreme aggressiveness and at the same time earned kudos for his achievement in his occupation.

Now that he was blinded, he was caught between his vaulting ambitions, which he had hoped would carry him to a pinnacle of independence, isolated above all the others, and helpless dependence upon the others. He resisted the attempt to resolve this old dilemma, each horn of which afforded pleasure that he was reluctant to give up. His work assumed even greater importance than it had before; the gratification that work afforded him was less anxiety-provoking than the satisfaction he received from his aggressive demands to meet his passive wishes. Moreover, the need to distinguish himself, always present previously, had now acquired an urgency compelled by the increased narcissistic demands that his illness produced. The loss of function had inflicted an injury upon his vanity from which he had to recover. The effort to learn braille, to show himself that he was succeeding over his limitation and exercising an effort that would reestablish his worth to himself, was directed toward his search. It also served as an exhibition of his infirmity and helplessness. In this way, both horns of the dilemma might not be removed but at least they would not be so pressing. The fact that he seemed to be rehabilitating himself quickly was not wasted on his narcissism. One difficulty that his impaired vision had created was its contribution to his feeling of isolation. This, together with his increased preoccupation with himself, made loneliness intolerable. His dependence and reliance on others increased and served in part to overcome the sense of isolation, but it was in a regressive and narcissistic fashion that this was achieved. He inadvertently made himself appear pathetic, bumbling and unkempt. He sought help, pity, approval, and indulgence for his ineptness, posing as though he were preoccupied with profound problems upon which commonplace realities only intruded. This behavior was quite similar to that which he displayed before his illness, but it was all merely intensified unconscious exhibitionism.

The psychosomatic aspects of his illness, the compulsive elements characteristic of much of his behavior, the fact that the eyes are organs both of perception and of erotism, the alterations in body image and the quality of the object relations, are all significant considerations which make up the totality of this disorder. They are common problems that have been dealt with extensively in a large literature that must here be set aside in favor of an important and as yet undealt with facet of disorders related to loss of function. A review of this man's disorder, as related to loss of function, shows that it has followed the course of a clinical depression with remarkable fidelity. The florid features of depression were not so much in evidence as were their psychodynamics. The clinical findings did not resemble mourning his loss of vision or grief; rather, and most importantly, they resembled a *melancholic losing*. This diagnosis was confirmed by the presence of lowered self-esteem coupled with a feeling of impoverishment, intensification of sadomasochism, and increased narcissistic concern with the self in hypochondria; and also by the high degree of self-absorption displayed and the paranoid reaction to others in which he combined, on retrospective reflection, self-accusations with complaints that he felt himself to be scorned, in disfavor, and perhaps even abused through collusion among others [1].

One of Freud's most important single contributions is overshadowed by the massive proportions of the science of unconscious functions which he established. Nowhere in his extensive writings are empirical observations of the emotional determinants of human behavior better demonstrated as a basis for psychoanalytic theory than in his paper, "Mourning and Melancholia." When this work appeared one of the commonest experiences that man undergoes, mourning and depression, was removed from the level of description, where it had been since the time of Aristotle, to the level of explanation. The three generations of psychoanalytic students since Freud have added many contributions to the psychology of depression. Their contributions have been derived from an elaboration of Freud's theory of its intrinsic defense mechanisms which has been gained from an increased knowledge of ego psychology and, more recently, from direct psychoanalytic studies of children. An incidental illustration of how far-reaching and useful this work of Freud's has been is the fact that such widely separated writings as the *Confessions of St. Augustine* (in which St. Augustine described his despair at the loss of his friend) and *Mark Twain at Work* (Bernard DeVoto's dynamic description of that great writer's melancholy which for a time all but destroyed him) are now understandable in a way not hitherto possible.

Freud wrote that

. . . the distinguishing features of melancholia are a profoundly painful dejection, cessation of interest in the outside world, loss of the capacity to love, inhibition of all activity and a lowering of self-regarding feelings to a degree that finds utterance in self-reproaches and self-revilings and culminates in a delusional expectation of punishment. This picture becomes a little more intelligible when we consider that, with one exception, the same traits are met in mourning. The disturbance of self-regard is absent in mourning; but otherwise the features are the same [3].

Freud discovered that the reaction, depression, referred specifically to the "*loss* of a loved person, or the loss of some abstraction that has taken the place of one, such as fatherland, liberty, an ideal and so on" [3]. If we consider loss of function as a loss of part of the self, we observe the same reaction as has occurred with the loss of a loved person. The reaction to such a loss resembles depression or melancholia more than it does grief or mourning. The distinction between the two lies in *what* has been lost. There was nothing unconscious in the young editor's loss of vision; his vision had obviously been impaired. But he reacted as though a loss of a love object had occurred. It was when he lost a part of himself, his vision — when he incurred the loss of the function of his eyes — that the morbid reactions were invoked. The significance of the deprivation is that it is a narcissistic loss. A loss of function means that a part of the self has been forgone. A narcissistic interest in the self, that is, in its parts and its functions, has been compromised. A loss of parts and functions of the self may be expected, from this point of view, to have a melancholic effect.

In mourning it is the world that becomes poor and empty; in melancholia it is the ego itself [that is impoverished]. The patient represents his ego to us as worthless, incapable of any effort and morally despicable; he reproaches himself, vilifies himself and expects to be cast out and punished. He abases himself before everyone and commiserates with his own relatives for being anyone so unworthy [3].

The young editor revealed all these qualities. He showed little or no restraint in exhibiting himself as pathetic and undeserving, and in acting guiltily when he received the favors he had solicited. At the same time, he expected censure that he believed was well earned. Freud's main point was that awareness that the loss he suffers is in himself is central to the understanding of the melancholic. The dissatisfaction with the self on moral grounds is "by far the most outstanding feature. We get the key to the clinical picture . . . by perceiving the self-reproaches are reproaches against a loved object which has been shifted to the patient's ego'' [3]. This means that a type of regression develops in which one turns back on oneself, taking oneself as the object upon whom the focus of dissatisfaction is placed. The conflict is expressed in ambivalence toward oneself and is made manifest in self-denigration, disparagements, regression in the ego, and attacks on the self from the superego. This completes the picture of clinical depression. The loss of functions that involve mastery becomes particularly significant when we bear in mind that the process of acquiring them was an achievement of the ego. Since realization of executant functions of the ego promotes narcissism and the fulfillment of the ego ideal, and also helps to meet demands of the superego, then losing a function or a part of the self affects the ego profoundly in a way that is similar to the effect caused by losing an object.

Although we have cited the example of the young editor, it cannot be said that the psychological effects of a loss of function are peculiar to the loss of vision. That vision was the function lost only gave the reaction to the loss its particular characteristic, just as the loss of hearing or any other function, or of a part of the body, would produce its individual effect. Ordinarily the loss of the use of the organs of perception has a more profound effect than would a broken arm. In some individuals, however, a fracture or even the removal of a blemish may have devastating consequences [6]. All who suffer a loss of function embark on a common course set by the significance of a severe injury to narcissism. Illnesses of whatever sort, whether minor or grave, threaten the integrity of the self and therefore the body image. What determines the expression of the threat to self and body image is not to be found in the image *per se* but in everyone's readiness to narcissistic injury.

Naturally, succumbing to melancholia or to clinical depression takes place in the organization of the individual's narcissistic development. Perhaps the commonest loss of function, and one which epitomizes a narcissistic injury, is impotence. An exceptional basis for impotence is organic disease. It would be too narrow a view to explain the narcissistic injury arising from impotence simply in terms of castration fears and thereby fail to take into account the many other psychological phenomena related to impotence. A study of impotence shows us that a loss of function can bring about the same emotional effect as illness, whether it is due to organic disease or not. The specific cause of the loss of function is not as important for understanding these psychological effects as is generally thought. It is true that the proclivity to look for specific causes rather than for the significance of the effects, especially in terms of the self, is as old as the child's conception of causality. There is no doubt that real events, such as actual disease or pathological tissue changes, as any physician has learned, seem to his patients preferable to a self-accusation as an explanation for disorder. This is clearly illustrated by the hypochondriac who seeks and demands a cause for his illness that would seem to leave him personally exonerated. To judge by his discontent with the explanation that his illness has no physical basis, he would prefer to find that he had in fact an organic disorder. The hypochondriac is above all severely narcissistic. The fact that he may select one set of organs rather than another because of their unconscious importance to himself should not distract attention from the fundamental fact that narcissism is ruling the hypochondriac.

Freud [4] compared hypochondria with organic disease, both having their effect in distressing bodily sensations. The difference, of course, is that while both patients suffer, only one has a physical disorder to account for his ailments. Although there is a vast difference between the two, the patient with hypochondriasis and the one with organic disease resemble each other strongly insofar as the effect upon the ego is concerned. Patients with demonstrable organic pathology suffer not only from their actual disease but also from the fact that the significance of the illness is directed at the individual's narcissism, unconsciously affecting it as an injury to his self-esteem, body image, or body ego. The behavior and the emotional content of both types of patients thus bear a remarkable similarity. This is evident especially in comparisons of the chronically ill patient and the hypochondriac, whose state involves more or less constant attention to oneself.

From these observations we may conclude that depression, commonly known to be associated with illness, and especially with those illnesses in which a loss of function occurs, may be best understood psychodynamically as a clinical depression. It is due not *only* to the unpleasant reality of the illness itself (to which the reaction is conventionally attributed), but as well to the importance of the loss of function in terms of the narcissistic process. Furthermore, illness produces hypochondriacal effects that express the activation of narcissistic preoccupation and withdrawal into the self. *Psychodynamically,* therefore, little distinction can be made between the patient with organic illness and the hypochondriac without physical illness, except that in the latter the degree of narcissism and the limiting of object relations are often more extreme. While the unpleasant physical reality may be ample explanation of the grief and despair that are unfortunately the accompaniment of illness and physical disorder, if we confine ourselves only to a consideration of the physical reality as the basis for the depression, which is associated with a loss of function, we shall not be able to account for those psychological features which are regularly present: loss of self-esteem, heightened narcissistic preoccupations, self-accusations, and all the other characteristics that are more indicative of melancholia or clinical depression than they are of grief or mourning. Moreover, when reliance on a denial of reality is the last resort in warding off despair, cheerfulness, a seeming acceptance of dysfunction or loss of function, euphoria, elation, and mania are part of the spectrum of responses that may be found to be associated with the loss of function.

—————

The extreme opposite of hypochondriasis, that epitome of narcissism or self-absorption in impaired function in the absence of physical disorder, would be the denial of an existing disability. The phenomenon of a "phantom limb" is perhaps its most notorious example. Since phantom limb is known to occur in a wide variety of personalities, there is little to suggest that it is peculiar to one type, the hysterical, as is generally believed. Probably there are only differences in the degree to which phantom limb actively or persistently exists. The term is literally applied to those people who have lost either a part or the whole of an arm or a leg by amputation, and yet experience sensations from the missing parts. The same concept should also be applied, although so far it has not been, to the deaf and the blind. They too have been commonly reported to experience seeing and hearing long after such functions have in fact ceased. Hemiplegic subjects attempt to ignore their severe disabilities. Stengel and others [7] have described such patients who insisted that their two paralyzed limbs were healthy, and who attempted to carry out acts as though they were indeed healthy. Patients with pathology of the peripheral nerves and the central nervous system which caused complete loss of sensation, although not loss of their limbs, also have claimed no loss of sensation.

It is generally agreed that the inability to accept important changes in the body as a result of illness and multilation (surgical or accidental) relates to the image of one's self. The recent studies on phantom limb by a variety of investigators suggest that in most instances all the sensations of the phantom limb may have their origin centrally, that is, in the brain. Regardless of the extent to which these experiences may be attributed to some continuing activity of a particular tissue of the brain, the resistance that is offered to acceptance of the loss and the resort that is made to defenses consisting of denial cannot be accounted for on a neurological basis [8]. Phantom limb phenomena are more satisfactorily explained as manifestations of a significant disturbance of the ego which shows how little the ego can tolerate a loss of function or a change in body configuration.

The ego does not accept alteration in the image of the self, nor will it comply with whatever suggests alteration of the self image, however real such a change may be. A "disruption of the body scheme" cannot be accepted, whether it is due to accident or design (surgery). It has been claimed that the aged are far more disturbed by their disabilities than are younger people because the old are nearer death and such experiences regularly bring awareness of the end. Although younger people may indeed respond somewhat differently, because depression in the young is not apt to be as profound as it is late in life, they also become very disturbed by similar experiences. Age of itself is not, therefore, a necessary factor in reactions of the ego to disruption of the body scheme. It seems that there is no time in life at which the ego fails to resist change in the image of the self, body scheme, or body image, especially when those changes imply a loss of a part of the body or a loss of a function. It will be recalled from an earlier chapter that a little boy fought against having his hair cut. While that example referred largely to castration fears, it also referred to what, to him, was a loss of part of himself that he was loath to do without.

The episode that follows illustrates a loss which impairs the image of the self, ego demands that are heightened, a superego that becomes more critical and resorts to projection, and a depressed state which develops. Recovery comes about as compensation for the loss is found.

A physician's routine physical examination which in-

cluded laboratory tests showed that his thirty-five year old
patient was a healthy vigorous man. Though there were no
symptoms, the laboratory tests revealed that under indeterminate conditions the blood sugar may become abnormally
elevated and suggested therefore incipient diabetes. Despite
the fact that there were no indications of an illness at
present, and while it is a presumption that an increased
blood sugar, with time, may lead or prove to be a source of
physical problems, the physician, as a precaution against
what he anticipated might happen, prescribed an anti-
diabetic medication for his patient.

On the way to the pharmacy with his prescription, the
patient behaved in a furtive manner. He feared that he
would be seen making a purchase of medicine, thus revealing
that he had some defect. Believing that he had a stigma,
he was loathe to reveal his condition to anyone. He
imagined that he had done something to himself to bring
about this condition. He said, ''I have lost a valuable image
of myself. Now I must make every day count. The actuarial
tables say that my life is to be shortened, I must find some
compensation for my loss, my self-esteem has to be compensated. I want to be indulged now. But how long I live
depends on whether I indulge myself. I have to give that up.
I want to hide the stigma from the others and hide this [self-
indulgence] from myself. In five or seven years from now
you may hear I dropped dead from a stroke. You will say
the wishes to indulge himself killed him. It will be a just
punishment. You will be able to say he is responsible, it is
not accidental. I want to hide my complicity, my guilt in
bringing about my fate. I want to keep this image of myself
a secret, now that it has suffered a defect or impairment. It
is a secret infirmity; I don't want to reveal it and lose
esteem in the eyes of others. I don't like what others would
think. I hate to hear any talk now about diets, infirmities or
impairments of any kind. It makes me disgusted with my-

self, I am ashamed of how others would think of me and I am guilty over what I think of myself.''

The patient followed the doctor's orders by observing the demands of a moderately regulated diet and regularly took medication. The results showed in an improved physical appearance. He eagerly responded with private gratitude to notice that was taken by others of the change which, although not marked, nevertheless served in dispelling his fears of criticism and to a degree in relieving his guilt over the self-inflicted injury he attributed to self-indulgence, which he still had the impulse to act on. Social invitations, while always important as a mark of approval by others, now were given added meaning that he was desirable. They also offset the fears that he would lose the esteem that others held for him. To the same ends his added effectiveness in work helped restore self-esteem.

This clinical example shows how the entire process of loss and restitution need not depend upon palpable findings. It also illustrates the important distinction to be made between shame, which is governed by external approval, and guilt, which is controlled by internalized values. The importance of being esteemed by others is developmentally earlier than self-esteem. It reaffirms that narcissism is not self-sustaining except under severely pathological conditions and then it is not wholly self-supporting, as we have observed. It suggests furthermore that the internalization of the approval of others contributes heavily to the image of oneself. It compels and gives added significance to the social relations with others. Their disapproval is a loss to the ego ideal as well as to the superego. The consequence is that the ego is demeaned and the effect is felt in despair. Recovery depends upon how and to what extent narcissism is restored.

The following excerpt of a case is cited to illustrate a healthy man's emotional reaction to the serious impairment of a vital organ. His reaction is characterized by its commonness, by its transience, and by its demonstration of a particular psychopathological process that is readily rationalized in terms of the obvious circumstances, which only obscure the motivating conflicts. In each case the self image is no longer intact; its integrity is threatened, with the result that an urgent need for restitution finds expression in an increase in narcissism and also in an intensified need for a dependent relationship to others.

An active middle-aged man, whose accomplishments were significant and had been achieved without great effort and through many talents which had been put to good use, was stopped suddenly in his career by a coronary occlusion. He had no history of previous illnesses other than minor infections and considered himself to be in good health and not particularly limited physically either in his work or his pleasures.

He was married and the father of three children. His relations with his wife were those of an indulgent man given on occasion to outbursts provoked by his own or his wife's failure to meet his expectations. His anger with himself was often projected upon her by taking some shortcoming that annoyed him as an excuse to abuse her. Except for these episodes, they had a harmonious life. Their sexual relations for many years were a source of continued satisfaction with relatively few periods of disappointment. The children regarded him as a fond but demanding father who was deeply attached to them but perhaps too easily bored by their foibles. He enjoyed his physical youthfulness despite his growing older and derived pleasure from tennis, skiing, and fishing excursions with his family. Both friends and people at work saw him as a stable, warm, witty man who characteristically exercised good common sense. Changes in his mood were not easily brought about because of a tendency to optimism which suggested that the ability to deny what was painful came rather easily. Under unpleasant and adverse circumstances during the war as an infantryman, for example, and later in his work or with his family, he would become aloof and withdraw into a self-contained isolation until he found some relief from his distress. It usually took the form of work as a distraction, but at such times insomnia, restlessness, and ruminating occurred.

His recovery from his cardiac impairment was rapid and uneventful. It was uncomplicated because the occlusion had not been severe. There were no signs of cardiovascular disease elsewhere. In the fourth week of his convalescence (a seven-week period), it became evident that he was frequently tearful and was easily moved to sentimental expressions and comments that he did not deserve the care and the kindliness everyone was showing him in his disability. None of these reactions seemed typical of him. They continued to persist. He had not been given to sentimentality before, and in fact disparaged its display. Now, however, he expressed feelings of unworthiness in which he referred to his heart impairment and the likelihood that he would not be able to work as before. Although it would have been appropriate to be optimistic as he ordinarily would have been, as the stay in the hospital was coming to an end, he became depressed. While most of his complaints were attributed to his recent infirmity and were considered a transient phenomenon associated with the reality of his cardiac lesion, they were nevertheless inappropriate. When he was asked to accept psychiatric help, he readily agreed. This, too, was unusual for him since, when discussing with his wife the psychiatric help that friends required, he had asserted that he could take care of himself.

The visits that began at his bedside revealed that in the period of recovery his compliance with the reality of his condition was genuine. He had, in addition, many other ideas that were disturbing and about which he had spoken either not at all or only in a limited and cryptic way. They

were given voice by his sentimentality, his obvious gratitude for the efforts made on his behalf to keep his affairs in
order, and by contrast self-reassuring comments that he
would be able to continue his active life with little modification. Thus superficially he was a cooperative, model patient.
A sensible man before, now under the stress of a serious
illness he seemed reasonable. Privately he dreaded returning to work. He feared others would regard him as a
cardiac cripple, and the thought that he might indeed be one
seemed unbearable. His impaired body image was damag-
ing to his vanity and compelled him to regard himself as
damaged, whereas previously he had prided himself on his
good health and physique. Now he was no longer desirable,
either to himself or, therefore, to others. He feared having
to give up sports. His reason was not that he was an avid
sportsman but rather that he would have to forgo what
previously he had been free to choose. No choice meant no
self-assurance. It was the loss of the freedom to choose that
he complained of rather than the loss of what he had to give
up. Though he longed to return to work, the need to be
cautious worried him. It will be recalled that when he was
angry or upset, he turned to his work. In working he had
been able to restore his self-esteem; now he believed he
might have to limit his working. Although he was not aware
that it was his narcissism which was restored and replenished by his work, he was aware of his need to work and of
his dependence upon it for his well-being. But the anticipation that his cardiac condition would limit his working
brought out his present sensitivity to being hurt and made
him aware that it had always existed and that he had
thought primarily of his own interests. The selflessness of
his family and his friends made him tearful, thinking that
they were much better people than he. He was troubled that
in years past he had been aggressive and selfish. That made
him unworthy of the devotion he saw being given him

freely. He could not be as generous as his family and friends and he felt he probably never had been.

He very reluctantly admitted his fears of impotence. These were due in part to a fantasy in which he feared he could not carry out intercourse; he wished to exert himself sexually to affirm that he had lost none of his vigor. He was fearful of trying and failing, although he had not previously had a period of impotence. He was preoccupied with it during convalescence. It, too, was a function that he was losing or that he feared would be limited. He would appear less a man and could not prove that he was adequate, he thought. The persistence of self-criticism was for a time unremitting. He kept to himself the associated suicidal wishes that were fleeting, expressed in regret that his heart attack was not fatal. The frankly phallic aspirations in this man were too obvious to require more than mention.

Self-denigrating thoughts were not confined to his anticipation of diminished sexual prowess but led to a review of his work. Since there remained a difference between what he expected of himself, his ideal, and what he actually accomplished, even though it was of high quality, he took the discrepancy as a basis for lowering self-esteem. And with that he became tearful. The expressed senimentality and the otherwise unaccountable tearfulness, the feeling that everyone was too kind and that he did not deserve such generosity, were directly attributable to self-demeaning fantasies. Superficially, he appeared to be mourning over the reality that with no warning an impaired function affected a vital organ that in fact did constitute a threat to his life. But what tended to be obscured and what his grief did not account for was his loss of self-esteem and his self-denigration. The manifest mourning masked a more far-reaching reaction, melancholia or clinical depression. Granted that it was mild and of short duration, nevertheless the mental content was not to be distinguished except in degree and the hold on reality from a typical serious psychotic clinical depression.

He returned to work within a relatively short time and became as active as he had been before his infirmity. He gave up athletics and smoking. They remained as disquieting signs of his limitations. He appeared to be more driven into productivity in his work. That activity in part compensated him for his concern over exerting himself. He had no period of impotence as he had feared. A readiness to be tearful and a residue of self-demeaning briefly persisted. Since they were minimal signs they were easily balanced by his productivity in work and by the lack of concern over his masculinity. This transient psychotic episode, related to the loss of function, did not recur during the next five-year interval in which the patient was seen periodically in a follow-up study undertaken with his consent.

In cases involving serious brain pathology, in which judgment and other higher functions are significantly impaired, the phenomenon of the denial of any disability has been frequently observed and has been puzzling because it could not be explained upon the basis of a brain defect alone. A conclusion drawn by Weinstein and Kahn, who wrote a definitive paper on the subject, is that "it may be best described as the manifestation of the patient's drive to be well" [8]. Doubtless, a denial of illness expresses a wish to be well. But since all wish to be well, what information is divulged by the one who is very sick and who categorically denies it [7]? Some hints by these and other authors are provided by their recognition that changes in the body, which are literally alterations in the self image or body image, are abhorrent. Not only does everyday common sense easily confirm this, but there is a vast literature on the subject of body image and the conflicts arising from its alteration. Left in question, however, are what compelling psychodynamic processes dictate denials of illness or an impairment of function. They appear to repudiate an unmistakable reality, even when the brain is badly damaged and when other intellectual functions show severe deterioration or crippling. The processes of denial seem to survive unscathed. The wish to be well is natural enough and obvious. Underlying it, however, is a resistance to recognizing or accepting bodily changes. The unconscious conception of the body image tolerates no alterations, and allows no doubt to be expressed in the wish to be well; it also denies illness that exists. In short, the wish to be well speaks for the image of oneself as intact.

If we understand that all people wish to remain intact, that is, to suffer no damage, no alterations, and least of all no loss of function or of a part of themselves, then the behavior directed toward these aims leaves little mystery. The common occurrence of depression during or after illness or mutilation is not surprising. Depression develops when it is no longer possible to deny the reality of the conflict over the loss that has been experienced. We know, from ample clinical evidence, that when denial gives way, depression is exposed. In short, impairment of any kind and violation of the integrity of the body image may be complied with, but it will not be accepted. Losses that are sustained are dealt with emotionally on a *quid pro quo* basis.

And illness is dealt with on the same terms. Only full restitution may be accepted. Hence, the wish to be well commands the need to be restored, to be again intact. Denial of reality, one of the principal defenses against what is odious, is the earliest defense to appear in the course of development, and it seems to be one of the last to go. It is of special service in illness. Its use is to preserve the status quo, to admit to no effects that an altered reality might enforce. Since the first components of the ego to develop are the body ego, that is, the body image, changes in it are met with the strongest emotional resistance. Alterations, losses, and changes in the body have always been comprehended as representing a danger. In fact, our first encounters with and recognition of discomfort are equated with danger and anxiety, and are comprehended as a change in the body. This conviction remains.

In view of these findings, one should ask if the hypochondriac, by his insistence upon a physical infirmity, differs from all others who are ill. Does he accept a change in the body image that is abhorrent to others? The hypochondriac directs attention to a loss of function or an impairment of one that he has perceived, one that in reality cannot be substantiated. His claim, however, can be made valid if it is not directed against an organ that has failed or a part of himself that does not function, but rather against his self-esteem that has been lowered. This is what he unwittingly refers to, and what creates his despair. It tends to be generally overlooked that in hypochondriasis all the manifestations of clinical depression are present: egocentricity, narcissistic preoccupation, lowered self-esteem with a sense of loss and an aggressive reaction aimed sadistically at others and turned masochistically on the self. What differentiates hypochondriasis from clinical depression is that typically, in depression, "dissatisfaction with the self on moral grounds [are] by far the most outstanding feature; [and] self-criticism much less concerns itself with bodily infirmity, ugliness, weakness, [and] social inferiority" [3]. But in hypochondriasis the entire process shifts to an emphasis upon physical infirmities, impairment and loss of function. In short, in hypochondriasis regression has taken place and to a greater degree than is usual in depression, although when severe regression does occur in depression, hypochondriasis often appears to express it. Self-esteem is not the direct focus of attention in hypochondriasis; instead, it is the body ego at which the superego with its prohibitions and decrees aims. Self-deprecatory and denigrating remarks are addressed to the body image and demean it. For example, "I berate myself for not being active. I feel tired, I ache and feel weak. I hate myself for it.

One part of me whips the other part that should work and pull'' are typical hypochondriacal comments from a patient who, when he is not focused on physical complaints like these but has reason to deprecate himself, becomes depressed. Whether he becomes depressed or hypochondriacal depends upon the degree of regression and the involvement of the body image as an object of self-attack or self-criticism.

There is a remarkable similarity between suicidal wishes, which so commonly express aggression turned on oneself, and the self-attacks which the hypochondriac expresses by his insistence on illness. That hypochondria is a self-affliction seems to be overlooked. An analogous attitude would be to disregard self-inflicted wounds as expressions of suicidal intentions.

What the hypochondriac experiences is a loss in relation to the body image. This is a change that is deplored, and is what the hypochondriac unconsciously refers to when he insists that he is suffering from the loss of a function. He despairs of the changes in the body image that he believes have developed and protests against them just as vehemently as do the organically ill. The conflict seems to be the same in both; one has a real disability and denies it while the other has no real disability but deplores his state as if it were real. Neither finds his loss acceptable. The lame, the halt, the blind, and the hypochondriac all protest their lot; they wish to be *intact*.

The cases cited above as well as those referred to in the literature lead to the conclusion that loss of function, illness, or loss of a part of the self, regardless of the cause, of the circumstances, and perhaps of the extent of one's culpability in having brought it about, produces the emotional conflicts found in depression. But a shift occurs, due to the fact that the sense of loss converges upon the body and hence upon the body image, and depression is replaced by hypochondriasis. The body ego, and particularly the body image, threatened and altered by illness, impairment, or disability, becomes the object of attacks by the superego, which demeans it for its defects. The patient who suffered a coronary occlusion had a sequel, a narcissistic injury. His body image had been damaged as well as his cardiac muscle. The self-denigration that stemmed from this experience not only was based on the neurotic moral grounds characteristic of depression but also was founded on devaluation of the impaired body ego and image. It is significant that while the melancholic aspects, that is, the depression, cleared away, rudiments of the hypochondriasis remained. It may be argued that the reality of the cardiac disease constituted a danger about the future, and is therefore a matter of tangible concern so that the ensuing depression was not precipitated by unconscious motives at all. However, such a conventional formulation does not account for the persistence of disappointment in the self, and of self-reproaches and devaluation directed at the self-image.

Insufficient attention has been paid to the fact that the conflict between the ego and the superego which is the key to understanding the psychodynamics of depression needs only to be shifted to a conflict between the superego and the body ego to explain the dynamics of hypochondriasis.

One critical factor of illness or disability which distinguishes the emotional reactions that accompany illness from grief, and which prevents grief or mourning reactions from taking place, is that in grief a disengagement from what has been lost is possible. In grief or mourning the ego disparages or denigrates the lost object, thus loosening the libidinal attachment to it until finally the lost object is given up. Its value is referred to the past and no longer to the present. But when the self is taken as the lost object, denigrated and demeaned, its destruction entertained in suicidal wishes, loosening the ties to oneself is not so readily accomplished. This difficulty may account in part for the persistence of depression and also for the persistence of hypochondriacal complaints. In hypochondria the accusations, although addressed to the self, are more specifically shifted to the body, its organs, and its functions; in other words, to the more archaic part of the ego — the body ego. To relinquish the ties to the body when it has become the focus of attacks would be most difficult if not impossible.

In 1917 Freud asked: What brings melancholia or depression finally to an end [3]? His question has remained unanswered. The same question and its answer also apply to hypochondriasis. Freud may have actually provided the answer in part when he stated that we never relinquish anything willingly, and in any case only when we can find a substitute for it. Depression comes to an end when a substitute for our disappointment and our lowered self-esteem is found. Restitution for impairment or a disability must be made in order that the ensuing process of lowered self-esteem and depression may terminate. But for many individuals with physical disorders restitution is not possible, and therefore a residue of hypochondria and depression remains, as we have noted in the clinical material cited. A denial of our limitations provides a way out of hypochondria that is commonly resorted to; but, as we have seen, this is a precariously balanced solution.

Injuries, impairments, or disabilities for which full restitution is not possible leave a gap between the wish to be intact and the fact that it cannot be realized. We have learned that without restitution depression remains. When the body image cannot be restored the residue of depression results in hypochondria. That is to say, a disorder of narcissism develops specifically involving the body ego.

We give up nothing of value without a substitute to take its place. But the inevitable loss of what is valued gives rise to conflicts that require resolution. Ordinarily the familiar denigration and demeaning of what was valued and lost put to an end grief or mourning over what has been given up. Such reactions to loss begin in childhood and go on throughout life. When life itself is in danger of being lost, however, the old defenses which are useful in relation to other values are not effective. Only a belief in immortality or an afterlife can substitute for the loss of life, but these substitutes rest essentially on wishes. They lack certainty; they are hedged with conditions whose fulfillment depends in part on the will of the gods. However strong one's faith, the unpredictability of death keeps the believer in a precarious position. An effort to demean the value of his own life is a remarkably ineffectual device and one which operates better in relation to the need to disengage oneself from others who are lost amd mourned. But any such defenses when directed against the self are confronted by narcissism, which resists attempts to devalue self-esteem. We have seen that what brings about a lowered self-esteem increases narcissism. As a result of attempts to devalue oneself, egocentricity is concentrated. To show that the foregoing suppositions are not theoretical or abstract, the following clinical demonstration is cited.

Janice Norton recently reported an extraordinary experience in treating a dying young woman. The case began with "the fact all those on whom we usually rely to spare us the necessity of listening to dying patients, family, clergy, friends, other physicians had already relinquished their roles and could not be induced to resume them" [5].

The patient, a thirty-two-year-old married mother of two sons, was visited by her sister, who became alarmed at the patient's obvious depression and frankly suicidal wishes. The patient felt no need for a psychiatrist, "as both depression and the wish to commit suicide seemed to her to be entirely reasonable under the circumstances." She knew that she had only a short time to live, because of a widespread carcinoma. Soon after the gravity of her illness left no doubt about its outcome, she attempted to return to a religion that she had long since neglected. At her request a minister came to see her, who engaged her in lengthy con-

versations on immortality. These discussions were actually
not as important to her as the feeling that she was falling in
love with this man. She confessed it to him. He responded
by "telling her this was unrealistic, that she was sick," and
with that he sharply curtailed his visits except for perfunc-
tory calls upon her. "Her depression and suicidal preoccupation began at this time." At this point, it will be well to
recall that a bleak reality does not necessarily produce such
reactions as depression and the desire for self-destruction.
One should note that the patient turned to a minister to
help her extend her life, to transcend the limits that were
being placed upon it and thus, she hoped, to restore what
she was losing. One need not make such a transaction only
through a minister, but for this young woman seeing a minister meant something more than returning to religion for a
lease on life. She was turning to someone who clearly
represented her father, who was himself a minister. When
she confided to him what was more important to her than
talk of immorality, she was saying that under the extreme
conditions that faced her, she sought and needed a relationship, and particularly to mend a relationship that had been
broken off. As an adolescent girl she had repudiated her
oedipal incestuous wishes about her father by withdrawing
from him and giving up all interest in religion. The minister who rejected her with the admonition that she was sick
said in so many words that she was not worth an involvement. Thus demeaned at this point, she developed a disorder which has at its core a loss of self-esteem, injured
narcissism, guilt, and wishes to carry out an attack on herself as denigrated: depression and suicidal wishes.

She had had recent experiences in which others had reinforced the reactions of her disorder. Her parents, her
husband, her children could no longer endure the intense
feelings of grief that she evoked in them as she lay dying.
In their own defense they withdrew. "Her doctors, increasingly frustrated at her lack of medical response to their

various forms of treatment, became hearty and hollow.''
She probably could have tolerated the physical consequences of the disease, but her distress at loneliness was far
more difficult to bear in the face of the feeling that she was
being abandoned by everyone whom she valued. Her anger
and then her guilt were mobilized in turn. "She endured her
illness, that is its discomfort, painful treatment and even
realistically attempted to adapt herself to the adversity of
her circumstances. The only demands she made were that
they allow her to share her experiences with them. It was
only [as] she became aware of their increasing withdrawal
from her that she became suicidal.'' Norton emphasizes
her patient's search for help that she could not find. Another aspect of depression that her patient brought out was
that she could not tolerate isolation and the ensuing sense
of acute loss.

But the sense of loss was not a grief reaction nor mourning (as Norton and others to whom she refers suggest) because the response of mourning does not account for the
presence of suicidal wishes that accompany a fall in self-
esteem; such wishes do not occur in mourning or grief. It
was the fall in self-esteem which in each instance drove this
young woman further and further into depression and to
suicidal wishes. Her illness, she believed, demeaned her as
did those who fled away from her in their grief. To her their
withdrawal meant far more than grief or sorrow on their
part; it meant that she was no good. Angry at those who
left her to die, and to whom she was deeply attached but
who, in their mourning, gave her up as devalued, she felt
the denigration directed at her (which implicitly it was),
and with that she wanted to destroy herself. She agreed, in
so many words, that she was worthless. Taking herself as
the object of her rage, which was deflected from those whom
she loved, she became suicidal.

The necessity to disengage oneself from one who is dying
has not been given sufficiently eminent consideration in the

psychoanalysis of grief. It is naïve to suppose that mourning or grief begins only with the death of the loved object.
It is a denial of the need to withdraw cathexis from an
object that is going to be lost to suppose that such self-
'sparing defenses are operative only after the fact and not
when the loss is anticipated. Janice Norton's case corroborates a similar finding in other cases that close and
immediate members of the family of a dying person are
thrown into the distressing conflict of withdrawing from
and attempting to give up the loved object while needing to
hold on to it. The interest of psychoanalysts in the inevitable ambivalence about an object has obscured the fact that
the process of devaluing the loved object is a means of
freeing oneself from it and an inevitable defense. Although
the defense resembles and may be difficult to distinguish
from ambivalence, it does not pertain to ambivalence, but to
the process of narcissism instead, and hence to the relinquishment of an object in whom an investment had been
made and from which it needs to be withdrawn. Because
the need to withdraw from an object may be regarded or experienced as hostility toward the object, guilt is thus promoted. Hatred present in the prior ambivalence is revived.
Therefore, the one who withdraws cannot distinguish between denigration of the object as his defense in grief and
hostility toward the object as part of his earlier ambivalence.

The grief reaction in relation to the sudden death of a
loved object differs from the mourning for one whose death
has been realistically anticipated, as occurs during a grave
illness. With the sudden death of a loved object withdrawal
has not taken place in advance of the death. The period of
mourning tends to be briefer, since the conflict over giving
up the one who has died has not been heightened by the
withdrawal in advance. The period of mourning that occurs
following the slow and often agonizing death of a loved
object is made all the more difficult for the survivor. His

need to withdraw and to give up the object often coincides with awareness, on the part of the object, of the gravity of the situation. This awareness compels placing increasing demands, generated from fears of isolation, upon those who are depended upon. The mobilization of hostility from previously existing ambivalence is compounded with current anger at the demanding object who is being lost. As a result, a long period of mourning in these instances is needed to undo the burden of such an animus. Self-accusations that we should have given more to the one who died (which in a sense is true because of the withdrawal), that he should have been given more charity and kindliness and patience, in other words, that one's aggressive impulses should have been more effectively repudiated, lead the survivor toward depression and away from grief. While the elaborate system of denial is operative, it is often only partly effective to give the survivor only a measure of relief from these conflicts. Relief comes more fully only when the past history of the relationship can be rationalized and the memory of past hostility diminished.

Norton devoted herself to her patient with singular generosity, and was able to bring about a profound change in her. It is of central importance that as the intimacy grew between Norton and her patient, "many discussions brought out . . . that she was afraid of dying alone, of becoming less and less attractive, sick [that epithet of rejection by the minister] and having people lose interest in her . . . she also feared a sense of helplessness." From these remarks by the patient that Norton recorded, is it not noteworthy that a dying woman, fully aware of her plight, is not so much concerned with what is killing her as she is with fears of loss, injured vanity, self-denigration, a sense of limitation, and the loss of function? These, in fact, are the issues vital to a dying woman whose maturity and ego development were previously not in question. "She began

to share with me,'' says Norton, ''her grief over dying
. . . mourning continued . . . until her final coma.''

The phenomena that Norton refers to as mourning are
explained more completely in terms of melancholia or depression. This conclusion is reinforced by the fact that the
patient remained in a depression and was suicidal until her
relationship with Norton raised her self-esteem, relieved
her fears of being abandoned, and assuaged her guilt for
her hostility and for having driven her family away (she
interpreted her family's leaving her as being her own fault
because she was no longer attractive and was too sick for
them to have sustained interest in her). She recovered emotionally as her relationship with Norton proved to her that
she was worthy of attention and care. ''She began to reveal
how hurt and angry she was at the injury the minister inflicted when she needed him and he deserted her. She was
similarly injured by her husband's seeming neglect, at his
withdrawing because of his grief.'' To her it meant to be
abandoned. This was correct. The husband did indeed try to
disengage himself as from one who had died. To the patient
it meant being discarded as worthless. It led, moreover, to
her expressing her fury that she was being deprived by her
untimely death. In this complaint two issues were joined:
her despair at having to give up those whom she loved and
her despair at being abandoned by them. It would be an
oversimplification and even an error to reduce the conflicts
in her complaint to an issue of ambivalence, which, while
present, fails to take into account the conviction of her own
lowered self-esteem. She reasoned that she would not have
been abandoned had she been more valued.

Her dreams of childhood pleasures and activities without
restraint are not entirely to be accounted for as so-called
''simple wish fulfillment dreams of childhood,'' as Norton
and others conventionally label such productions which appear under these conditions. They emerged as the patient's

functions were further reduced by the progression of disease. As she became more acutely ill, dreams appeared which referred to a time of life, latency, when conflicts are held somewhat in abeyance and when unlimited activity is a natural solution to the oppressiveness of the previous oedipal phase that constituted a rejection. It will be recalled that the oedipal phase had been particularly oppressive for this young woman, who had repudiated her father in a stormy adolescent struggle with him. The patient confirmed this not only through her dreams but also when she spoke retrospectively, when she frankly admitted her envy of Norton who, she said, was young, vigorous, and healthy and who might replace her as her husband's new wife, while she herself would go to an ignominious death.

In its final stages the spreading malignant cancer became more centrally located and perception was severely impaired. The signs were intermittent blindness. Norton calls attention to them as indicating to the patient the proximity of death. No doubt this was the case, but of further significance was her patient's fears of her loss of function. These fears were chiefly emphasized in her feelings of anxiety over the isolation, rather than emphasized in her awareness of the serious visual disability that she now suffered. Moreover blindness, which would entail a further test of whether she was worthy of being cared for, made her apprehensive. She was not certain that she would continue to be cared for. It is of consequence that her physician supported her in the virtually childlike care that she required. It was her wish to have the 23rd and 121st Psalms read to her over and over at this time, a wish with which Norton complied.

The 23rd Psalm speaks to the renunciation of animus, rewarded by soothing and comfort. The 121st Psalm is about giving oneself up to one's Keeper. These psalms further plead that giving up hostility will be rewarded. At the same time they address themselves to fears of separation, the giving up of object relations. A loss, in other words, is emphasized in which one is not simply impoverished, as in grief, but in which one is demeaned, as occurs in the despair of melancholy, but one is offered the elevation of self-esteem by a relationship with the Lord to whom one surrenders oneself. It has become conventional to reduce these complex regressive forms of behavior to their so-called infantile antecedents, as Norton does by describing them as "infantile forms of separation anxiety." It is to be expected that the physician's relationship would reveal but also reduce or diminish the anxiety. Of special significance, however, is that the physician's relationship also seems to effect a relief of the conflict over self-denigration. This relief appears to be an empirical event which a valued relationship will not fail to show. Many authors tend to regard regressive behavior in the adult as a return in fact to that individual's infancy. But Hendrick and others have warned, as has been noted above, against the temptation to interpret adult behavior, however regressed it may be, as merely reproducing a vignette from childhood.

What signified peace and contentment to this patient in her last hours was the secure conviction, held up by her fantasies, dreams, and wishes, that her physician, Norton, was constantly with her: "She felt as if I were always there comforting her, assuaging her pain or physical discomfort and telling her she need not be afraid, that she was not alone . . . she had long since taken my presence during her death as an established fact . . . she no longer worried about what was to happen . . . more importantly it had occurred to her that I would share this experience (death) with her, although not at this time. She said she would miss me terribly." These last statements were made just before the patient lapsed into a final coma. They show that to the very end there could be no real or supposed giving up of a relationship. The fantasy, which was expressed as "I'll miss you terribly," says that after death she will feel lonely; death has separated them for the time being and she will be obliged to wait alone for her physician's arrival.

Eissler [2], Weisman and Hackett [9], Norton herself, and others believe that dying would be eased by the giving up of object relations prior to death. In other words, they suggest that if mourning one's losses could be resolved in advance of death, then dying would be simplified. This theory proposes that those who are dying should renounce what they hold to and value. All of our life, as we have observed and learned, is organized to do exactly the opposite of what these authors suggest. To reverse the process would require a psychological system that does not exist. At the time of dying, far from being able to give up what has been valued, namely, human relations, we cling to them more steadfastly than ever before. Throughout life, the more thoroughly we are deprived of a relationship, the greater is the need to find another or a substitute; the human condition does not exist without that need. The proposal that to repudiate human relations is a solution to a human problem is perhaps answered poignantly by Norton's patient, who at the very end of her life was "taking me with her in death."

This patient was not an exception. There is no evidence to suggest that a dying person can mourn either his own loss or that of those whom he loves and values and will give up through dying, and behave as one does in grief by accepting the verdict of reality and relinquishing what was valued to the point of being left with nothing. Relationships that are valued cannot be given up without grief and restitution. To renounce objects increases narcissism and leads, at the very least, to the finding of substitutes for those who are gone or who have been given up. Where the loss of a function is concerned, and in dying, a similar process is operative, restitution, often as tenacious, hypochondriacal preoccupations with functions. Those who are dying show an intensified need for objects. When they appear to have disengaged themselves from others, as occasionally is the case, the unconscious process of denial and repression best accounts for their behavior. It is conceivable that all affairs may be disposed of in advance of death, with the exception of the relationship with others and abandoning oneself.

Life is not conducted alone, nor for that matter is death. Life after death is not conceived of as a lonely existence, except as a punishment. Otherwise life after death is conceived to be a joining with others either in heaven or hell, or if one returns to roam the earth in a reincarnation, such an existence is not thought to be a lonely one. These persistent beliefs are brought up not to argue that Heaven and Hell are crowded but to show that the solutions that man finds are in terms of his relations with other people and especially with those who are personally important to him, whether these solutions are addressed to problems that exist when he is alive or to those that he believes arise when he has died.

Norton's patient was outspoken in her belief that the doctor's role was to spare her further attrition of self-esteem and the self-denigration which she felt in her case stemmed from object loss and the loss of function. Moreover, Norton's patient was willing to be treated because treatment led to reaffirmation of her worth, which had been undermined by self-devaluation caused by disease and desertion. The patient's self-demeaning impulses found their aim in self-destructive wishes that not only expressed anger with her present illness but probably stemmed from obscure past conflicts which we know arose from her struggles with her parents. Now she turned her rage on herself as being an utterly worthless creature. Up to her final coma this woman was concerned, as her various functions each failed her in their turn, with whether each disability that followed would render her less worthy. This is not so much a pathological as a human condition. It demonstrates what illness, disability, impairment, or a loss of function signify to everyone. When the patient became blind for periods of time, her first anxiety was that she might lose Norton rather than her vision. "The tenacity with which she clung despite all the vicissitudes," writes Norton, "was extremely impressive." It should be stated that it was because of the vicissitudes rather than despite them that the patient clung to Norton so tenaciously.

Insufficient data precludes a discussion of the patient's developing hypochondria.

The important clinical details of Dr. Norton's unique and valuable report are of special worth because in large measure she has provided the reader with enough material to understand the patient and the views which she herself took of her patient. Norton's formulations are inclined to be the conventional ones that are currently being put forth by a number of writers. She does not make as full use of her material as it permits, but this in no way detracts either from her important contribution to clinical work or from an appreciation of her extraordinary devotion to a patient who needed her and whose needs she fulfilled.

REFERENCES

1. Blank, Robert H.: Psychoanalysis and Blindness. *Psychoanal. Quart.*, 26 (1957), 1–24.
2. Eissler, K. R.: *The Psychiatrist and the Dying Patient* (New York: International Universities Press, 1955).
3. Freud, Sigmund: Mourning and Melancholia. In *The Complete Psychological Works of Sigmund Freud*, Standard Edition, edited by James Strachey (London: Hogarth Press, 1957), XIV, 244, 246.
4. ———. On Narcissism: An Introduction. In *Collected Papers* (London: Hogarth Press, 1948), IV, 40.
5. Norton, Janice: The Treatment of a Dying Patient. In *The Psychoanalytic Study of the Child* (New York: International Universities Press, 1963), XVIII, 541–542.

6. Rochlin, Gregory: The Loss Complex: A Contribution to the Etiology of Depression. *J. Amer. Psychoanal. Ass.,* 7 (1959), 300–301.

7. Stengel, E., *et al.:* Unawareness of Physical Disability. *J. Ment. Sci.,* 42 (1946), 379–388.

8. Weinstein, C. A., and R. L. Kahn: Syndrome of Anosognosia. *Arch. Neurol. and Psychol.,* 64 (1950), 772–791.

9. Weisman, A. B., and T. P. Hackett: Predilection to Death. *Psychosom. Med.,* 23 (1961), 232–255.

8

IMPOVERISHMENT

It has been said that the descent into Hades is the same from every place, and that it is not death but dying which is terrible. While dying is indeed terrible, aging is the tortuous path to dying. Therefore, the subject of this chapter is not so much the experience of dying as it is the experience of aging. The distinction to be drawn between this period, age, and all those preceding it is that the conflicts or the residues of conflicts that continue into this last phase of life are no longer experienced as loss and restitution but as loss and impoverishment. The loss of personally important objects who are neither replaced nor substituted, the losses of functions that cannot be restored, and the alterations by aging in oneself that perceptibly contradict the latent self image all convey a sense of impoverishment. Therefore, we do not find in aging the course of resolution of conflicts that was typical in other phases. The sense of impoverishment becomes increasingly prominent and plays a definitive role in aging. Becoming old is not mere physical fact. It is also an emotional process. The reactions to aging may come with the first signs of the climacterium, or with the waning of the accustomed erotic interests and pursuits, or with the indications of a decline in physical or intellectual powers. In other words, the universal omens of an involutional phase signify a process of impoverishment.

The variety of the signs of aging is great. They all point in the direction of no return. These harbingers evoke a reaction which is similar to that which takes place in the process of transition from one phase of development to the next. It will be recalled that failures or disappointments in an earlier period of development have an important effect on behavior in the period to follow. We have learned that the solutions found to the problems or conflicts in a particular phase are significant not only for the phase in which they occur but perhaps even more for the period which is in preparation. In each phase of development, beginning with the earliest, we observed that a thrust of activity took place. Its principal function was to help make the transition from one phase to the next. This is to say, activity was put into the service of the ego functions, in order to influence, alter, or modify the environment, thus gratifying the self and, in so doing, effecting a better adaptation to it.[1]

The thrust of activity also often marks the period of change that, without it, might not have been so easily identified. There is always a heterogeneous group of people who shrink from the thrust. In part they do so because they abhor change, because changes invariably bring anxiety and uncertainty and a renewal of aggressive wishes and fantasies even though some relief from a present dissatisfac-

---

[1] It will be recalled that the observation of the "thrust of activity" was first introduced by Helene Deutsch in her *Psychology of Women*. She considered it significant in those phases of development with which she was concerned, namely, puberty and adolescence of girls. We observed the same phenomenon in earlier periods of development and referred to it in Chapter 6, The Psychology of Failure. We shall show that it is also present in the last phase of psychological development — aging — just as we demonstrated it to be present in the earliest phases. A personal discussion with Helene Deutsch on the subject now, about twenty years since the publication of her famous work on female psychology, brought out her concurrence that in all likelihood the thrust of activity had a much wider application than she had thought. Although she had no clinical experience with young children and hence would not know of its appearance among them, yet, from the clinical histories of older patients she has had since the publication of her work, she would be inclined to confirm the extension here of the thrust of activity into the other periods, that is, the earlier ones as well as the last ones. She has suggested that some such activity or thrust takes place in relation to the climacterium.

tion may be desired. Theirs is, in part, a reluctance to relinquish the gratifications of the present for dubious gain to come. In those people the pleasure principle rules, frequently to such a degree that the reaction to each change of phase is challenged by the pull of regressive wishes. The satisfaction afforded by earlier sources of gratification constitutes a serious obstacle in adapting to the uncertain conditions that the reality of the new phase requires. Aging people who especially resist the social and physical changes over which they can exercise little or no control appear to lapse into manifest complacence or isolation and a seeming apathy. While they appear resigned they are in fact often in a ferment of regressive wishes and behavior, which is aimed at mitigating the deprivation that changing or aging means to them and which should be distinguished from impoverishment. Their behavior, as one might anticipate, tends to be directed toward the fulfillment of primary needs. These may be expressed in preoccupation with eating and body care, in greediness and hoarding of possessions, and in turning away from frustrating problems in a desire to resolve them by avoidance or by helpless dependence upon others accompanied by insatiable demands.

The thrust of activity mobilized in the aging individual usually poses a divided issue which has been observed in other periods also. The question again raised is: Will the thrust of activity only entail a new mobilization of aggression with attendant regressive desires and acts, or will it initiate an elaboration of functions and continuing sublimation? The distinction is no sharper than it was in earlier phases.

Aging is the only phase of human development which is characteristically, generally, and regularly resisted. The resistance to aging reveals an awareness that impoverishment well understood in advance leads to the end of life. Among persons whose characters are more primitively organized, it is not chiefly impoverishment, however, so much as deprivation that is feared. It is a fear that is always responded to with regression. Although recognized as having its own characteristics, aging has been neglected as a developmental phase. It has been regarded instead as a static terminal period in which psychological functions fail or shut down, as does the sclerotic arterial system. Even more frequently overlooked is the dynamic importance of aging as an experience in which limitations will not be transcended nor losses restored. Life is made more precarious, when it nears its end, by the replacement of a promise of restitution with the disquiet of impoverishment, to which, in some cases, the danger of deprivation is added.

Any loss of what is valued, we have come to appreciate, brings an increase of narcissistic defenses. As restitution occurred in earlier periods of development, narcissism was correspondingly reduced. We know that a loss which one believes cannot be restored may lead to a lowered self-esteem and paradoxically also brings an increase in narcissism. It is a process that is no better illustrated in any period of life than in aging, which is typified by highly egocentric reactions to loss of functions or their progressive impairment. While the inroads of aging affect memory of the recent past, leaving remote memory intact and often even embellished, it is curious that the behavior resulting from the defect in memory closely fits in with the vanity upon which the aging depend. For them the present, now distressing because of its frequently uncompensated losses, compels attention to a past which they actively endow with a luster it often never had.

In aging as in other periods, the thrust of activity is a reaction that mobilizes aggression and also inevitably brings out ever-present, but usually unconscious, sadism. Even though the old sadistic wishes, impulses, and fantasies may be but faintly revived, they nevertheless activate masochistic defenses and behavior. The activation of masochistic defenses affirms the guilt that is associated with destructive acts and wishes. To behave destructively in this phase of life, where there is less hope for restitution, restoration, or redress, increases both anxiety and guilt, however. Although the readiness to make amends for hostility and thus to avert the threat of guilt is present in other periods of life, in aging the harboring of hostility and its resulting guilt feelings are of primary concern. The super-ego in those who are aging increases in severity and is often expressed only by projection in scoldings and criticism of others. The self-sacrificing and self-suffering acts which appear more commonly in this phase than in previous ones are not due, as has been naïvely assumed, to the fact that one is nearing the end of life and offering a final newfound wisdom in which a lesser price is placed on oneself; rather they represent attempts to atone for aggression or hostility. These reactions to feelings of aggression or hostility may account for the higher incidence of depression that occurs in old age.

The thrust of activity, when expressed as aggressiveness toward personally important people, and when associated with deaths of members of the family or close friends, leads often to depression rather than simply to grief or mourning. Depression is therefore particularly frequent among the aged. When the thrust of activity becomes expressed as aggression or as the oppressiveness of depression, it is in turn relieved by the unconscious use of denial of one's culpability in thought and deed. Correspondingly, guilt is more actively (albeit unconsciously) denied in age than it was in previous periods. Thus in age hostility is most frequently displaced to others or to circumstances, to relieve the depression which arises from one's own onerous hostility. The projection of hostility, although fostering masochistic suffering, serves not only as a denial to mitigate self-accusation, but also to elevate self-esteem. The overvaluation of the self in aging buttresses a progressively precariously held self-esteem. It draws more upon the past than upon the present to do so. All these defenses against impoverishment — masochistic suffering, denial of hostility, overevaluation of the self — are not effective if narcissism cannot stand the severity of the superego. Hence, in old age, the search into the past for self-elevation is in part engendered by a severe superego. It risks finding instead ignominy that prevails and brings on depression.

The many facets of the development of clinical depression in age do not differ from those involved in the dynamics of the depressions of other periods; nevertheless the simpler equations that explain depression in the earlier phases of life are not adequate to explain the depression that develops late in life.

Despite the great increase in their numbers (and a vast literature devoted to them), what is known about the intimate life of old people is principally legendary. Psychoanalytic study has been conducted throughout the world on a wide variety of people, with the exception of those who are old. There is little direct knowledge about aging individuals. Psychoanalytic studies of the aged that have been reported are rare. There is no important body of literature of the aging based upon clinical material of everyday psychopathology that one can cite.

A sixty-four-year-old man, who was very successful in his work, which together with his relationships remained unimpaired by age, became moderately depressed and required treatment. He had a variety of physical symptoms that were appropriate to his years, such as a limited degree of arthritic changes in the joints of his hands and neck that caused him some discomfort but no disability, a slightly enlarged prostate, and a few other similar indications of age. None of his physical disorders could be considered significant at his time of life. He had been depressed approximately a year and showed no signs of recovery. In the past there had been depressive mood changes, lasting for a few days or as long as a week, that were uncomplicated and uneventful, and were relieved spontaneously without a residue. He was generally an evenly compulsive man who, although occasionally subject to brief neurotic, self-correcting depressions, made good use both of his talents and of his neurotic needs, which had brought him a successful history of work, army duty, and family life. If his past neurotic conflicts had had a serious effect upon his achievements, career, or domestic life, it was not evident. This was not due to a lack of perception about himself, but rather to the fact that he had adapted himself well enough so that his personal neurotic conflicts were sufficiently satisfied to give him little cause for complaint.

During the past year he had been increasingly preoccupied with the coming of his obligatory retirement from work (which was less than a year off). Since he did little except work, without his work he believed he had nothing. He felt that he was unable to give up his occupation. Currently he was enjoying the distinction he had earned, except for the increasing anxiety and the deepening despair which were overtaking him. Clinically he showed two principal reactions: first, depression with lowered self-esteem, expressed in a lengthy review of his past life in which he criticized himself; and second, inflated self-importance, which he expressed in a review of his past that recalled the triumphs over adversity and the accretion of accomplishments. He often felt compelled to extend his record of successes to include, with pride, some sexual exploits of the past. The pleasure he derived from retelling his successful experiences in the past furnished him a measure of self-aggrandizement in the present — seemingly more pleasure than they had given him decades ago when they were fresh encounters. These ruminations anticipated the loss his retirement would cause him; they were a premature reaction affording him narcissistic gratification in compensation for the loss before it had occurred. While his vanity was partly supported by his actual success in work, it was increased by the meaning he gave to his sexual prowess.

His conscious conflicts focused on continued jealousy of his siblings, with whom he still vied unconsciously for his mother's favor, even though she was long since dead. He unconsciously defined success as that which he believed would earn his mother's approval. The course of his success had brought him to triumph over a slightly older brother, his father's favorite, and it made him appear more heroic to a sister two years younger to whom he was deeply attached. He was contemptuous of his ineffectual father who had been a braggart and whose accomplishments were little more than vain aspirations, whereas our patient, perhaps no less boastful, had made his strivings into true achievements.

During this period of anxiety over his forced retirement, the intrusion for the first time into his consciousness of incestuous fantasies about his daughter and displaced to his secretary was alarming him. Occasional masturbation that he could not resist followed these fantasies. The thinly disguised erotic daydreams about young women which accompanied this act made him very remorseful and anxious. But what was most disturbing to him was not that he had dreams, wishes, or fantasies that were incestuous and that led ultimately to his mother (after having been displaced from his daughter and sister, respectively); what upset him was that he was acting out his impulses. He feared he was losing control of himself. He was not aware of the extent to which his narcissism compelled him to this behavior. In his dreams, fantasies, and acting out he was never an elderly man.

Two conflicts are illustrated by this aging man. One is that loss leads to impoverishment. He believed he had nothing to replace the occupation that he would lose, although he was healthy, intelligent, skilled, and should be in demand for his services — even though not in his previous capacity. As later events were to show, he feared deprivation and impoverishment. The second conflict was caused by the rapid increase in narcissism that came as a reaction to the decline in self-esteem. As a secondary phenomenon the mild physical disorders which were previously noted took on a somewhat hypochondriacal character which also indicated an increased narcissistic preoccupation.[2]

Narcissism increases at critical points in the earlier decades of life when self-esteem is in jeopardy. Narcissism is thus important, we have learned, in averting profound depression and at times may avert it altogether. When narcissism is carried to a still further degree, as is frequently the case with age, it leads to those self-deceptive and at the same time plausible states in which a renewed and welcomed vigor appears with increased interests, seeming self-disregard, and lack of concern with impoverishment. This heightened affective narcissistic state frequently is a reaction to the death of a loved object (a wife, a husband, a child, or a friend). It is actually a mild hypomanic state that unconsciously masks grief effectively and often depression as well. It often leads to constructive, profitable, and satisfying work in old age in which narcissism is again served by the executant functions in yet another period of development. No attention has been paid to this period of life as one in which this development may take place. A deeper understanding of psychological phenomena has perhaps suffered from being conceptually bound to the realistic state of the aging tissues.

Close examination of unsuccessful attempts at sublimation in the aged frequently reveals that there has recently been an increase in aggression or hostility because narcis-

[2] The inclination to reduce the experience to a return or persistence of fears of castration would be an oversimplification and an example of the application of a pansexual theory that Freud, Hendrick, H. Deutsch, and others have warned against but which nevertheless tends to be given support it does not clinically merit.

sism has intensified. Previous strong and even latent sadistic impulses and wishes, with corresponding masochistic reactions, have been activated and are expressed in self-attacks, self-suffering, and self-sacrifice which are often clinically betrayed in agitation with depression.

In a recent and as yet unpublished work, Maxwell Gitelson states: "Its interest resides almost entirely in the fact that the subject is an elderly woman." She was sixty-six years old, "depressed and suffering from severe insomnia." Following her husband's death six months before she commenced treatment, she experienced a recurrence of erotic memories, about one man in particular. All the memories were associated with prohibitions; nevertheless she desired them. Her depression did not follow her husband's death. She denied the importance of his death on the basis that her marriage had been unrewarding and that her husband had a lingering illness from which his death released her. The depression appeared with the return of erotic wishes associated with past and current prohibitions. With the resurgence of sexual fantasies, a phobic symptom appeared for the first time, "a fear of physical violence and rape . . . she became afraid of being out after dark." She was somewhat derisive about a woman being erotically excited at her age. Recalling that such remarks suggested prohibitions and admonitions against sexual wishes with guilt and similar past inhibition, she became anxious.

The course and content of her conflict as revealed directly through analysis of dreams were not remarkable insofar as she focused upon sexual wishes and upon conflicts in the past which she transferred to Gitelson. When she was convinced that he was not critical of her she gave up her initial resentfulness toward him and also gave up being severely self-critical. Her self-esteem raised, she began to recover from the depressed state which had brought her into treatment. She was seen nearly two years later for a few months. During the interval the patient had so improved that she

was busily engaged in many activities, but Gitelson remarks: "Sometimes it seemed to me that she was somewhat
hypomanic and there were a number of visits in which she
seemed depressed." Her improvement continued and the
depressive episode evidently gave way to increased activity, which was directed toward current realities rather than
to the past with its inevitable disappointments. The patient
is now in her seventies.[3]

Gitelson's elderly woman patient demonstrates some
phenomena which are of interest although they were not in
the direct focus of his concern. If his patient's age had not
been furnished the reader, the content of her fantasies and
wishes, the nature of the defenses, and her symptoms that
were associated with the fear of rape would not have betrayed her age. Only a few specific elements in relation to
the fantasies were more typical of a woman her age, namely
the depression. Gitelson tells us, that this woman's conflicts
were focused on the "survival of the unresolved oedipal
conflict." Despite the fact that the evidence for his point is
clear, his explanation of the onset of the disorder, the depression and insomnia, is not; nor is the process of her
recovery dealt with except within the narrow and modest
limits Gitelson set forth. Some questions which he raised remained to be answered. A clue to the nature of this woman's
difficulties is gained from the fact that she did not grieve or
mourn following her husband's death, but was depressed.
Also significant is the fact that her recovery began with the
return of her self-esteem, which finally was restored. Therefore, what led to the lowering of her self-esteem is at the
crux of her disorder. The disorder followed only indirectly
from her husband's death. Her hostility toward him was of
long standing and wishes for his death, in lieu of his lingering mental deterioration, were freely admitted. The reality
of his death did not consciously constitute a loss. Her

[3] Dr. Gitelson was very generous to offer the use of his unpublished
manuscript [4].

initial complaints and her fears that her symptoms of depression were signs of senility pointed to an identification with her dead husband through his disorder. Her identification with the lost object, even though her relationship to the object was hostile, reveals more of the dynamics of a depression than Gitelson considered to be present. Her husband's death ushered in erotic but prohibited wishes to have illicit relations with men. The fusion of her aggressive and erotic wishes is expressed in the phobic reaction.

This elderly woman resembled a girl in puberty when she expressed fears of the dark and of a sexual assault by an unindentifiable man. But there is a significant difference between the emotional experience involved in this aging woman's erotic enterprise and that of the girl in puberty with a seemingly identical interest. The girl, no less harassed by conflicts, anxious, and phobic, does not become depressed, while the woman does. The young girl's fears of sexual attack by an anonymous man, notwithstanding the great anxiety about the brutality of such a sexual experience, reveals that she herself secretly, that is, unconsciously, is a passive, willing partner who masks her wishes behind her protests and fears. Her guilt, which is expressed in the phobic prohibition, is derived from the unconscious wishes in her dreams and fantasies that contain the masochistic longings that will satisfy her passivity, the desired gratification of which she must protest.

The same fantasies and fears to be found in a girl erupted in the elderly woman that Gitelson describes. What is evident is that in the elderly woman their activation is in large measure due to a sense of impoverishment rather than to libidinal longings, which are the primary motive in the girl's fantasies. For the aging woman whose prospects of fulfillment are poor (rather than for the girl whose prospects are good), "the prominence of the narcissistic elements in the erotic fantasies is in itself a triumph over the masochistic element. Many women retain these masochistic

fantasies until an advanced age'' [2]. As women age, however, while masochistic fantasies, fears, and phobias may
remain or may be evoked, as in the case cited here, an essential element of their character that was not as conspicuous.
previously becomes increasingly important. Narcissism
typically does not diminish with time, it tends to increase;
and aggression that accompanies it is also heightened.

As this example of a woman in the final phase of life
shows, the old rape scene is there, the participants are
the same, but its meaning differs. The woman's aims have
changed. No longer does passivity, with its corresponding
masochistic longings, motivate her, as they do the girl who
renounces aggression for the sake of being loved — which is
the key to her behavior. The erotic wishes from the past
remain as does the narcissistic wish to be loved. But in
expressing them the woman is active and aggressive. Her
purpose is to restore her narcissism. That the unconscious
scene from girlhood which Gitelson's patient revives may
have persisted unwittingly throughout her married life is
suggested by the fact that she had feared a close relationship with her husband and had retained fantasies about a
union with another man. These fantasies were not acted out.
On one occasion in early middle age an episode occurred
which gave her the opportunity to carry out some of these
wishes. Opportunity only put her to flight; she did not
fulfill her guarded fantasy. In her present intention to
meet these wishes she felt more destitute and strongly
wished for what she had little expectation to realize: not a
real sexual experience with the meaning it may have once
held, but one in which her egocentricity, self-satisfaction, or
her vanity would be uppermost. The eruption into consciousness of forbidden erotic wishes which were partially
released by her husband's death brought on lowered self-
esteem and with it depression.

Gitelson showed that only when his patient was relieved
of her guilt did she begin to improve rapidly. The guilty

response had arisen not only because of her wishes to satisfy herself with men who were prohibited or because of inhibitions about entertaining sexual desires. Such conflicts, which stem from libidinal forces and involve prohibitions respecting the objects with whom gratification is sought, are rooted in earlier periods of development. When a woman of advanced age, like this one, shows guilt, it is related mainly to her narcissism that seeks satisfaction by way of aggression. In the old drama of rape, she has projected her aggressive wishes onto the assailant-seducer. It is, in fact, she who unconsciously is the real seducer, the active and sexually demanding aggressor.

Gitelson did not report the unconscious wishes that were underlying the phobia in his patient. She had never ceased to remember the sexual fantasies which she recalled from early adolescence, and she willingly accepted Gitelson's interpretation that her phobic symptoms referred to an actual "childhood episode with boys who had accosted her in the alley." There is ample indication that this was a correct interpretation of the origin of the scene that the phobia draws upon. There is an inclination in older women to dissemble unconsciously, and also deliberately at times; to deny the changes that take place in their erotic aims. The fantasies of girlhood do retain some of their original significance when carried forward into later phases of development. In this case the "alley" encounter was periodically revived and allayed with some gratification, only to be reactivated again at a future occasion, as this patient rationalized was the case. The girlhood fantasies, although intact, had arisen, however, to serve the aims of narcissism and aggression. The assignment of roles in the rape scene is therefore reversed. The aging person is eager to rationalize and to comply with the conventional consignment of a current erotic fantasy to some past period, as though it were a *déjà vu* experience, as if no new, more pointed significance could be assigned to the old fantasy. To fail to take into account the fact that impoverishment has an essential effect upon narcissism in the involutional period would be misleading. This case and that of the man cited before it demonstrate that aggression is mobilized in the form of activity and is at the disposal of narcissistic aims.

When Gitelson's patient turned away from the role of being sexually aggressive in her fantasies in order to satisfy her heightened narcissism, toward something that was to be more acceptable to her and hence less guilt-ridden, she was no longer depressed. She went into a sustained period of what for her was better sublimated activity. A final report fifteen years after he had seen her revealed that she had resolved her central conflict. Gitelson wrote that she had become "active in civic affairs . . . and highly respected. . . . Most interesting, however, is the new career she had built for herself: *mirabile dictu,* she had become a group therapist and for the last six years [probably she is near 80 years old], has been a leader and instructor of other laymen in this work" [4].

A. I. Goldfarb and J. Scheps [5] have written a series of reports on their experience in homes for the aged with the management and care of hundreds who were sixty-five to ninety years old. These aged people showed some remarkable uniformities in their psychological reactions to aging. Their characteristic reactions were heightened aggressiveness and increased helplessness, accompanied by anxiety and a lowered self-esteem expressed in complaints of worthlessness and reaction formation tendencies of self-aggrandizement. The erotic or sexual life of this group has not been reported by the authors and hence permits no comment. The similarities in a large group of aged people to the principal reactions in the individual cases reported above are striking.

The greatest test of narcissism is aging or old age. All that has come to represent value and with which narcissism has long been associated is jeopardized by growing old. The skills, mastery, and powers, all painfully acquired, which provided gratification as they functioned to effect adaptation wane in the last phase of life. One's resources, energies, adaptability, and functions, the intimacies of relationship upon which one depended, family and friends, are continually being depleted and lost. The longer one lives (as the longer one gambles), the more regularly one loses. Aging is an assault upon narcissism. Just as in early life the precariousness of existence is made clear to the child, so the friability of what is valued is made plain to the aging. Narcissism, therefore, has no lesser a role in aging than it had in the years before.

The substitute for losses, or restitution that is found for them, appeases the heightened demand for narcissism, but when restoration of objects lost or reparations for resources depleted is no longer possible, as is the case in old age, narcissism becomes intensified but not placated.

With an increase of narcissism, interest in others is correspondingly lowered. Narcissism is expressed in taking the self as an object in which to invest one's libido, as others and the substitutes were taken in earlier phases. Freud's essay, "On Narcissism," illustrates the point being made here: "Libido and ego-interest share the same fate and have once more become indistinguishable from each other. The familiar egoism of the sick person covers them both. We find it so natural because we are certain that in the same situation we should behave in the same way" [3]. A parallel process takes place in aging. If we were to substitute the word "old" for the word "sick," Freud's statement would remain valid. We have observed that the aging man gives up his previous critical judgment of himself and overestimates his value, just as he avoids everything that would diminish the importance of his ego. He unconsciously refurbishes his past to be better than it was, just as he retouches his body image so that it becomes impervious, invulnerable, and ageless. To some extent he becomes his own ideal, exalting himself: ". . . where libido is concerned, here again man has shown himself incapable of giving up a gratification he once enjoyed . . . and if . . . his own critical judgment is awakened . . . he seeks to recover the early perfection . . . the lost narcissism of his childhood" [3]. In old age narcissism and aging are indivisible. He no longer projects forward, as his ideal, that which represented or substituted for the given-up narcissism of childhood. An unremitting need results therefore to press for satisfaction perpetually, by countervailing what may be valued and lost, by taking as the substitute himself, *faute de mieux*.

A modern clinical document that would convey the personal experience of old age is not in existence. Fragments which have appeared, from the time of Plato to that of Poe, are brief comments, reflections, or contemplations of old age: its active voice has not been heard.

A unique exception recently appeared. During the last eleven years of his life, Bernard Berenson recorded in diaries the span of his eighty-second through his ninety-third year, the one in which he died [1]. The reader is provided with an unequaled and revealing clinical report of Berenson's experiences in his advancing years. He also comments on the "passing scene" and sometimes wittily on the many and famous people who continued to visit him at his beloved villa, I Tatti. His fears of being neglected and unwanted seemed to heighten his need for personal attention and visitors. To the last he remained remarkably active and was confined only for short intervals by the extremes of illness and infirmity. His entries in the diaries, many in the form of vignettes, have the dimensions of sketches. Famous for his perceptiveness throughout life, Berenson retained the faculty for it even when aging restricted him in ever-narrowing circles.

The combination of being especially perceptive with aging and an increasing narcissism was a goad for him to set down countless details of his own disintegration. Here the vignettes give way to an intimate portrait of himself. Somewhat objectively he describes one system after another in his body that falters, and to a degree, subjectively, he records his encounter with some of the processes that bring on his end. Berenson's diaries, although personal documents, are in many respects unselfconscious ones, because they reveal far more of himself, as an aged man in the throes of dissolution, than he could have been aware of. He spared neither himself nor his reader the clinical details that authenticate the subject he portrayed.

The diaries are thus a valuable, unique source, useful to the study of the psychology of loss, of aging, of the emotional significance of the depletion of faculties, the loss of functions, and the melancholic effects that are associated with the feeling of impoverishment on growing old and dying. The result of Berenson's efforts, therefore, is a matchless account, extending over a decade, of the many vicissitudes on becoming very old.

Berenson commences his diaries as an octogenarian frightened by both his advanced age and his frailty. His fears about being old seem to have arisen with his beginning first to age rather than coming toward the end of his life. They appear at the outset of his entries and are reaffirmed throughout the entire decade. Berenson tells us in his opening comments of how affected he was by a close glimpse "many years ago of some old men sunning themselves who merely existed . . . even then they made me ache to turn away." He evidently saw himself in them and fled. He briefly escapes the burden the years have put upon him when, for example, he relates that an old man came to visit him and treated him as a peer. One of his reactions is to make a quick mental calculation that reveals the visitor to be ten years younger than himself. Pleased that his guest, in taking him as a contemporary, thus made him ten years younger than he actually was, Berenson found the visit more enjoyable. He aches not to be old: now he was eighty-four. Still striving for these aims, in a comment two years later, he reports a fragment of a dream he enjoyed: In some fashion he is in collusion with the police, who although arresting him for publicly molesting women are friendly and do not prosecute him. The episode is pleasurable. In the dream he is no old man, nor is the exhibition of his active sexual behavior subject to censure, because the authorities are not severe; on the contrary, they are well disposed toward him. This fragment from Berenson's unconscious permits no further interpretation without going beyond the limits of the meager material. It nevertheless clearly reveals that the dream succeeds in satisfying an unconscious wish that reverses reality, that is, that his aging, a pressing problem, not be manifest; social judgment of himself is held in abeyance, so that he does not regard his public behavior seriously (a matter which when awake always concerned him), and thus a second wish is met; the sexual liberty he takes fulfills for him a third wish.

Berenson commented that the "Freudian interpretation would be simple — a common, ordinary sexual ferment." He was correct that the Freudian interpretation would not be difficult. The interpretation goes far beyond what he naïvely suggests, however. When he dreams of making a conscienceless public display of his aggressive sexual aims toward women, it is his own narcissism which is being gratified and his self-esteem which is elevated. The wish to satisfy narcissism and to raise self-esteem is consistent with old age as well as appropriate to what Berenson reveals of himself. In the same vein he writes, "I enjoy flirting with women over forty, stirring the remains of sex in them." His expressed wish to "look backward toward what one has been looking forward to" is part of the fantasy of reversing the clock and thereby lifting the oppressiveness of the present — old age. Thus when he was nearly eighty-six he wrote, "Dream sexuality . . . preoccupies me as much as physiological sexuality ever did." The assertion of the durability of a function, a faculty, or a perception appears often in Berenson's diaries, usually after the report of some disability or limitation that age has imposed. Typically, Berenson is prompted to write, "My mind is clearer than ever," as though the changes that were taking place in him were restorative rather than deteriorating.

Despite the variety of his intellectual interests and the stream of stimulating visitors which tended to make Berenson feel that his "mind was living up to his expectations," he is required to pay increasing attention to his physical needs. He records, "Part of a tooth gave way at dinner . . . made me feel dejected and humiliated . . . is it a sign of disintegration?" He comments from time to time that he regards deterioration of his body as a punishment. It appears from many other similar remarks that what he regarded as punishment was really the deprivation, and hence the frustration, that aging forces on him. His description of life reminds one of Tantalus, tortured by unappeased appetites. In order to relieve or to mitigate the punishment and to wring still more satisfaction from life, he pursued wishes with tenacity. He notes at the age of eighty-five: "Keeping alive is now my career, and it is a whole-time job. It scarcely allows leisure for any occupation and of course, no vacation. Every morsel of food, every mouthful of liquid must submit to its purpose . . . keeping alive at all cost. It is an adventure keeping alive against all the invading powers of destruction."

These defiant declarations yield to a description of the disorders that have no regard for his demand and he writes, "Memory for names is gone entirely, vocabulary in English even diminished, absentminded, restricted horizon, aches wherever I touch my body from skull to toe, shooting pains in my insides. Hernia, threatening hemorrhoids, repletion, . . . nose dripping or sneezing. Throat, coughing and spitting . . . melancholy reflections on my incompetence . . . eyes watery . . . almost drives me to despair." Following these complaints in which he was clearly depressed, self-demeaning, and denigrating were many remissions and respites so that at ninety-one years Berenson muses that he is perhaps boastful to say that few at his age would "keep a parcel of their wits."

He remarks on a landscape ". . . visually more poignant, more beautiful than ever . . . I feel the machine going to pieces . . . my mind is clearer than ever. . . . Everything else, physical and mental, seems to diminish; the appreciation of beauty is on the increase. . . . I see clearer and deeper than ever before and enjoy it in actuality and artifact as never before. May this remain and increase!"

Berenson asserts that he perceives with greater clarity, that his powers increase and his enjoyment is without precedent. He thus demonstrates unequivocally that his struggle against being diminished or "going to pieces" is countered with unconscious, self-elevating efforts. He attempts to raise his self-esteem, to achieve self-aggrandizement, and thus longs to restore himself.

Berenson's extended preoccupation with aging gradually gave way to more pointed expression of the same ultimate problem, death. Until his deterioration reached a point of frank infirmities that his narcissism could no longer surmount, he found aging abhorrent and wrestled with it, as his diaries amply indicate. But as he grew very old, dying became the chief issue; it appeared to replace aging as a conflict. Even at the age of ninety-one, when he had barely recovered from a severe bout with intestinal illness, he laughs aloud to the staff of I Tatti and teases them, "Why do you try to hide from me that you despair of keeping me alive? If you think I am dying tell me so, for I have various matters to attend to before I die." Actually, Berenson showed no inclination to hear of dying, despite his preoccupation with it, which was becoming more pervasive. "In fact," he declares, "the expectation of death . . . I did not believe it." Having gone through a most trying time of illness, on his recovery Berenson noted, "Knowing [if not believing] that probably I was dying . . . strange that I took no interest whatever in death . . . the end of all things for me." Then he inquired about the mail that had in the meantime accumulated. Such occasions as these showed Berenson's use of the mechanism of negation and denial as conspicuous defenses which become more widespread in the very old.

Little activity was left him when he became very old. What energy remained was expended in defending himself against the progressive deterioration he perceived to be obviously taking place. Whereas in the earlier period of old age the thrust of activity may have served further development to relieve his anxiety of impoverishment, Berenson demonstrates that if one lives long enough this, too, will be relinquished for the sole activity of keeping alive. Too little remains to be invested elsewhere than in his narrowly centered, wholly narcissistic aims of the final and terminal period.

Having virtually outlived his struggle with aging, he was confronted with conflicts over death, "that end of all things for me," as he called it, and became more obsessed with fears for the future. He appeared no longer to be concerned for himself as he was in the earlier years of his last decade. Most of his fears for himself were displaced from those of dying to fears of what would take place after it. Paradoxically, he seemed thus less directly concerned with himself although he was nearer to death. He feared that his beautiful Florentine Renaissance villa with its valuable contents and the lovely gardens, with all of which he had so intimately identified himself, would after his death show "gardens neglected, indoors necessarily institutionalized. All the odds and ends, the flowers, the trinkets that give intimacy to a room, will have disappeared . . . a dreary abstraction will reign . . . and who will preside, what kind of biped will replace me and mine?" With a picture of I Tatti a ruin and its

contents scattered if Harvard should fail to accept his possessions as a legacy to be kept intact and preserved, Berenson's final plans for the future, that is, his own immortality,
were in question until he was assured during a visit by the
Dean of Harvard that the University had accepted I Tatti.
The relief this gave Berenson, now at last certain that continued attention to I Tatti would prevent it from being neglected or abandoned, suggests that Harvard's action allayed fears he must have suffered through his long life and
against which he needed to defend himself even after his
death [1].

Miss Nicky Mariano, editor of *Sunset and Twilight:
From the Diaries 1947–1958,* began working for Bernard
Berenson in 1919 when he was fifty-four years old. She re-
mained with him until his death forty years later in 1959.
Miss Mariano very generously and promptly replied to in-
quiries that I made regarding Mr. Berenson.

The questions were based upon issues or conflicts that
Berenson himself had brought out in his diaries. The main
one was about his almost exclusive preoccupation with himself in the last decade of his life. Did this reflect a previous
hypochondria and surrender to infirmity and discomfort
that with advanced age simply had become more pronounced, or was the excessive concern with himself more
consistent with his old age rather than with his attitudes in
previous periods? Was his denied concern with death significantly present before the last decades? Did he seem troubled
at the prospect of aging when she first knew him? Was he
fearful of infirmity or illness?

Miss Mariano wrote about her early association with Berenson that "B. B. might easily catch colds and had an un-
usually delicate digestion. . . . Yet at the same time [he
was] able to overcome such physical ailments by severe self-
discipline and a stubborn determination to carry out what

he planned.'' She had ''never seen him morbid over his health.'' This would suggest that he lacked hypochondria; but a reference to death which she reports — ''He was always very conscious of walking on the edge of a razor'' — confirms that the references in the diaries to losing his faculties and his worry over the experience, which at the same time he denied, when admitting that he was only beginning to feel old at seventy-nine, indicate a long-standing anxiety about aging, infirmity, and limitations. It will be recalled that one of the first notes Berenson entered in his diaries was that he fled from the sight of old, idle men who could only sun themselves. Her views further confirm the belief that heightened narcissism developed with age — ''he always observed himself but not as closely as toward the end.'' In fact, keeping a diary of one's disintegration, recording for oneself and for others the loss of one's powers, while no doubt a masochistic enterprise, also exhibits a mounting narcissistic preoccupation. Berenson's diaries reveal it as his main focus. Narcissism is the first of the qualities of character to sustain a human being, and it seems to do so to the last.

REFERENCES

1. Berenson, Bernard: *Sunset and Twilight: From the Diaries 1947–1958,* edited by Nicky Mariano (New York: Harcourt, Brace & World, Inc., 1963).
2. Deutsch, Helene: *Psychology of Women* (New York: Grune & Stratton, 1944), I, 255.
3. Freud, Sigmund: On Narcissism: An Introduction. In *Collected Papers* (London: Hogarth Press, 1948), IV, 30–59.
4. Gitelson, Maxwell: Survival of the Sexual Impulse and the Capacity for an Erotic Transference in an Elderly Woman. Presented before the Boston Society for Gerontologic Psychiatry at a conference on the subject of Emotional Disorders of the Aging Process, on November 3, 1962.

5. Goldfarb, A. I., and J. Scheps: Psychotherapy of the Aged, *Psychosom. Med.*, 16 (3) (1954), 209–219; A. I. Goldfarb, Psychotherapy of the Aged, *Psychoanal. Rev.*, 43 (1956) 443–449; A. I. Goldfarb, Patient-Doctor Relationship in Treatment of Aged Persons, *Geriatrics* 19 (1964), 18–23.

INDEX